DPH SPORTS SERIES

SKIING

H. C. DUBEY

1999
DISCOVERY PUBLISHING HOUSE
New Delhi-110002

First Published-1999

ISBN 81-7141-452-4

© Author

Published by:
DISCOVERY PUBLISHING HOUSE
4831/24, Ansari Road, Prahlad Street,
Daryaganj, New Delhi-110 002 (*INDIA*)
Phone: 3279245
Fax: 91-11-3253475

Printed at:
Arora Offset Press,
Delhi-110092.

PREFACE

The need of having a sports series felt because today's situation of the world is not conducive to peace, all round there is destruction, despair, conflict and war; war if not between two nations then within the country itself. In a world where there are some 820 million people unemployed or under-employed, and where 86 million people are born every year, it is not surprising that one out of every four individuals lives in absolute poverty. The *Discovery Publishing House* by Publishing this series seeks to get positive response as—to means by which sports can promote and propagate peace and international cooperation. Sportsmen form a large identifiable cadre. We visualises a situation where a conscious efforts is made all over the world to train the sportspersons to spread the message of peace and international cooperation. Instead of peace keeping efforts through arms and army, the sportspersons may be used as soldiers of peace in a subtle manner. The effort is to make the realize the contribution of sports as a factor for sustainable development, peace keeping and international cooperation.

In developing countries, sports development cooperation is still in the need of justification and steadfast arguments. Many people ask the question "why invest in sports in developing countries for which water supply, health service and agriculture projects are much better suited? An apt reply to this question may be "for many of the people of a developing country,

Preface

Sports is the only 'Sweaty' Leisure-time activity. Sports represents a moment of joy in the midst of hard poverty-stricken and dirty everyday life. Doing sports even makes one's work go more smoothly the next day.

This series will be useful to the sports promoters, organisers, coaches and other persons related or interested in sports.

Editor

CONTENTS

Preface

1.	Fundamentals of Skiing	1
2.	Principles of Skiing	15
3.	Teaching Technique	66
4.	The Drills and Exercises	110
5.	The Tools	162
6.	Skiing the Steeps	187
7.	The Counter Turn	217
8.	Powder Skiing	229
9.	Recreational Skiing	245
10.	Ski Touring	295

1
■ FUNDAMENTALS OF SKIING ■

Skiing is one of the many sports that tempts you to figure out approximately how it's done, so that you can go out and do it. You're apt to progress more rapidly and painlessly toward consistent skiing performance, however, if you take the time required to learn fundamentals at your own pace. This book assume from the beginning that you already ski and have a love for the sport, and that you want to learn the basics not of how to ski, but of how to becomes a high performance skier. That is what this book is all about. The basics of high performance skiing are a blend of your technical skiing skills, the physical attitude with which you ski, and the powers of your mind. The three-part concept of the fundamentals of high performance can be stated briefly.

1. *Technical skills*: this includes being balanced over your skis with independent legs/skis; having a muscularly relaxed stance; being versatile in the use of different kinds of turns and the linking of these turns; having edge control in varied conditions; controlling speed (acceleration and deceleration); using poles appropriately; moving efficiently; being versatile in using the whole length of the ski as well as the inside and outside edges; and relying on *ski feel*.

2. *Physical attitude*: This includes being reactional; at times feeling fearless and aggressive as you really work your skis; at times, feeling very loose and light on your skis with very few inappropriate movements or contractions in your muscles and little pressure on your skis as they actually ride of glide atop the snow, at times; feeling playful and adventurous.

3. *Mental powers*: This includes first, confident followed by a sense of pride and accomplishment; goal setting and determination; self-acceptance and inner-direction; desire to learn; acceptance of personal growth; control over the fear of failures; and kindness to oneself and others.

Next, you'll be skiing the steeps and jumping off cornices; and in subsequent chapters we'll take you skiing in moguls, powder, the race course, crud, slush, and more.

High performance skiers ski at all levels and in all conditions. You needn't be an Olympic racer or expert skier to ski at a high level of performance. Rather you have only to Purdue high performance in all levels of skiing be it your 5th or 5000th time through the race course mogul field groomed run trees or wherever. Unless you have sense of there being fundamentals to every step towards higher levels of performance you may be disappointed with your lack of progress even though you're trying hard to improve.

Regardless to whether you're an intermediate, advanced-intermediate, expert, or super expert skier, there's always that hill, mountain, or mogul run that presents trouble or difficulty for you. If you *perceive* *difficulty* with a slope or condition, you will *experience* difficulty; you reinforce the difficulty with the power of your mind.

One of the best ways to find out if you are really advancing to high performance skiing is to test skills and confidence by returning to those slopes or conditions that intimidated you the last time out. In the meantime, ask yourself these five questions about your skiing.

1. Are you relaxed mentally and physically?
2. Do you feel confident with your turns?
3. Are you able to make subtle adjustments of speed with-out making erratic moves?
4. Do you keep your attention focused downhill, skiing the fall line without hesitation?
5. Experience the feeling of effortless control as you move your skis in a pendulum-type fashion, reaching out side to side beneath you, moving your weight from ski to ski while skiing an efficient line down the mountain?

If you answered "yes" to all of the above you're a high performance skier! To those of you who answered "no" or "sometime" to at least some of these questions the information this book should help you to work on your skiing so that you can eventually answer "yes" to all of the above.

What you might find amusing, or embarrassing, is how teachers and coaches can read the level of your performance simply by watching certain aspects of your skiing. In a conversation with Christian Cooper, she gave her impressions of the high performance skiers coming down the mountain. "They're really solid on their skis, and dynamic. They work from ski to ski while playing with the terrain and remaining relaxed. Their basic position," show emphasized, "is balanced over the middle of their skis. This provides the control without the risk of their skis. This provides the control without the risk of their skis getting away from them." As she concluded, " You can tell when skiers have a lot of miles behind their skiing, and when these miles have included a lot of disciplined training doing the basic."

Curious about this point, we asked Mike Iman if he thought there was an observable difference between a high performance skier and a less passionate skier. He answered, "Simply, the high performance skier's last turn in a series is as relaxed and smooth as his or her make a series of turns. All you have to do is sit and watch skiers make a series of turns. This alone will tell you a great deal about their skiing ability."

What enables the high performance skier to remain relaxed until the last turn or the last gate in a race course?

The answer is confidence, built on experience in a variety of conditions. When skiers get enough exposure to, for example, powder, the steeps the bumps or racing they naturally develop confidence in these areas. As they develop confidence, skiers acquire versatility and a dynamic attitude about skiing. They are better able to relax or to ski aggressively according to the demands of the conditions and those placed on the development that each skier goes through at his or her own pace. Thinking like a high performance skier early in your skiing will get you to ski with more purpose and dedication. With this sense of purpose you can progress rapidly to the point where the changes in your skiing are subtle and small. It is at this point in your skiing when the real perfection of certain skills takes place; the refinement of your skiing in varied and difficult snow conditions. Through this development you become reactional in your skiing, no longer needing to think about what you're doing.

Reactional Skiing

Is there really a great need to take the thought out of your skiing and just go with the flow of the terrain, that is, ski reactionally? For high performance skiing, yes. Of course you always put some thought into your skiing; the curse of too much thought in your skiing is to become overfocused on one aspect, to the extent that you forget about other aspects and end up fighting with balance. You may find yourself bracing against the environment as opposed to flowing with it, when what you really want to be doing is the latter. When you start down any hill you want to feel as though the terrain is doing much of the work for you, the skis are doing the work they're designed to do, and you're enjoying the ride.

Ultimately, through drills, exercise, and time on skis, you want to get to the point of skiing very reactionally; that is, making a very quick read of the terrain. You look at it and see that it's crusty, cruddy, icy, bumpy, or poorly lit. Instead of panicking, you are reactional: Your knowledge of appropriate skills is combined with your sense of how you want to ski this condition. You react and respond to the condition. The result: The skis work for you, and energy expenditure is minimal; you can actually feel the skis do more of the work; and the conditions help your skis to perform at a high level.

Skiing reactionally never involves being in a static position. You flow with the changes in terrain, and your upper body is quite and very still while your legs do the work. As you keep your upper body relaxed and headed down the fall line, your lower body moves by reacting to the cues it receives from the terrain and the messages it receives from your brain. The brain is instantaneously interpreting the sensory information it's receiving from your hands, face, ears, inner ears, eyes, and feet. When you ski reactionally, you are efficient and ready to attack any situation for which you have the skills to ski.

Being ready to attack any situation sounds exciting, but are all skiers ready for this?

May be not at first, but they can be with the right mind-set and technical skills. Assuming the skills are there, it's self-confidence that allows skiers to be relaxed and aggressive in any situation. They're confident when they start down the hill, and often have a mental picture of how they are going to ski the hill. This image is so vivid, skiers can almost feel the run before they physically ski it. Skills development leads to their knowing they can do with their skis what they imagine in their minds. Confidence, perception, and imagery allow skiers to be aggressive, knowing that they can adjust to any changes in conditions. This mind-set allows skiers to stay in balance while in motion, a critical prerequisite to versatile skiing.

Ski Feel

High performance skiers have keen ski-snow sensitivity: *ski feel*. They have the skills to respond to their perception of how to ski a particular run and feel relaxed doing it. Swimmers who are not relaxed look like tanks going across the water. Runners who are not relaxed have no stride or length in their movements. Look at skiers who are not relaxed in the race course; they can't function. All of these athletes are performing their sport statically.

What does Mike have to say about this concept of ski feel?

Ski feel is a concept like balance, which is instinctual to individual who are athletic, but which can also be developed by others who approach skiing more socially than athletically. Athletic skiers are naturally light on their feet and regularly engage in a host of recreational sports. Ski feel can be developed in a sense, through any sport that has to do with angles of balance and the sensitivity of pressure from any outside force, which can be either gravity or the resistance of water, ice, ground, or snow.

A good example of this is running. When runners land on the balls of their feet, they roll their feet forward. The last thing to leave the surface of the terrain is the runner's sensation (feel) rather than the shoe. Through the shoes, the feet and toes identify the terrain and send messages to the brain.

These skiers have more fully developed ski feel and a high degree of *ski-snow awareness*. From years of skiing and thinking about the sport, these skiers instinctively know when to put pressure or when to eliminate putting pressure on their skis, and when to angle their ankles, knees, hips, or shoulders to create or relax the edging of their skis. Their sense of the snow comes in part from their naturally acquired degree of ski feel, time spent experiencing the different sensitivities and pressures of their skis on variable snow surfaces, and time spent manipulating their skis on these surfaces.

Former U.S. Ski Team member and downhill medalist Pete Patterson says you learn to ski by feel and stay balanced over your skis by skiing in the worst of conditions. "Sometimes," he goes on to say, "you can get too involved with the technical aspects of skiing and forget the most important thing is to make sure you get out regularly and have fun. When you have fun, you relax and enjoy yourself-you're much more into the feeling of skiing, and you don't make it hard on yourself by being too tense. You can concentrate on having fun by skiing efficiently, but not so technically that you get blown away with the preciseness of it all. Just enjoy skiing, and you'll develop the feel for it."

Overall, when you think about ski feel think sensory: *sight*, the look of the snow and conditions; sound, the sound of your skis against the snow reveals much about the conditions and your mastery of skiing skills, tough, the tactile messages you receive through the tips of your skis/ poles from your feet/hands to your brain, and, of course, *sense of balance*, recognizing that the more relaxed and confidently you ski, the more your balance helps to naturally correct your ill-chosen reactions to unexpected snow conditions or poorly executed moves. The result is that you fall less often after making clumsy maneuvers. Ski feel: Work on it!

Is there a way to get the mind and body to work together on the acquisition of skills that build the confidence required for ski feel and reactional skiing?

Goal setting is not a bad way to set your sight on greater skills acquisition, but skiers goals must be complemented by a willingness to go through the process of skill development are patience and fitness. If skiers are patient, their learning process can take its natural course; if skiers are fit, and if they are in skier tone (Cardiovascular fitness along with strength and flexibility training,) they will have the stamina to persevere with practice. Given these factors, it is easy to develop a healthy mental attitude to complement your physical willingness. You can't have one with out the other.

This is like a balance in effort. If skiers ski with an aggressive mental attitude, yet lack physical readiness, they may find frustration. Mental desire and output overwhelm the capabilities of the physical body. If, on the other hand, they are physically strong enough, yet haven't the attitude to push themselves and work toward goals, they will similarly be frustrated with their progress. The best approach is to blend their mental evolutionary development of their skiing skills through experience and exposure.

Types of Skiers
Make is found of saying that there are essentially three types of recreational skiers with respect to their use of muscles, skills, and skeletal bracing. What does he mean by this?

The three types of recreational skiers are the inefficient skier, the efficient but tricky skier *and the* disciplined athletic skier. They expend too much energy, too much of the time. The ill-result is often muscle soreness, strains or more serious joint and bone injuries.

The second type of skier is at midpoint in skills acquisition, mental perspective, and physical attitude. For the most part, these skiers ski technically well and, with their naturally developed muscles, ski with a blend of muscular control and skeletal bracing along with a collection of technically sneaky tricks. They have an inborn ability to stay in balance and their movement pattern seem very precise. They look very smooth, yet do not really espouse high performance skills.

The third type is the *disciplined athletic skier* who knows how to ski highly proficiently. This skier, is technically sound, physically fit, aggressive, confident, and committed to skiing and off-season training. This is the essence of the high performance skier!

Skeletal Bracing

Skeletal bracing is what many children use when first start skiing. If you watch children skiing a wedge or snowplow position, they seem to be hinged back, their legs straight and bodies bent at the waist: They are braced. Instructors, parents, and friends encourage the children to bend their ankles and knees. Due to their immature muscular development, children need to use structural rather than muscular strength. When the children stand and brace against the skis and hold that position, they are using their skeletal structure. This means that they have their legs straight forming a natural bracing against the skis and the snow. One of the things that happens with adults is that they stop using skeletal bracing. Skeletal bracing is one skill that, when used properly, allows for most efficient skiing. Skiers who don't occasionally rely on this tax their muscle strength unnecessarily. If these skiers stood up, kept themselves tall, and used angles from their shoulders to their hips, knees, and ankles, they would ski more efficiently. You can create angles throughout the skeletal structure. By using these angles you're not using as much support to hold any one position, or more properly, any series of positions.

Blocks to Becoming a High Performance Skier

What might keep a good skier from ever becoming a high performance skier? How can this be addressed to recreational skiers?

What keeps any skier from becoming a high performance skier is tentativeness and the avoidance of new skiing experiences. A very good recreational skier who can ski most conditions may become stagnant. This particular skier may choose to ski powder only when it's very light and four to five inches deep; or choose only small, developing moguls, only when the lighting is good and there is no real hard pack or ice. This skier prefers the familiar, new situations are often dismissed as too difficult. Because new challenges are avoided, skiers like this keep themselves from the opportunity to express greater skiing potential. It's important to challenge the things that hold you back. Ski the runs that trouble you; ski them the best you can.

Overall, it may seem like you're doing more things awkwardly and inefficiently than properly. If you keep trying those new runs as many times as you ski the familiar ones, eventually those new runs will becomes your forte; if you continue to add different runs, conditions and situations to your skiing, you'll break out of your tentativeness. If you avoid the challenges, you're likely to stay in a skiing rut that keeps you from becoming a high performance skier.

Another problem that good recreational skiers have is the low average number of days they are able to go skiing in a season. Infrequent skiing can lead to hesitation and ambivalence; there's little room for either in high performance skiing.

Many skiers measure their performance in terms of the carved turn. Isn't the perfectly carved turn really a myth?

There is no such thing as a perfectly carved turn, except in reference to a turn with a very long radius. It would take you can entire run to make that single turn. There are, however, relatively perfect, carved turns in which there's a subtle, continuous, and patient steering of the inside ski, and a patient foot guiding of the turning (outside) ski into its edge until a certain point when it's time to get off of edge to minimize skidding, and get onto the other ski.

We teach skiers to make *skidded turns* because these help beginner and intermediate skiers control their speed and turn. In a skidded turn, the skier emphasizers rotary, rapid steering first, then pressures the downhill or outside ski, and finally uses the edges of the skis to control movement or speed. As skiers advance to higher levels of skiing we want them to largely abort the dynamics of a skidded turn, and embrace the dynamics of a carved turn. In the carved

turn, and finally rotary motion or ski steering (constant steering with both inside and outside skis) to finish the turn.

Fig. 1: Steer or guide the inside ski into your new turn to increase the carving of your outside or turning ski

When you examine the phenomenon of the carved turn in Figure 1, you realize the inside (uphill) ski has to be constantly moving away from the turning ski to effect a truly carved turn. There are many levels of carved turning you can create with inside-ski steering:

- You can accomplish beginning carving with your downhill ski/by lightening the inside ski, relaxing the pressure of your leg/foot/boot, and letting the ski glide stop the snow rather than through it.

- You can accomplish more advanced carving with your down-hill ski by steering the lightened inside ski away from the turning ski, directing the knee of this inside leg uphill.

- You can accomplish extreme carving with your downhill ski by diverging the inside ski away from the turning ski, radically pushing off of your downhill and directing or stepping the inside ski diagonally uphill.

Certainly, whether or not your turns are carved and to what degree, says a lot about your level of performance.

2
PRINCIPLES OF SKIING

The majority of skiers use only the Basic Technique and more up within that category. The steps of the ladder of skills (called *final, or demonstration, forms*) are based on seven principles.

Natural positions. The relationship of the anatomy to balance on skis. Under normal conditions the skeleton, rather than the leg muscles, carries the body weight. The skier should maintain a relaxed stance.

Total motion. This is intended to imply that muscle action is a product of the entire body. Body motion should be continuous throughout the maneuver.

Unweighting. The reduction or elimination of the skier's weight on the snow. This can result from traditional up-unweighting or from down-unweighting.

Axial motion. Motion about the body's axis. This includes both rotation and counter-rotation.

Edge control. The adjusting of the angle between the ski's running surface and the snow.

Weight transfer. The movement of the body weight toward one ski.

Leverage. The effect produced in ski turns by a skier's moving his weight forward of back in relation to the centers of the skis. This principle applies primarily are advanced levels of skiing.

Before you venture onto the slopes for the first time, we suggest that you spend a few moments familiarising yourself with your skis and poles. Put them on and take them off a few times indoors or on your lawn. In this way, you will find it easier to practice and get the feel of the basic positions without slipping around on the snow.

To carry your skis, place them bottom to bottom. With the tails pointing away from you, hold the tips with one hand, and with the other hand swing the middles and the tails over in an arc to rest on the nearer shoulder. The hand that was at the middle of the skis movers to the front. Now the other hand is free to lift your poles to the other shoulder under the skis.

When you are ready to go skiing, it is important to get the skis accustomed to the outside temperature. Many skiers take their skis out of warm cars, heated lodges, or rental shops, and lay them directly on the snow. The result is that the snow, contacting the warm skis, melts into water or moisture which then freezes again to ice on the running surfaces of the skis. This condensation and freezing process will occur even if your skis are lacquered and waxed. Then you will have the hard task of scraping ice from the bottoms of the skis. Beginners, especially, are never aware of this condition, and it makes their first try on skis almost impossible. The skis will not move, since the ice under the ski acts as a brake. To remedy this condition it is not necessary to bury your skis in the snow overnight. If you stand the skis up against an outside ski rack or wall for at least 16 minutes before putting them on in the morning, you will condition the running surfaces of the skis to the outside temperature and keep them from icing up. Also be sure to remove snow and ice from boot bottom. An ordinary plastic ice scraper, the type given away at most gasoline filling stations, becomes a very handy item to carry in your parka pocket for this purpose. The scraper is also very handy when the snow conditions change rapidly, causing unwaxed ski bottoms to ice up. One swipe of the blade is usually all it takes to clean them.

Hold your ski poles correctly. Place your poles in the snow, a bit in front of and to the sides of your boots. Open the straps so that they lie smoothly, without any kinks in the leather. Usually, the rough side of the strap will face toward your hand. You will note that, at the point at which the strap joins the pole, one end of the strap usually overlaps the other. Always keep the overlapping strap to the outside as you face your poles. In this way, you can tell which poles. In this way, you can tell which pole fits your left hand and which the right. Using them in this manner will prevent chafing and give and a comfortable grip. Walking and gliding. Walking on skis involves a step somewhat shorter than the one used in normal walking. There is also a pronounced shift of weight, from the ski to be moved forward the ski remaining in place. This weight shift momentarily "sets" the ski, enabling you to push off on your step. Also make use of your poles. The pole and arm opposite the forward-moving leg move forward as the leg is moved forward and the pole planted in the snow. This enables you to pull against the pole in the first of the stride and to brace against it when you bring the other leg forward. Practice following an imaginary straight line and walk relaxed. Practice on flat or almost flat terrain. When walking up a slight incline, you can prevent backslip by more bracing against the pole and by slightly edging your skis. By "edging" we mean the controlling of the sideward slippage of the skis by setting the skis at an angle to the snow so that they "bite" the surface.

A more vigorous form of walking is gliding. Each gliding step is preceded by your going into a slight crouch. As you take your forward step, you rise out of your crouch and propel yourself forward and upward, using the pole as an aid. The skis are then allowed to glide for a distance before the next step is taken. Actually, gliding emphasizes swift movement and introduces up-unweighting. The body is propelled forward and at the same time up-unweighted by the springing action of the propelling leg and by a simultaneous sharp stroke of the opposite pole.

Step around. Skiing in the modern sense means turning. An the simplest way to turn around or change direction from a stationary position is to step around. You should practice this first on level ground where there is no danger of your skis slipping away from you in either direction. Starting with your skis parallel, place all your weight on one ski. Lift the tip of the other ski and, using the tail of the ski as a pivot, swing the tip a foot or two to the side. Then place it back on the snow, shift your weight to it, and bring the other ski parallel again, lifting the tip and pivoting on the tail. Keep your poles in the snow for balance and move them only when necessary. Note that the tails always remain on the snow and that the movement of your skis resembles the motion of the hands of a clock. If the snow is soft, you will leave a pattern resembling a large fan.

Another variation of this turn is to move the tails of your skis and pivot around the ski tips. You will find that you will able to use this turn on gentle grades, opening the tips if you are facing uphill and opening the tails if facing downhill. By edging your skis inward and using your poles for support, you will be able to turn without slipping. The important aspect of practicing the steparound turn is the weight shift. In order to move a ski, weight must be removed from it and transferred to the other ski. This is an almost automatic reaction, but it must be emphasized in skiing. In the step-around there should be a conscious transfer of weight to the stationary ski before the other ski is moved.

The kick turn. The kick turn is another method of turning around from a stationary position. It is usually taught only after a skier has gained more experience, since it requires a close coordination of skis and body and a conditioning of the skier's muscles and sense of balance. However, on steeper slopes, it is often the only practical method of changing direction from a stationary position. For the sake of keeping the climbing turns together, we will consider it here. Again, this turn should be practiced first on the level where you can stand firmly without slipping. Stand with your skis planted solidly on the snow. Place both poles in the snow, one near your ski tip, the other near the tail, on the outside of the same ski. Now put all your weight on that ski and kick the other one forward—up into the air so that it is perpendicular to the snow surface. Place the tail into the snow near the tip of the weighted ski and, using the tail as a pivot, let the ski swing around to the outside until it faces in the opposite direction, parallel to the weighted ski. Now shift your weight to this ski, pick up the other one and bring it around too, parallel to the one you moved first. You will have to pick up your pole too as you complete the maneuver. If all goes well, you will be facing in the opposite direction, ready to traverse. A word of caution, though—be sure that each ski is securely placed directly across the hill before you weight it completely. Otherwise, you will find it sliding out from under you as it is weighted.

The secret of completing the kick turn from the ski's vertical position is to follow the moving ski tip with your shoulders. As soon as your ski rests in the snow you can easily transfer your weight of it and finish the turn by lifting the other ski around. Timidity and lack of vigor are the major problems in executing the kick turn. To get the ski on its tail, the leg should be swung up briskly and the rest of the action should follow quickly. Another problem is that skiers often tense leg muscles during the kick turn. This makes it impossible to complete the turn easily. So, in order to relax, make sure of your balance by doing this: Kick the ski up to the vertical position, then bring it back to the starting position. If you can do this well in balance, then you will have no trouble with the turn. If you find the exercise uncomfortable, then check the position of your poles and the point at which you rested the tail (close to the first ski is correct). Try it again, several times, until you find you can do it easily. Then do the kick turn from start to finish.

The climbing steps. In the early days of skiing, before the advent of ski lifts, climbing was a necessity. To day, it seems impossible for the modern skier to visualize himself climbing to the top of a mountain two or three times a day just for the trips down. However, the satisfaction gained was well worth the labor, although it probably deterred quite a few people from taking up the sport. But even with modern lifts, a little climbing is not only necessary but advisable, especially for the beginner. It is still one of the best ways we know to warm up the skiing muscles and condition the body to the demands of the sport.

Begin by walking up the hill, using your poles for support, just as you would when walking on the level. As the hill gradually becomes steeper, you may have to keep your poles more to the rear to support you from behind. When the slope becomes too steep for this, you must resort to one of the following climbing methods:

1. *The Sidestep.* Stand with your skis across the hill so that they will not slip either forward or backward. Place your poles in the snow, well to each side, and then step sideways up the hill. Put your weight on the downhill ski, edging it slightly into the hill if necessary to prevent slipping. Lift the entire uphill ski off the snow and place it up the slope a bit. Then shift your weight to the uphill ski, edging again if necessary, and bring the downhill ski up to it. Now move your poles back into position again and repeat the entire process. If you find that you are slipping sideways down the hill, edge your skis a bit more. By "edging," as was previously stated, we mean placing the skis on their uphill corners so that the steel edges on the bottoms of

your skis will bite into the snow and give you a grip. This is most easily done by pushing your knees sideways toward the hill. The more you edge, the more you will grip. Do not try to edge too much by rolling your ankles into the hill. Most ski boots are purposely constructed to prevent lateral movement of the ankles for better support when the skis are edged. If the slope is very steep, the skier can support himself with his poles. However, care should be taken not to rely on the poles to the point where they substitute for positive weight shift. The weight-shift rule applies in sidestepping particularly. There must be no weight on the ski to be moved.

A frequent error in sidestepping is to be ambitious. Too large steps result in an awkward position; this makes sidestepping more tiring that it already is and may lead to a all.

2. *The Traverse Sidestep.* The traverse sidestep is the most practical method of climbing. It differs from the sidestep in that you climb not only sideways but forward as well, moving your skis up and forward whenever you lift them off the snow. You climb, therefore, in a zigzag manner, "tacking" first in one direction, then in the other as the edge of the slope is reached. This means that you must also turn around on the hill as you complete each "traverse" and switch to the other direction. Until you have perfected your kick turns, you can change direction by stepping around, using both poles set firmly in the snow behind you for support and to prevent slipping. Normally the kick turn is used in this method to link your traverses on steep slopes.

A frequent error in this approach to climbing is to

move the ski up the hill too much for comfortable walking. The uphill motion of the ski is usually less then in the straight uphill sidestep. If the slope is very steep it may be necessary to make several traverses before the destination is reached.

3. *The Herringbone.* Another climbing method is the herringbone, which is quicker than sidestepping but quite tiring, especially on steeper slopes. Face straight up the hill and spread your ski tips into a wide V position, making sure that your skis are on their inside edges to prevent slipping backward. Keep your poles behind you and to the sides so that they can give you necessary support. It helps to slip your palms up onto the tops of your pole grips instead of grasping them in the usual manner. Maintaining the V position, lift one ski and step it forward and outward, far enough to clear the tail of the other ski, and set it down firmly on its inside edge. Shift your weight to it and repeat the process with the other ski. The steeper the hill, the wider your V must be. Be sure that the tails of your skis clear each other as you lift them alternately up the hill, creating the herringbone pattern for which this maneuver is named. As in most skiing motions, keep your knees flexed and try not to let them stiffen. You may wish to alternate side-stepping with the herringbone, since the latter is tiring. It is best to learn the other climbing steps first until your skiing muscles develop.

Straight running. Straight running means sliding downhill without turning. Though it is the simplest form of skiing, it can become difficult at high speeds on rough terrain. It is the first thing a beginner should try after walking and climbing but, of course, only on the slightest hill. That is, straight running should be practiced on a very gentle slope with a level runout at the bottom so that you can come to a natural stop without falling or turning. Learn the proper downhill position thoroughly because it is basic to all subsequent maneuvers that you will perform. It is important that you learn to stand on your skis properly now in an easy, relaxed manner. It is always easier to learn to do something correctly from the beginning than to have to unlearn a bad habit later on.

Straight running should be done with your feet fairly close together and the skis parallel to each other. Keep your knees and ankles bent forward enough to absorb irregularities in the snow. Bend slightly at the waist, but be careful not to overdo it or you will have difficulty maintaining balance and control. Keep your weight equally distributed on both feet, and try to keep your feet and skis fairly close together.

Keep your poles off the snow with your hands slightly forward of your body and the rings trailing to the rear. Let your arms hang naturally with the forearms help in "ready" position, almost parallel to the snow surface. In this way, your poles are out of the way but still available should you wish to touch them to the snow for balance. One thing you should be sure to avoid is trying to stop yourself with the poles. This is a common mistake which can be dangerous.

Keep your body relaxed and flex your knees as you descend so that they absorb the shocks going over bumps and hollows. Keep your head up—look where you are going, not down at your feet or ski tips. The faster you move, the farther ahead you should look so that you are prepared for any terrain changes that you might encounter. To help overcome the tension that most beginners feel, start to slow down at the bottom of the slope. Most people are literally "scared stiff" their first time on skis. Any movement to prevent freezing in one position in helpful. If you feel tense, try flexing your knees as you descend.

Another good exercise to familiarize yourself with your skis and to develop your balance while running is to ski alternately on one foot and the other, getting used to the reaction of your skis as weight is applied or released. Or occasionally try reaching down with both hands and touching the sides of your boots. These are good tricks for improving balance and promoting relaxation. You should be skiing only on gentle slopes at this time, but when you graduate to steeper hills you must always keep your body perpendicular to the slope, not "plumb" as you would when walking down a flight of stairs. Proper indoctrination now, concentrating on balance, relaxation of tension, and proper flexing of the knees and ankles, will help you to achieve a natural and correct position. In other words, the sole major principle of straight running is one of Natural Positions. The skier is in a comfortable, balanced, relaxed stance over the skis.

The snowplow (Wedge). The snowplow (or "wedge" as it is called today), while mainly a beginner's tool, is often used by even expert skiers because it is the only way to slow down on skis without changing directions. However, it should be considered more than basic elements of edge control, which are so vital to advanced skiing.

In the straight snowplow position, the tips of your skis should be close together, while the tails are separated and held at equal angles from the fall line. (The fall line is an imaginary line marking the shortest route down a slope). Weight is even on both skis, and the skis are on their inside edges. Your ankles, knees, and hips are slightly flexed; arms, head, and eyes are the same as in straight running.

Practice the snowplow position on level ground. Then, when you have the feel of it, climb up the slope and step around into the downhill running position, placing both poles solidly in front of you to arrest your forward motion until you are ready to move. Slide both heels out into a wide, inverted V position, keeping the ski tips together. Edge both skis slightly inward. The push off with your poles. Concentrate on maintaining an even plow with both skis at the same angle, weight equally distributed on both feet. Keep the tips together and push your heels outward to maintain the wide V. Bend your knees more than is straight running. The universal mistake is to stand too straight. Your skis should be on their inside edges because they will not slow down if they remain flat on the snow, but be careful not to edge too much or your skis will cross in front. Govern the amount of edging by the position of your knees. To edge more, move the knees toward each other; to flatten your skis, move the knees apart. Avoid extreme bowlegged or knock-kneed positions.

Stay loose and try not to freeze up. You can maintain an even speed down the hill, controlling your skis by the width of the plow and the amount of edging. To stop, increase the bend in your knees slightly and release the edges. Practice this until you can control your speed and your ability to stop at will on a gentle slope. But remember that the slowing action from a snowplow does not come immediately and it will take a few yards for the braking action to take effect. So anticipate your speed to slow down.

Basic problems with the snowplow

Problems	Causes	Cures
Too fast, cannot slow down of stop	Insufficient edging	Press knees forward and in; roll ankles in.
	Insufficient snowplow	Increase angle of snowplow.
Skis wander or cross	Unequal edging	Press knees forward and in equally; roll ankles in equally.
	Unequal weighting	Center weight squarely over each ski with equal knee bend.
Skis separate, cannot maintain snowplow	Improper weighting, sitting, back, stiff knees, or standing up	Center weight equally over each ski, bend knees, and press forward and in. Push heels out; keep tips together.
Inside edges catch	Overedging or knock-kneed position	Roll ankles out; press knees forward.
Outside edges catch	Insufficient edging or bow-legged position	Press knees forward and in; roll ankles in.
	Loose boots	Tighten boots, or inquire at ski shop about need for new boots.

Cannot control edges	Stiff knees	Bounce to loosen up. Press knees forward and in.
	Loose boots	Tighten boots, or inquire at ski shop about need for new boots.
Cannot hold direction	Unequal weighting	Center weight equally oven each ski with equal knee equal knee bend.
	Rotation of upper body	Keep hips and shoulders facing in direction of snowplow.
	Unequal edging	Press knees forward and in equally; roll ankles in equally.
Forward fall	Extreme bending at waist	Straighten upper body; press knees forward.
	Extreme forward lean	Keep weight on balls of feet.
	Loose bindings	Have bindings adjusted by ski shop.

The basic beginner's fall is first. While traveling slowly across a gentle slope covered with soft-packed snow, prepare for the fall by holding the ski poles about parallel to the snow, with the points away from your body. This position of the poles is important and basic to all controlled falls. It ensures that you will neither stab yourself nor catch a pole in the snow which could cause a wrenched shoulder. As you move your poles to the safe position, begin to sit back, as if you were going to sit on a low chair. As you sit back, twist your hips and shoulders so that your upper body will face downhill. Your hands should remain about the same distance from the snow at all times. There is a good reason for this. You should avoid all uncontrolled movements of the arms, since a jerky arm movement will throw you off balance. Your hips should be just a few inches away from the snow and well to the uphill side of the skis. Now, prepare to land.

As you sit all the way down, lean back. At the moment of impact lie flat on the snow keeping your head from receiving a possible hard knock. Slam your forearms against the snow just as your back is about to hit. Such a slam takes up any undo stress which your back might receive. This basic beginner's fall is painless and easy. Therefore, it is ideal for learning some of the characteristics common to all falls. For example, after a few preliminary warm-up falls, never let your muscles go limp. Your must not overrelax, nor should you cause your muscles to stiffen. To fall safely, your muscles must be in good tone; they must be supple and relaxed. Gymnasts use the phrase "stay pulled together with your muscles ready for immediate action. This takes practice.

Another common rule for a safe tumble is this: Keep your eyes open when you fall. You will always have better balance and react faster is you can see. When you "know where you are" (to borrow another phrase of the gymnasts), you can usually make the right movements to come back right side up. Perhaps you have read of the psychological experiment in which a cat is dropped upside down from a few feet above ground and always manages to land feet first. Yet, when the cat is blindfolded and again dropped, it is as helpless as a bird in a blizzard. So it is important always to keep your eyes open when you fall. Actually, there is a good deal of truth in the statement that if you do not fall, you will not get hurt. But it is also just as true that if you do not fall, you are not learning a hard fact of skiing. It is one thing not to fall because you are a great skier, but it is quite another thing if you never all because you avoid all challenges. You will never become a really good skier, or good at anything for that matter, if you constantly avoid challenges. To become a good skier, accept challenges, and as you gain confidence and skill in overcoming them, you will become an expert. You may lose your footing along the way, but you will pack up many tricks to regain your balance before a fall actually occurs. Let us look at a few of these.

Suppose you catch an uphill edge and it looks as if you are going to fall into the hill. There are at least two things that you can do to prevent a tumble. If you have control of your arms, you can quickly stab your uphill pole into the snow to prop yourself back to a balance position. Or you can make a quick, forceful push-off from the leg on which you are standing. Then, while your skis are free of the snow, you can swing your legs back under your hips to land in a balanced stance.

If you caught a downhill edge, you could use a ski pole, outrigger fashion, to prop yourself back up. Or, you could quickly push off form your standing leg, swing your skis and feet under you, and land in a good, balanced position. The next time you are on the slopes, try there exercises. You will be well rewarded for your efforts in terms of new confidence.

The trickiest of all falls to cope with are those in which you cross your skis in front, dig a tip, or somehow get your skis caught on a twig or rock. These clobbers pitch you forward and happen so fast that you have seldom much chance to try to regain balance.

When you feel you are about to be thrown forward in an ungraceful dive, the safest thing to do is to go with the momentum of the fall. Do not fight it. When you get thrown violently forward into the eggbeater type of tumble, just strive to keep your legs together and your skis parallel. Try to attain a compact, pulled-together feeling. With a little practice, you will soon become an expert at recovering from a forward fall. And once you completely lose your fear of falling, you will find skiing any slope easier and much more fun.

Getting up from a fall sometime required a little special technique. It you find that you can rise from a fall without difficulty, they perhaps this paragraph is not necessary for you. If you do have trouble, try this method: First, arrange your skis so that they are parallel to each other on your downhill side, pointing directly across the slope so that they will not slide away when you put your weight on them. Now, draw your legs up underneath your hips and, if the snow is well packed, push up from the uphill side with your hand. Edge your skis into the hill to prevent slipping. If the snow is soft, lay your poles on the snow and push from them. When the snow is really soft and deep, leave the poles on your wrists and place the downhill pole across your chest with the basket in the snow on your uphill side. Place your uphill hand over the basket and push down, at the same time pulling up on the pole with your other hand. It also helps to throw your knees downhill to help support your weight. Beginners often make the mistake of trying to rise with their skis on the uphill side or in a position where they can slide forward or backward. It is much easier to spend a few seconds more and make proper preparations.

When you fall, try to get up as soon as possible so that you will not endanger yourself or others coming down the slope. Do not lie motionless any longer than is necessary. Others may think you need assistance and summon the ski patrol on a false alarm.

After a fall when your ski has come off, it is sometimes difficult to get the ski back on. It may be that you are on a steep slope, or that the snow is boiler-plate hard. In either case it is easier to put on an uphill ski than a downhill ski, so, if it is possible to do so, turn yourself so that foot that lost the ski is uphill. Then start putting on the ski. From this position, if the ski should start to slide sideways, you can stop it. Jam your poles is the snow to act as an obstacle. Once you are in position to replace the ski, put your mittens on the snow under your loose ski. Then the ski will stay in one place while you are scraping the snow off your boot sole (this should always be done) and putting the boot back into the binding. It is always a good idea to stamp the newly refastened ski on the snow a couple of times to make sure your heel and toe fastenings are well seated on the boot. Then press the leg forward; this is a final test of the security of the binding. Lastly, do not tear off in a hurry as if to make up for lost time. The fall may have been a warning you are getting tired. Make one or two nice rounded school turns in perfect control before you decide to open up again.

The snowplow turn is a devoutly-to-be-wished-for consummation of the first day on skis, because it means that not only downhill speed but downhill direction can be controlled by the skier, enabling him to negotiate trails and slopes rather than shooting down them in an uncontrolled fashion.

Snowplow turn. From a snowplow position, all you need do to turn is to place your body weight over whichever is to be the outside ski of the turn. Very shortly you will find yourself turning in a broad arc. The important thing is to wait for the turn to occur; do not try to force it. To place your weight properly over the ski, pull back the shoulder slightly on that side and lower it toward the heel of the foot, at the same time bending the same side knee a little more to keep the ski on edge and fully assure the weight transfer. To return to the fall line after you have turned enough, simply return your body to its normal snowplow position directly between the skis. With both skis equally weighted, you will find that you drift naturally into the fall line again. As long as you wish to turn away from the fall line, keep your weight over the outside ski—and do not lean forward at the waist.

If you wish to turn left, lean over the right ski, accentuating the bend in the right knee. Turn right by leaning left and bending the left knee. Do not lose the correct plow position while turning. Keep your ski tips even and close together, the tails wide apart.

Hold your poles in a ready position, as in downhill running, but be careful that you do not rotate your arms or shoulders in the direction of the turn. In fact, do just the opposite; keep the outside shoulder slightly back during the turn. This is a good habit to acquire early in your skiing, since it is important in the advanced turns that you will learn later. Right now, however, the important thing is to get all your weight over one ski at a time. It is also important that you edge the ski that you are weighting. If it remains flat on the snow, you will slide without turning. Edge the ski by moving the weighted knee inward until the ski bites into the snow and holds.

Snowplow turns can be linked very easily by placing your weight alternately over one ski, then the other. It is necessary, however, to move through the normal snowplow stance en route if the maneuver is to be carried out smoothly. This will permit you to drift gently toward the fall line for the start of each new turn. Do not hold yourself in the straight snowplow—simply pass through it with a gently up-and-straighten motion of the shoulders. The whole motion should be slow and rhythmic, first to one side, then the other.

Remember to concentrate on putting nearly all your weight on one ski when you turn. The instinct of self-preservation is strong and it usually works against you in skiing. Your normal reaction will be to lean into the hill. If you obey this impulse, it is quite likely that you will fall without turning. Therefore, you must concentrate on leaning out—away from the hill. We think your ability to learn quickly is based largely on how well you can overcome your natural instincts.

It is neither necessary nor advisable to master snowplow turns before going ahead with the traverse, the next basic position that must be learned. As you advance and acquire more proficiency, it will proved beneficial to your skiing technique to go back and perfect your snowplow turns. In fact, practicing them is still one of the best cures we know for those who continually place too much weight on their uphill ski. For the beginner, the snowplow and snowplow turns offer a quick method of learning to control speed, change direction, and come to a stop at slow speeds. There are better and easier ways of skiing at higher speeds on steeper. They should be learned now without delay.

The principles of natural positions and edge control apply in the same manner as in the snowplow. Weight transfer is also present as the turning force. With total motion the entire body is involved, and all movements are smooth and uninterrupted.

Traversing. In skiing, the work "traverse" means to ski across the hill. This is always done with the skis parallel to each other, much the same as in straight running. Now, however, the skis are not equally weighted. The lower ski should carry most of the weight. The uphill ski should lead the lower ski by about 4 inches (or approximately half the length of your boot). There are fundamentals that must be kept in mind, for a violation of these rules will literally start you off on the wrong foot.

The knees and skis should stay fairly close together as in straight running. With the uphill ski advanced and unweighted, and with skis close together, the possibility of crossing them is remote, since the upturned tip of the downhill ski acts as a barrier. The lower knee will necessarily be slightly behind the upper one. Knees should be flexed, but do not bend them too much. You will need some reserve for use in turning and absorbing bumps.

If the snow is hard packed, you will have to edge both skis into the hill to prevent them from slipping sideways. To do this, press the knees tightly together and into the hill. This will make your skis act as unit, rather than as two separate skis, with an equal amount of edging on each ski. This is what you should strive for. It is the correct approach to modern ski technique. Move only the *knees* toward the hill. Keep your weight out over the lower ski by facing the upper body slightly downhill with a slight bend at the waist. A common mistake is to lean the entire body into the hill instead of just the knees. This only puts weight on your uphill ski and results in loss of control of the skis. You must get your weight out over the downhill ski by leaning the body downhill in opposition on your knees. This will also automatically place your shoulders and hips at a slight angle toward the downhill side, away from your line of direction, so that the uphill ski, arm, hip, and shoulder will always be leading. This double bend of the body is known as angulation, and it is best achieved by twisting the chest and hips toward the valley. This twisting has the further advantage of pushing the upper ski slightly ahead, the position it must ride in a traverse to prevent the tips from crossing. In all but powder snow, it is necessary to carry most of the weight on the downhill ski, and this is done by increasing the angulation of the upper body. Despite the apparent awkwardness of the stance, it can be adopted in a relaxed manner with practice. Think of a corkscrew in action avoid forward or backward lean, and keep the legs flexed loosely.

Practice the traverse on a wide slope that will allow a long running distance. Be sure to ski in both directions, not only in this but in all maneuvers, since all skiers have a "preferred' side that they constantly favor. Remember to keep your weight rather forward from the ankles. This is true when you are pressing them inward to edge at the same time. If you can, make your track straight and narrow by keeping your feet and knees close together. But the main thing is to feel comfortable, and if this means your feet are slightly apart to create a wider track, so be it. Should your downhill ski start to slide away, tip your upper body laterally downhill and press the knees into the hill.

To prevent the common fault of leaning the whole body into the hill, practice lifting your uphill ski off the snow as you traverse on your downhill ski, or reaching down and touching the calf of your lower leg. Looking at the heel of your downhill boot will help you to find the proper body position too. These exercises will give you the correct feel, but the only real cure is confidence, gained through experience and practice.

Skating. One maneuver for every level of ski ability is skating. (1) It offers inherent value as a way to move and to change direction on skis. (2) It is a fine balance exercise. (3) It is one of the best possible aids in learning weight shifting and the feeling of edge control. In fact, beginning skiers might consider skating a further development of the step turn in which the ski tips are moved around ahead of the tails.

The real secret of learning how to skate on skis is to analyze the way the ski edges work. In slow-motion photography, for instance, you would see that the ski touches the snow first on its outside edge, rolls to a flattened position, and then to its inside edge, from which the skier pushes off. You can begin to learn skating by practicing these simple edge changes on level ground without moving forward. Then gradually combine edge changes with forward motion.

It is at this point that you should analyze the other components of skating. One leg is your power leg, the other your gliding leg, alternation back and forth. Bend the power leg, put all your weight on it, and push off from the inside edged of the ski. At the same time, step the gliding ski forward with the tip pointing outward. Move your arm and shoulder forward as body weight is transferred onto the gliding ski.

If this seems confusing, think of how a fencer lunges forward from his rear foot with his arm and shoulder moving in unison with his forward foot. Once you have made forward progress on flat terrain, you can try skating on *very* gentle slope. Moving downhill, your skating steps need not be as precise as those on flat terrain because the slope provides forward momentum. However, your glide on one ski will have to be longer, requiring more accurate balance. Naturally, at first your balance may be precarious, but a little courage will keep you going.

When you want to stop skating downhill, make several steps to one side. This maneuver introduces "skating into the hill": that is, repeated push-offs from one foot with repeated shifting of your weight—from the downhill ski, which acts like an exploding spring, onto the uphill ski, skis together in an edged traverse, then another push with the downhill ski. As your skill develops, you should be able to skate in one traverse, go down the fall line, skate in a traverse in the opposite direction, and finish skating into the hill. Exercises like these will eliminate any leftover fear of the fall line.

A final skating achievement is to do figure eights, either on level terrain for intermediates or on a fairly steep slope for experts. To do a figure eight on a steep slope without losing altitude, take several short, strong parallel steps uphill at the crossover point before making a tight turn downhill.

A final word of advice: Do not try to reach perfection during your first attempt to skate. But, whenever you find the right terrain, try it again and think consciously about your movements until you are able to do them with ease. You will find skating games add to your confidence and control and to your ski fun.

The skier in the intermediate class is ready for more sophisticated maneuvers. The stem turn, sideslipping, and the uphill Christie will concern us here. The basic form of each is to be learned in order that the logical progression to the more advanced movements of the American Technique may be made.

Stem turn. This maneuver marks a milestone in the skier's progress. It combines the snowplow turn with the traverse, allowing for travel across the trail in a much more rapid manner than with the snowplow turn alone. In the snowplow turn, you are always braking. In the stem turn, you stop braking as you come into the traverse position and glide easily across the slope to the point where the next turn begins. The stem turn is used primarily to link traverses together into a continuous run at slow speeds. It should be practiced on a fairly gentle slope.

Start with a shallow traverse, making sure that your position is correct and that you have complete control of your skis. To make the turn "stem" the uphill ski by pushing its tail into a V position. This will put you accomplish the actual turn. Follow the same procedure you learned in snowplow turns but, as the turn is concluded, bring your inside (uphill) ski back to the parallel position so that you finish the turn in the traverse position facing the opposite direction.

You will find it helpful to bend the knees more during this turn. Then, as you bring your skis together at the conclusion, straighten up a little before settling down again into your traverse. This "up-and-down" motion is extremely important in more advanced skiing and should not be neglected at this stage. This advanced snowplow turn is used to develop correct habit patterns of body position and weight distribution. The two are inseparable and important. Do not fight your way around on skis—let the weight of your body do the work for you. You will make smoother turns, not just in these preliminary stages but in advanced skiing as well.

All skiing pupils make the same mistakes—using protective motions for self-preservation which are contrary to good skiing technique. They forget that people who are not afraid learn to ski quickly. This has nothing to do with natural ability or coordination, for often an otherwise good athlete finds skiing difficult. These people will become good skiers when they gain more confidence. For instance, the basic fear is of falling downhill, so beginners automatically lean back and toward the uphill side. The next false move is to edge the skis in an attempt to stop. Done while trying a stem turn, this results in either a fall toward the hill or a clumsy stop with the skis crossed in front. If this happens frequently, practice skating steps on the nearflat, using both poles simultaneously. The skating makes you shift weight, and the poling gives support and tends to bring your weight forwards. Using the combination of poling and lifting your skis, you develop relaxation, a better knowledge of edging, and a neat way of uncrossing skis and correcting other mistakes. In the stem turn, all the basic principles involved in the traverse and the snowplow turn also apply here, in exactly the same manner.

The sideslip. The sideslip is the transition from a steered or stemmed turn to the fine feeling of sliding or slipped turn. Learning the sideslip is to unlearn the hard bite of the edging that the good traverse position requires. Sideslip edging is relaxed. The ski must slip sideways down the hill. Sideslipping is also a useful maneuver, since it often affords the easiest descent over a given spot. The skier who spends some time getting his ankle muscles accustomed to the feeling of letting go has made the best possible investment in his future on skis.

The sideslip and the traverse are almost identical. The body and ski positions are the same in both. The difference between the two maneuvers is that the skis slip sideways down the hill in the sideslip, whereas they slide only forward in the traverse. The amount of sideslip is controlled by the edges of the skis and determined by the steepness of the hill and the condition of the snow surface. There are three kinds of sideslips: the vertical slip, the foreward slip, and the backward slip. The vertical slip is a complete broadside skidding of the skis down the hill. The other two are similar but include a simultaneous forward or backward slip with the sideslip. All three are performed with skis parallel and together, the upper body in the traverse position. They should be practiced on a fairly steep slope and on well-packed snow.

Start the sideslip from the traverse position. Although there are several ways to initiate the slip, many skiers prefer to use an up motion, creating a momentary unweighting of the skis by the rising movement from the knees. During the unweighting, the skis will start to slip sideways, provided they are not edged. Sideslipping always feels insecure at first, and it is only natural to edge the skis for security. However, you must learn to keep them flat on the snow during the slip. Keep your knees and feet as close together as you can so that both skis work as a unit. Control the edges of your skis by moving your knees either toward the hill to apply the edges or away from the hill to release them. The flatter the skis lied on the snow, the easier they will slip. To slow the slip down or to stop the slip, simply apply your edges by pressing the knees into the hill. Be careful, however, that you do not flatten your skis so much that your outside (downhill) edges catch the snow and cause you to fall.

Be sure to keep your knees bent at all times, just as you would in a traverse. Try to stand more on the lower ski than on the upper one, and keep your weight evenly distributed over your foot, neither completely on your toes nor on your heels. You will find that nothing remains static in a sideslip and that you will have to make minor adjustments in your weight distribution constantly. A little more weight forward will cause the skis to slip forward and down in a forward slip. Shifting your weight slightly to the rear will cause a backward slip in a similar manner. Both maneuvers have definite usefulness in skiing, but you should also know how to control them when you desire to do a vertical sideslip. You will also find yourself varying your edging as the slope and snow surface change, and you might even find it desirable to shift a little weight to the other foot occasionally as you slip down the hill. As in the traverse, you will find it easier to slip in one direction than in the other. Do not neglect your weak side; all the more reason to practice it. Spend more time perfecting your sideslip than on any of the other exercises you have learned to this point. It is not as easy to do, but it is of more value in learning the advanced maneuvers.

Practice sideslipping only on a hard-packed surface on a relatively steep hill. Start it from a traverse, by making the skis flat on the snow. This is best done by a slight straightening of the knees in what is called an "up motion." Do not set the skis too flat, or you may catch an outside edged and fall. Good fitting boots will promote correct sideslipping. The inevitable mistake is to allow the downhill ski to advance ahead of the upper one. It does not work, because the skis may cross and you will stand on the uphill ski. Instinct will tell you to do this because it seems the safest thing to do. It is not.

The following suggestions may help: Though the uphill ski should properly be advanced only about half a boot length, try to keep it a foot ahead. This way it will not cross the lower one and it will make you stand more on the lower one. You can correct this exaggeration later. Facing the whole body more downhill, and looking downhill, will help too. An occasional push with the upper pole can be useful in starting a skid, but do not lean on the pole. Once you can sideslip consistently, try stopping quickly by edging the skis. You must be skidding nearly broadside to the hill, or you will continue forward. Move both knees toward the hill to edge, but remain dominantly on the lower ski, withe your weight mostly on your heel. A good skier will plant his downhill pole at the same moment he edges his skis. Later you will notice that edging (or checking, as it may be called) with simultaneous planting of the downhill pole is standard procedure.

For the first time the principle of Unweighting is present when the skier unweights his skis with an up motion. The skier may also release edge pressure by a simple down motion, which will unweight the skis for a split second.

The Uphill Christie. This is the very first taste of "Christie skiing." The uphill Christie is actually an application of the forward sideslip and is a parallel turn executed from a slip and is a parallel turn executed from a traverse which brings you up into the hill instead of around and down the hill. When completed, your skis will face somewhat up the hill, which will bring you to a stop. It is generally used for stopping and as a training exercise for more advanced skiing, since it is actually the last part of both the stem and parallel Christies. It can be performed from various angles of traverse, from across the fall line or from down the fall line. When used from a steep traverse down the fall line, it is often referred to as a "Christie into the hill!" or "Christie off the fall line." The execution is the same in all cases.

Start with a traverse, rise into a sideslip, then, on sinking again, thrust the heels downward and outward. Power rather than speed is what you need. Just sink, slowly but purposefully, holding your chest slightly facing downhill and pushing down on your heels as though you were grinding a pair of cigarette butts into the ground. Be careful, however, not to let the hips move outward from the hill. Although they will rotate slightly in the direction of the turn, the hips, together with the knees, must always be held farther into the hill than the upper body. Otherwise, your weight will go onto the uphill ski and your control will be lost immediately.

There is some delicate coordination involved here that takes a considerable amount of practice. Most people forget to maintain their traverse position and almost invariably allow the uphill ski to lag behind the lower one. This puts their weight on the uphill ski, resulting in crossing the skis or falling in a spread-eagle position. Remember to keep your knees and feet as close together as possible, preferably with the lower knee actually touching the side of the upper knee. This will keep the uphill ski ahead, where it should be at all times. Never allow it to lag behind the lower ski. Remember, too, to keep your upper body in the proper traverse position: downhill hip, shoulder, and arm held slightly back so that you are facing slightly down the hill. Maintain this position throughout the maneuver. The only change or movement necessary is in the knees and ankles. And make doubly sure that almost your entire weight remains on the lower ski throughout the turn.

At this point, begin using your ski poles as aids in making the turn. This should be done without effecting any change in body position. When turning left, touch the left pole lightly top the snow just before the up motion. Do just the opposite in a turn to the right.

Remember, left turn—left pole; right turn—right pole. If you use a pole when you when you turn, do not lean on it. Merely touch it lightly to the snow to act as a sort of pivot around which to turn.

If you are making an uphill turn to your right, you would start it by touching the right pole, but would stop by facing to your left and planting the left pole. Usually, people who are right-handed have more difficulty with the left turn than do left-handed people. So be sure, when practicing a left turn, that you are weighting the right ski and keeping the left one forward, with the upper body facing toward the right, or downhill, side. In other words, do not neglect practicing turns to you weak side. You cannot ski by turning in one direction. To do so would require either a lot of kick turns to reach the bottom or a hill built like an ice cream cone. Learn your uphill Christies in both directions and vary the steepness of your traverse until you can even do them off the fall line. Once you can make good uphill Christies to a complete stop under full control, you have conquered many of the problems in your progress to advanced skiing.

In the uphill Christie, Natural Positions, Total Motion, Edge control, and Unweighting principles all apply. Axial Motion now comes into play in the form of slight counterrotation, which displaces the skis and starts he turn. The Leverage principle will often be involved in the execution of an uphill Christies as the skier moves his weight forward over the edged, carving ski to encourage the turn and control its arc.

The Stem Christie is a combination of the stem and the pure Christie.

The stem is actually similar to the advanced snowplow turn. The basic difference is that the stem Christie is a quicker turn, performed at higher speeds, in which the V or stem configuration (tips together, tails apart) is abandoned as the skier crosses the fall line of the hill and the skis are then allowed to skid sideways to some extent after they become parallel.

Begin your stem Christie from a traverse. Stem the uphill ski, dropping slightly with your knees and counterswinging your upper body as you did in the stem turn. However, after you have started the turn with a stem, you must bring the inside ski parallel to the outside ski and thrust out with the heels as for an uphill Christie. In order to make the down motion to thrust the heels, it is necessary to come up somewhat at the beginning of the turn. The up motion should be made at the moment you start the stem. To do it properly, you must get the feeling of stepping up from your downhill ski onto the stemmed one. This will also give you valuable experience in the up-unweighting and weight-change method needed for the more advanced turns that you will meet with later. To work yourself easily from stem turn to stem Christie, start out by going into the heel-thrust phase only when the turn is almost complete. When you have mastered the combination of stem and thrust, start the heel thrust a little earlier. Work it in by stages until you can bring your skis together as soon as your weight is over the stemmed one. As you become more and more proficient, reduce the angle of the stem and emphasize more the stepping of the weight from one ski to the other.

It is a good idea to use your poles in this

maneuver. On the first down motion, as you stem the uphill ski touch your downhill pole lightly to the snow about midway between your ski tip and boot. Then, as you transfer the weight and come up again, the pole is removed from the snow. Using your pole does three things for you. First, it gives you more stability during the critical phase of the turn as the weight is shifted, providing a point about which your turn can pivot. Second, it helps coordinate the timing of your unweighting and turning actions. Finally, it helps to keep your weight forward, particularly if the pole is placed will ahead of your feet. Be careful, however, that you do not place the pole too much to the side and that you do not permit it to lag behind your body as you accomplish the turn. Either of these mistakes will upset your timing and throw you off balance.

The most common fault in performing the stem Christie is permitting your weight to get too far back or onto the uphill ski. Your weight, as always, should remain on the downhill ski. After the weight is shifted, the new uphill ski (the inside ski) should be completely unweighted so that you can actually lift it off the snow during the turn. In all your practice exercises, strive to ski with your weight almost entirely on the lower ski.

Without question, stemming can become a habit that is not only unnecessary but a positive drawback to advancement. Yet very few beginners are capable of making a turn across the fall line with parallel skis. The only alternatives to stemming are to jump the skis around or to ski quite fast. For the beginner, the former is almost impossible, the latter is dangerous, so the stem lingers. Actually you should use the stem only long enough to get you "over the hump' into the fall line. Then make your skis parallel as soon as you can. As you become more familiar with the stem Christie, try to reduce the amount of stem you use and your dependency on it.

In the stem Christie, Natural positions and Total Motion basic principles are involved, as before. As the skier accelerates in the turn, he moves his center of gravity forward to keep his balance and to encourage the turn, thus applying Leverage. The skier unweights with an up motion while he applies Weight Transfer, the force that initiates the turn. Edge Control and Leverage determine the radius of the turn and finish it.

The goal is to make sure that the "residual stem" is completely removed, and that the skier's mind does not even think stem, but substitutes unweighting. Instead of stemming, unweighting becomes the key to bringing the skis around. Unweighting reduces friction, or the resistance of the skis to moving in a new direction. The lower body turn is accelerated by an opposite counterturn in the upper body. This "countering" supplies the force with which it is easiest ways of approaching the parallel Christie is by the sideslip garland exercise.

Sideslip garlands. Sideslip garlands derive their name from the track they leave in the snow. These exercises are most helpful in learning how to "set" the edges before a turn. This is an important part of modern ski technique take the place of your stem as you prepare for each turn.

Sideslip garlands are nothing more than a continuous series of traverses and forward slips repeated in sequence; traverse, slip. Start own a traverse, maintaining proper traverse position. With a very slight up motion, unweight the skis, release the edges, and go into a forward slip. Then stop the slip immediately and definitely by sinking down with the knees and edging sharply into the hill. This will "set" the edges (make them bite positively) and place you in the correct traverse position again. Resume your traverse, repeating this sequence as long as the terrain will permit—traverse, up, and slip—down and set the edges—traverse, up, and slip—down and set again.

Once you start in the correct traverse position, do not lose it. Try to make your garlands with rhythm and accuracy, neither too fast nor too slow, always correctly and with precision. Be sure that you get the feel of your edges and that you become accustomed to the amount of pressure you need to set and release them. This is not the easiest thing to do at first, but this exercise is a basic movement which must be learned. The more you practice it, the more natural it will become—and do not forget to practice it in both directions.

The parallel christie. The parallel Christie is the goal of all modern skiers. To be able to perform smooth, controlled turns with precision of all types of terrain in all snow conditions, keeping the skis together—this is what we are striving toward.

The best way to learn to make parallel Christies down the hill is to sneak up on them gradually. So, we start on a well-packed slope of medium grade. Traverse across, stopping with an uphill Christie. Starting again from the same point, make another traverse, and stop again with an uphill Christie—but this time make the traverse a bit steeper. Repeat this several times, making your traverse steeper and steeper, each one closer to the fall line. Soon, you will be starting straight down the hill and turning to a stop. Continue in this manner, making all your turns in the same direction. Eventually, you will traverse across the fall line and have to make a *downhill* turn that crosses back over the fall line again.

The flatter the traverse, the more difficult it will be to make a downhill turn with parallel skis. There are several aids to overcome this: one is to ski faster, another to use your pole, and a third to use plenty of "lift," which is just another word for up motion or unweighting. Since speed will always facilitate turning, ski a bit faster if you have trouble with parallel skiing, but make sure your basic technique is up to it. Using your pole, just as you did in the stem Christie, will help you to stay forward on your skis and will aid your balance. All advanced skiers use their poles in turning, particularly at slow or medium speeds and on steep hills.

To ski faster, you must head down the hill. This automatically puts the tails of the skis behind you, or up the hill. From this position, the fall line, its is quite simple to make a parallel turn, for the tails of the skis will slip off to either side with little effort. Those who hesitate to ski faster will find parallel turns difficult. It they have speed enough to make a parallel turn, they frequently lack the courage to shift the weight sufficiently to the outside ski to make the turn. For such people, rather short skis may help, for there turn in a shorter arc with less effort and this helps to give confidence.

Lift, or unweighting the skis, is of great help in starting turns too. Before you can unweight your skis, you must have a "platform" from which to push off. This acts as a springboard from which to launch the turn. Previous to this, we used the stem position, which offered a good base. But since a stem precludes the making of a parallel Christie, it is necessary to use some other platform from which to start the turn. So, we set the edges instead. This is, of course, done with parallel skis and in accomplished by a down motion (lowering the body and flexing the knees) and then edging the skis into the hill. As you sink with your knees, reach forward and touch the downhill pole to the snow. This is a very brief movement, followed almost immediately by the up motion, springing up off the platform, and a lateral displacement of the tails of the skis. More specifically, if you are making a left turn, drop down and touch the left pole simultaneously, then come up with the knees and push the heels of both skis to the right while unweighted. This will start the turn on its way. You then complete it on the newly weighted, outside ski of the turn.

Setting the edges in this manner prevents the skis from slipping away when you start to come up for the turn. Pushing both skis to the side replaces stemming and allows you to keep both knees and skis close together and parallel. Touching the pole to the snow gives you added stability and timing when most needed.

It is not necessary to lift the skis high off the snow when displacing them to the side after unweighting. Ideally, the skis should be unweighting. Ideally, the skis should be unweighted only enough to permit easy movement. If they are "lifted" completely off the snow, conditions must be unusually rough. The amount of lift required cannot be specifically determined, since it will always vary with your speed, angle of turn, terrain, snow conditions, and even with the flexibility of your skis.

THE PARALLEL FAN

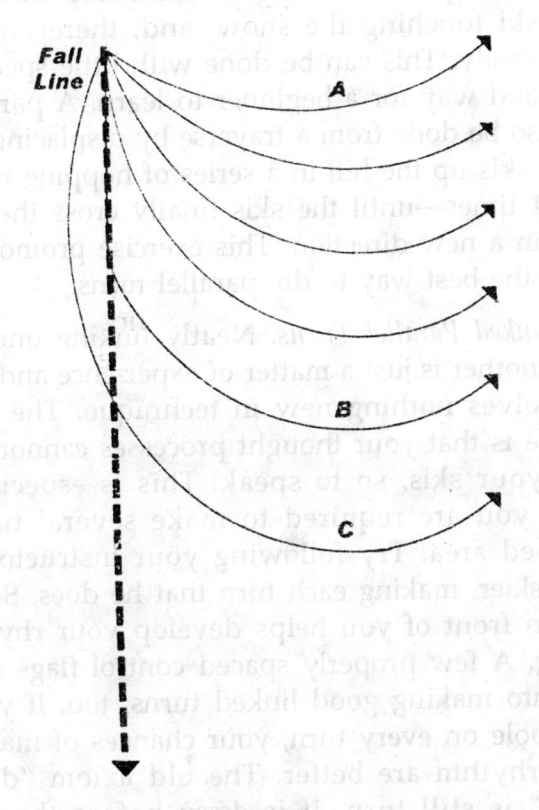

"Parallel fan" exercise develops parallel Christie gradually. It consists of a series of uphill Christies, each performed from a successively steeper traverse until you finally complete a Christie across the fall line. Start from a shallow traverse (A), increasing angle of descent until you make a Christie off the fall line (B). Now increase angle even more and make your parallel Christie across the fall line (C).

Once your skis have started in the turn, place your weight hard over the outside turning ski. This is the key to good skiing, and there is nothing more important, regardless of the technique used. It often works well to remember to draw the downhill hip back throughout the turn.

One easy way to make parallel turns is to turn over a bump. At the crest of the bump there is very little ski touching the snow, and, therefore, the ski turns easily. This can be done with little speed, sop it is a good way for a beginner to learn. A parallel turn can also be done from a traverse by displacing the tails of the skis up the hill in a series of hopping motions— 2, 3, 4 times—until the skis finally cross the hill and head in a new direction. This exercise promotes but it is not the best way to do, parallel turns.

Linked Parallel Turns. Neatly linking one parallel turn another is just a matter of experience and practice. It involves nothing new in technique. The common trouble is that your thought processes cannot keep up with your skis, so to speak. This is especially true when you are required to make several turns in a confined area. Try following your instructor or any good skier, making each turn that he does. Seeing the turn in front of you helps develop your rhythm and timing. A few properly spaced control flags can force you into making good linked turns, too. If you plant your pole on every turn, your chances of maintaining good rhythm are better. The old axiom "down-up-down" is still turn. It is *down* before the turn, *up* during the turn, and *down* at the end of the turn. If you make a long traverse between turns, stand fairly high again so you will have some knee bend left for the next down motion. Do not forget that down motions are done simultaneously with the planting of the lower pole and that your weight is always on the lower leg. The up motion is used when you turn and helps you transfer weight from one leg to the other. Never forget that shifting the weight from the inside ski to outside or turning ski is most important. This is done by angulation-deangulation-angulation. Except when the turn is being initiated, knees are toward the hill and upper body away from the hill.

If you have trouble getting an up motion at the right time, then maybe a little practice with the following hop turns will help.

Hop Turn Exercise. The unweighting of both skis normally is used in making parallel turns. Without stemming.

Be careful that you do not start to hop habitually like a rabbit just because you have learned to do these exercise will. Hopping is merely an exercise and not technique in itself. The good skier moves smoothly on the snow and hops his skis around only when it becomes necessary because of variations in snow conditions or terrain.

Parallel christie with check. On steeper terrain and in difficult snow conditions, the speed of the skis will be such that the skier will experience some difficulty in setting his edges. In these instances, a check prior to the turn is the proper remedy. The parallel Christie with check is the same as a parallel Christie except in its initiation. Instead of using a simple down motion to provide himself with a position from which to unweight, the skier uses a more forceful method. From the traverse, he begins a sideslip as though for an uphill Christie. Then, as the tails of his skis begin to slide out, he drops his body, increases angulation, and plants his pole. This sharp drop sets the edges of the skis very firmly into the snow, giving the skier a strong platform from which to push off vigorously into the unweighting phase of the turn.

By far the most important point to remember in the parallel turn with a check is: Do not try to compensate for the braking effect on the skis during the check by sitting back. The more forward your body is, the more quickly you can move the skis under it. In this parallel Christie maneuver, all seven principles are still involved, with more emphasis on Edge Control during the preparatory part of the turn.

Basic technique: VI

There is no longer a distinction between short swing and wedeln, since the two are so closely related. Actually, they are not really different turns from parallel Christies, but rather refined applications. However, for reasons of tradition and to demonstrate some aspects of edge application, they are treated separately here.

Short swing. The definition of the short swing is: "Consecutive parallel Christies without traverse, using the setting of the edges and pole plant." In essence, it is a series of parallel Christies with check, the heel thrust and finishing edge set of one turn being used as the platform for initiating the next. For the first time, the use of the pole becomes a stated requirement, for it acts as a means of bringing each heel thrust to a sharp end, leading to a quicker setting of the edges than would be possible in linked traverses or long linked parallel Christies. It is, therefore, used mostly for control on steep slopes. The upper body is kept facing down the fall line, the counter-rotation being only sufficient to balance out the twisting of the lower body. In point of fact, there is no sensation of counterrotation but only of a lower body rotation and resulting torsion at the waist. The mass of the upper body is used as a stabilizing factor, and the action is like that of a coil spring held fast at the top but coiling and uncoiling at the bottom.

In its extreme form, short swing leads to an actual hopping of the ski tails from side to side, with the skier's body continuing in a straight line down the slope. In this case, the ski displacement is used purely as a braking mechanism and not as a means of turning. At the other end of the scale, short wing mergers into wedeln.

Wedeln. The American definition here is: "Consecutive parallel Christies without traverse or appreciable setting of the edges." In fact, the main difference between wedeln and short swing is in the edge set. Wedeln is a smooth, snakelike motion in which the skis are kept almost flat on the snow. The tails are brushed from side to side by leg action, the body being kept almost motionless and used as a stabilizing mass for the leg movements. During wedeln, the legs are gently contracted and extended just sufficiently to permit the skis to travel beneath the skier's body in a side-to-side motion. Almost all of this action takes places in the knees and ankles. The upper body always faces down the fall line, and the poles are planted with the minimum amount of hand and arm movement. As a cat stalks its prey, so does a skier execute wedeln, perhaps the most graceful maneuver in skiing.

Wedeln performed in the fall line and is most early done on a medium-grade slope. If the hill is two steep, you will probably lose contract unless you have mastered the maneuver well enough to maintain a firm check throughout your descent. It is most important that your knees remain pressed together tightly so that both skis act as a single unit at all time. Start in the fall line and never turn far away from it. Touch your pole to the snow in each turn, but use no shoulder rotation. The upper body must face squarely down the slope at all times. Only the legs, hips, and skis change direction.

Rhythm and timing are important. You must use an up-and-down motion to unweight your skis, but it is not necessary to jump or hop. Bring your poles straight forward and place them about a foot behind your ski tips. Always do this on the down motion, which will be the end of the turn and the start of the next. Knees are together, flexed at all times, and stemming is taboo. Set the edges of your skis on each down motion, and change the lead of your skis as the weight is shifted on the up motion. Keep your arms and poles forward, close to the body, and do not raise your poles higher than necessary to clear the snow. Never let your hands or poles lag behind the body. Your weight must be mostly on one ski at a time. By sure that you make a definite shift in weight for each turn. This will help your turns to follow one another without a pause or break in rhythm. If necessary, control your speed with a little slip at the end of your turn, then set the edges, plant your pole, and unweight again for the next turn. Your edge control must be precise and subtle, changing on the up motion as you shift your weight and change your lead ski. Be careful not to overedge, or you will catch your outside edge and lose balance.

Wedeln can be done in almost any type of snow condition except breakable crust. Make use of bumps in the surface to aid your turning. Above all, keep your knees and skis together and do not stem. If you find that you are still troubled by a stem that upsets your rhythm and prevents you from doing a sustained wedeln, go back and check your basics: more up-and-down motion, correct edge set and change of edges, proper weight shift and distribution, timing of pole plant, change of lead ski, and sufficient unweighting to permit your tails to sweep around in each turn. Check to be sure you have enough speed to permit a natural flow of these basics without upsetting your rhythm.

Wedeln is difficult to analyze on paper. Even when seen, it is hard to distinguish the many subtle factors that appear to be happening at the same time. We have found these five points to be all-important in developing a good wedeln technique, and we suggest that you keep them in mind constantly:

1. Keep your knees and skis together at all times. Do not stem.
2. Use your pole on every turn.
3. Use unweighting (up-and-down motion).
4. Control your speed ad length of turns with your edges.

5. Keep the upper body facing down the hill at all times. Use no shoulder rotation.

Basic problems with the weldeln and short swing

Problems	Causes	Cures
Cannot link turns	Faulty rhythm	Check coordination of "down, edge, up, slip" sequence and of lead change.
	Insufficient pole action	Check timing of pole plant.
	Too much pole action	Check for too much arm motion, which delays pole plant and upsets rhythm.
	Traversing between turns	Shorten turn. Use quicker edge set at end of turn.
Too much acceleration in turn	Insufficient pole and edge action	Check timing of pole plant; do not let upper body lag. Use stronger edge action.
Faulty rhythm	Faulty pole action	Check for too much pole action.
	Faulty edging	Check timing and sufficiency if edge action
	Faculty unweighting	Check "down-up-down" motion for timing and sufficiency.
	Poor coordination	Check coordination of "down, edge, up, slip" sequence and of lead change.

Principles of Skiing • 61

Cannot check	Faulty rhythm	(See above.)
	Faulty pole or edge action	Check for too much pole action. Check timing and sufficiency of edge action.
	Faulty lead change	Check timing and point of lead change—In the up motion as weight is shifted.
	Sitting back	Press knees forward.
Faulty weight shift	Faulty rhythm	Check coordination of "down, edge, up, slip" sequence and of lead change.
	Faulty body position	Check for overexaggeration and overuse of comma.
	Faulty weight change	Check timing of weight shift—In the up motion as lead is changed. Unweighting follows down motion as the up motion starts.
	Sitting back	Press knees forward.
Cannot keep skis together; stemming	Faulty weight shift	Check timing of weight shift—In the up motion as lead is changed. Unweighting follows down motion as the up motion starts.
	Faulty edging	Check timing and sufficiency of edge action.

	Faulty body position	Check for over-exaggeration and overuse of comma.
	Faulty rhythm	Check coordination of "down, edge, up, slip" sequence and of lead change.
Inside edge catches	Edge change too late	Change edges earlier.
Outside edge catches	Edge change too late	Change edges later. Keep edges flat in turn.
	Faulty weight shift	Check timing of weight shift—in the up motion as lead is changed. Unweighting follows down motion as the up motion starts.
Skis cross	Faulty lead change or edging	Check timing and point of lead change—in the up motion as weight is shifted. Check timing and sufficiency of edge action.
	Sitting back	Move weight forward.
Instability, poor balance	Faulty body position, weight Shift, rhythm, late edge change	(See above.)

When doing the short swing and wedeln, all seven basic principles are employed. There is, however, great emphasis on Total Motion, so that rhythm is maintained. In fact, rhythm, as previously stated, is the key to both the short swing and the wedeln.

Emphasis on ski poles

Through the various steps of learning how to ski, we have made mention of the use of ski poles. Actually ever since man first began to ski, his basic equipment has always included skis and poles. As his knowledge of their use increased through the years, other items were developed that have become essential too. The emergence of various ski techniques necessitated advances in boots and bindings, and as these became modified, the importance of ski poles was often minimized. At one point, some people even advocated skiing without poles. Today, however, as we learn more and more about technique, the emphasis is again on poles. As in the early days of skiing, they are again considered essential. Modern skiing methods demand that the pole be used as an integral part of a skier's technique—not merely as an aid to balance, as they were first conceived, or as a "crutch" for the beginner to lean on as he learns to ski, but as a dependable aid to help him ski with greater ease and more proficiency.

In those early days, a ski pole was a necessary evil. The first skiers used a single pole hewn from a convenient branch or sapling. Long and heavy, its blunted tip was manipulated partially as a brake, partially as steering rudder, partially as a balance rod. Then someone discovered that *two* poles, shorter and lighter, with snow rings attached near the tips, not only aided in pushing forward on level ground, but also helped in climbing and provided more flexibility and balance while in motion.

At techniques made more use of the poles, they gradually evolved to their present size and appearance. First they became shorter, then longer; rings diminished in size; new materials, stronger and lighter, were developed. Today's ski pole represents the product of many decades of experimentation and enlightened knowledge.

In modern technique, pole work is an integral part of the learning process. The beginner first learns to use his poles in walking on skis. Here he learns the proper way to plant his pole into the snow and how to remove it. Only when he learns the proper cooperation of pole and ski action in walking is he ready to move on. Then he learns how to use his poles as an aid to the climbing movements and standing turns. During the snowplow and stem turns and the traverse, the pole is used primarily for balance. But in snowplow Christies and stem Christies, the application of the pole as an aid to turning becomes evident. Used as a point on which to pivot, it helps the skier to shift weight, to develop timing, and to master the all-important sideslipping movements necessary for advanced skiing.

In this stage, too, the skier learns to use his poles in a playful, relaxed. During the plant, the palm is slightly outward. As the skier comes up on his pole and shifts his weight, he brings the palm inward in front of the body. Otherwise, the hand would lay behind the body and pull him off balance.

The intermediate skier soon leans to rely less on his poles and more on weight shift and edge control for smooth execution of turns. But now the poles assume another role. Hop turn exercise, at first using both poles, then each pole alternately, substitute unweighting for the stem as the skier approaches parallel turns. The less stem he uses, the more Christie he gets. Substituting the hop for the stem helps to eliminate the "stem hangover" that plagues many skiers, since it gets the tails of both skis off the snow and across the fall line without dependence on the stem.

In the advanced stages of skiing, the pole becomes a somewhat secondary but nevertheless important factor, since it helps the skier to establish the necessary rhythm and timing required for short-swing turns and wedeln. Used properly, poles add the coordination demanded for smooth, effortless skiing. They also become indispensable in the execution of the various aerial maneuvers that are a part of any advanced skier's repertoire.

3
TEACHING TECHNIQUES

The most widespread and uniform of the new teaching system is the Graduated-length Method in which skiers start on two-and-a-half or three-foot skis, move on to four-footers, five-footers, and finally to their own longer skis all within one week of ski-instruction.

Clif Taylor of Squaw Valley, California, develops and refined the short ski technique in 1960. The following year he wrote his book *Skiing in a Day*, and his program was underway. Skiers found that in Taylor's School the first thing you learn is to slow down by making turns. They learned to make turns the easy way, standing in place, on the flat. There was no hill to contend with until they learned how to swivel the skis, using the modern body movement. With Taylor and his instructors out front showing how, the beginners were soon twisting their little two-and-a-half-foot skis left, and then right, in a rhythm: left-right-left. From there, the novice skier, within an hour of first putting on the skis, actually skied down the hill turning left-right-left in short turns.

In the next days under GLM, skiers abandon their two-and-a-half-footers for rented four-footers and then go on to five foot skis. They may still use the "twist-turn" they learned the first day. In a three-day weekend, they can "graduate" to near-normal length skin and can ski with more control than if they had started out in long skis. Actually, the present-day Graduated-length method is based on swiveling (twisting) the skis, rather than stemming, stepping, or hopping. Most ski school directors say they want their graduates to learn to stem the skis after they finish the week on short skis, and then as a safety measure for handling uneven terrain and difficult situations. The key is that GLM students are not learning from the beginning a stemming movement, which later they will consciously have to unlearn. They have no difficulty learning to stem after a GLM week, however.

There are some who claim a lower accident rate among GLM skiers, but this has not been proved. Certainly there seems to be less proved. Certainly there seems to be less chance for skis to cross if they are shorter and are kept parallel. And people who are not in top physical condition have a chance to develop muscles by working up from smaller, lighter skis to longer, heavier ones.

GLM has had such an impact on ski teaching that certain of its principles have been adapted by professional Ski Instructors of America (PSIA) for the American Teaching Method. ATM and GLM, in fact are the two ski-teaching systems used almost exclusively in the United State today.

ATM also uses a short-to-long ski progression but differs from GLM in using at the outset a gliding-wedge (exceptionally narrow snowplow) turn rather than the pivoted, skis-together turn of GLM. ATM emphasizes "wide track" skiing (skis slightly apart) for stability and, say its proponents, to gain a greater mechanical advantage in during. Skiers are started on skin ranging 130-160 cm, depending on the skier's ability and weight, and are then moved up to skis of longer length (170-190cm) as the student progresses. ATM starts the skier out with medium-long gliding-wedge turns, pivoting skis slowly rather than quickly as in GLM sequential leg rotation, one-two pivoting, is introduced to shorten the turn and open the skier's tips to bring his skis closer to parallel. The final parallel turn continues to emphasize independent leg action.

Some GLM schools claim that whereas GLM starts skiers turning parallel, and since experts skiers also turn their parallel, its easier to go from GLM to expert turns than from ATM's wedge position. Many students of ski theory, however, don't find this arguments convincing.

Despite the fact that the ATM turn doesn't start out with skis parallel, as does GLM, the mechanics of the ATM turn are closer to the mechanics of the expert turn: the skin are more on edge (because of the wide-track stance) and the edge is used more actively in steering the skin than in GLM.

NEW LEARNING APPROACHES

Quite apart from the changes in ski-teaching technique in recent years hate come new "approaches" to ski teaching that focus not so much on skiing skills as on the student's fears, apprehensions, and how he conceives of himself as a skier. Whether called "inner skier", "centered skier" or other such label, they deal with the psychological aspects of learning to ski keying on the skier's ability to not "think" his way through a turn or down the steep but merely to "do", to simply perform ski maneuvers without cerebral interference.

These programs focus on imagery, and the real benefit has been in the manner in which ski technique is today better communicated by the ski instructor. The human body, the ski establishment has come to learn, is a complex organism that is capable of learning ski maneuvers through more that one method. Many more programs that recognize this will undoubtedly appear in the future.

Ski schools

What motivates a skier's desire to learn? It is obvious what brings the beginner to ski dangerous because of lack of knowledge as to where and what to parakeets. It is common on weekends to see a beginner struggling for a couple of hours trying to get down a hill that he got up in ten minutes by chair lift. Such beginners often are misled by a friend or a ski movie, or they are just trying to do what the others skiers seem to be doing. When this happens two dangers arise; first, there is a possibility of injury from falling, and second, the person is discouraged from continuing to ski.

In early days it was necessary for a beginner to rise to the top of a hill to ski down. This gave him a chance to improve his skiing ability and climbing ability improved. Today, win gondolas, a person can carry his skis to the top put them on, and try to ski down.

Because of the obvious hazards, one would tend to mark that ski schools primarily teach beginners. In some areas this is true, but the average student in ski schools is in the advanced stem Christie and parallel classes. One of the reasons for this is that it requires very few lesson to teach the stem Christie levels

One tends to level off for a period of time, showing very title progress. Then there may be a sharp jump to a higher level, followed by a leveling off for a period of time. During the stages of the level period one may have good and bad days. These are caused by snow conditions, visibility, even your temperament for that day.

Again, the role of the instructor helps in shortening the time on these plateaus. Seldom is there a student on a level whom the instructor cannot help to move upward. The advancements tend to get harder and require more time as the skier improves. It is like trying to lower your golf score when you already play in the 80's. As in golf, progress in skiing is faster in the beginning stages. To get into the class of the top 10 or 15 per cent requires time. Sometimes the individual's goal may be too high for his circumstances. Never forget that skiing can and should be enjoyed at all levels. You may have perfection in mind, but more important are safety, stability, and maneuverability-then work on progress.

A typical ski school operation offers both group and private lessons. Group lessons last about two hours and usually begin at 10 A. M. and 2. P.M costs range around $6 for 6 for lesson, although discounts can be obtained by buying ticket books-eight lessons for $36 for example, Learn-to-ski weeks also lower lesson costs through package instruction plans. The size of a group can very according to the number of customers and instructors. Half a dozen pupils is coincided ideal. A dozen is a maximum. Any more create problems in learning. Private lessons are usually priced on the basis of one instructor and one pupil for one hour: $15 and up. Each additional pupil, to the limit of three, may cost $5 more. A private lesson for a half-day can cost $50, a full day $100. Although expensive, private instruction has its values because the teaching is direct and concentrate and a better safeguard against the learning of bad habits. On the other hand, however, the organization ski classes is a reflection of a single psychological fact: that at least seven out of ten of us will learn better in a group than alone. A ski schools class harnesses the competitive spirit of individuals. It permits you to observe others making the same mistakes that you are. This helps both to soothe your ego and to solve your problems because you can and what you are doing wrong, by watching others make the same mistake.

If you want to take a lesson, the ski school desk or the ski school house can easily be located at the ski area. Do not make the mistake of buying an all-day lift ticket before signing up for class. You may not need to use the lift for your lessons, or you may find out that the lift charges are included in the ski lesson. So, go to the ski school desk first.

Do not try to bluff your way into a more advanced class than you belong to. Answer the questions of the ski school honestly. If you do not understand the technical terms, simply say so. The ski school meeting place is usually well marked. Each spot in the meeting place is assigned to a different class.

In busy days, many ski schools have to the several classes under the same letter. The school will then use figures to identify deferent levels within the class. So if you find yourself in B-1, you probably have yet to learn the snowplow. If you are in B-2, you are in the second level of class B, and you very likely know how to make a snowplow turn and have begun how to make a traverse.

On behaviour; make sure you are on time. Nobody is going to wait for you. It is no fun to chase your class over half a mountain. The instructor will make sure that the group stays together on the slope. As long as you are with your teacher, you will not have to wait in the lift line.

To get your money's worth, pay attention to the demonstration and explanation of the instructor. Concentrate, but do not get all tied up in a knot. Free, relaxed moved, nets are more important than sheer muscles power. You will find your teacher patient and understanding: he knows what you are trying to do. You may have heard or red about the so called "natural" way to ski. In the beginning there simply is no "natural way". How can you make a natural movements when you are standing on an incline with the floor going out from under you? As in every other sport, it takes time, practice, and good solid instruction.

The ski instructor also knows the conditions in the area, and he will try to provide you with the best skiing available. You simply cannot struggle against bad snow conditions and still learn much. For the very same reason, you should ski on easy slopes after the lesson is over. While skiing easy slopes, try to work on the maneuvers you learned. Them move on to steeper trails or more difficult snow.

Skiing in class means skiing at slow speeds, under control. The ski instructor will not ask you to attempt exercise that you are not ready for. Since every major maneuver or "final form" can be divided on to parts, and since any known exercise may be used to teach you these parts, ski lessons will be varied.

No two teachers will use exactly the same method. The ski instructor is free to use whichever path to 'technique" he feels is needed, according to the individual student and to the snow conditions. This keeps ski instruction not only for the pupil but also for the instructor. Also remember that different personalities do exist. One instructor may be fine for a pupil, while the pupil's wife would nuts as soon take lessons from another. This is usually no problem. Most ski school directors are quick to recognize this fact. Instructor A "gets through" to pupil B, but not to Mrs.. B. "I do not know what he is saying", she may comment. She should by all means try instructor C.

Because of an association known as the professional ski Instructors of America, a skier can be assured of receiving fairly uniform instruction no matter where he goes in the United States-that is, if he takes his lesions from one of the more than 2,000 instruction who have passed the regional instructor association and are certified.

What does 'certified" mean? It signifies that the instructor is approved or qualified. He has taken an examination and met a high standard of ability. However, it has not always been that way. The movement toward certification took a long time. Before World War II, there were many self styled instructors. Ski instruction in some areas earned a bad reputation. But this changed to a degree when the U.S. Eastern Amateur Association established examination standards for would-be instructors in 1938. After the war, with the U.S. Forest service in the ski business because of their leasing of lands in many areas. USFES encouraged some type of certification procedure. Finally, in the 1950's a Utah instructor named William Lash and several others advocated a high national standard which led to the establishment of the professional ski Instructions of America, Inc, in 1960.

To be certified, a would-be instructor must pass a certification examination in which he must demonstrate his form, run a slalom, and show how to teach a class. There is also a written test in this day-long exam. To take this certification examination, a would-be in-structor must also have an advanced first aid card and have a knowledge of ski history, map reading, race-course setting, and-in some areas-even avalanche control and ski mountaineering. Actually, there are slightly different conditions and exams in the eight divisions across the United States. The reason is quite obvious; you would not expect the same approach to teaching from an Eastern instructor who copes with a 600-foot-long canyon.

How are would-be instructors graded? In one typical region, a student-teacher who wishes to become an associate instructor must have 12 to 15 points out of possible 20. A certified instructor needs from 16 to 20 points. The exam is not easy, and a high percentage of would-be instructors fail each year. In addition, to remain an instructor, he must attend a clinic every two years. Each season, more and more families are flocking to the slopes. Children can be taught to ski and enjoy it as much as adult. Over the past few years, the need to keep children of all ages happily occupied at ski centers has become very acute. Major areas have replied to this demand by installing nurseries for the "wee ones" and children's classes for youngsters aged four and over. These children's classes should not be identified with regular ski school, but though of, rather, as 'play school on skis", where the instructors use his ingenuity and colorful props to capture the imagination of the children. The youngsters respond quickly, following their leader around and thus learning to handle their skis in a playful and enjoyable way.

Skiing has much to offer a child. To be out of doors, playing in the snow, being warm and dry despite the cold, and going faster than he ever thought possible-no amusement park, television, or other game can offer such a thrill. The child's motive is simply it is fun. Take away the fun, an the most determined parent or the best teacher cannot make him learn. He will ski only if he enjoys it. Parents who want their children to ski should put aside dreams of eventual Olympic glory, and if possible, put them in a ski class before they lose patience. (Losing patience seem to be the inevitable result of trying to be both parent and teacher).

The child should away be warm and dry, and on skin he can manage-usually no taller than the child. A good age to start is before he is two, for as soon as a child can walk, he can walk on skis. Faced with snow up to his knees-say five or six inches-he finds that skis are easier than feet. For this reason a child of two or three years hence.

When he is ready for ski school (or parents are running out of patience), he should know how to cope with bathroom problems, or if he does not, one of the parents should watch from a discreet distance, ready to take him. A preschooler's mother who is not sure if her off spring will last should wait, too, Just as she would at nursery school.

Children exposed to bad weather and snow conditions becomes quickly discouraged. Ski lessons, therefore, though intent on keeping to a two-hour schedule, are semitones cut after one hour for a short trip to the restaurant. Hot chocolate or ice cream puts new enthusiasm into children, and the outdoor activities can then be continued for the second hour, unless the children, show signs of weariness. Remember that children are different from adults in their reactions to the ski environment. When a child says he is cold, believe him. A small child's skin area is more than twice as great as an adult's relative to body weight and volume. His heat loss is tremendous. He makes up foe it, partly, by a higher rate of metabolism, but this also means that when he feels tried, he is on the brink of exhaustion. A child cannot warm up by more activity as an adult can. He should go indoors promptly, preferably in front of a fire with something hot to drink, for him. Could registers as pain, sometimes quite intense.

Compared with an adult, a child's arms and legs are proportionately shorter, his center of gravity is lower, and his muscles are thicker relative to the bone structure. He also has better padding, his joints contain more cartilage, and his tendons are more flexible. All this works to advantage when he gets on skis. He has not far to fall, and when he does not long enough or thin enough to get tangled up. Skis of the proper length produces almost no leverage in any direction, and his flexible joints will give, even at extreme angles, with no discomfort. With a class of children, the instructor almost never has to say, "Don't do that, you will hurt yourself. It just would not be true. it takes a freak fall for a whiled even to bruise. In fact, falling is apt to be such a lark that he may have trouble progressing to anything else. For some, the merry thump in the snow is the most delicious part of the lessons. The rare youngster who is afraid of falling can be brought in the line with a ski lesions that resembles a tumbling class in which the instructor falls "accidentally on purpose."

The major cause of anxiety is the ski pole. Not only can poles be used as lances on others and self, they cause most of the black eyes, bruises, and tangles that can result in injury. Children have title use for them except in climbing. it is a good idea to take them away for downhill, lending them for slaloms, underpasses, making fox and geese circles, or race course on the flat. A well coordinated child without poles uses his arms to aid his balance and doesn't think about it.

A child has a different approach to balance anyway because of his proportions. The familiar wide-open stance of five-year-old is something that should not be interfered with too soon. It is probably the only way he can learn to turn.

Some children go up and drown a rope tow hill all day long and never get their feet closer than 18 inches. Awkward as they may look, they are in good shape. All you want to do is to get them turning faster, higher. On a steeper slope, when skiing with some speed, feet will drift closer together naturally. The child may use that weighty tail of his like a kangaroo's-stuck way out behind to steer with. The weight is not really in his fanny. His trunk is weighty and compact. With knees bent in a seat, or legs so straight that they seem to be bent backward, or at any angle in between, he can steer by shifting his rump behind him. You can give him good reason not to by clowning a little, showing him how he looks, and then showing him how he should look.

Although most children come to ski class because they want to, progress rapidly within the limits of age and coordination, and love every minute of it, there are occasional problems. Attitude is important. Some do not really want to be in class. Although they should get as much encouragement and comport as seems to be called for, never insist that they stay. They may go to the bathroom, get warm, and come back. Sometimes they stay close enough to watch and when convinced of the fun they are missing, rejoin the class. On the other hand, some competitive-minded children become discouraged when their friends pass in to higher classes, leaving them behind. Children do reach plateaus in skiing. If nothing much seems to happen for a lessons, parents and teachers can help by taking them to a race, a jump, or anything that will put new spark into their desire to learn. A little boy of seven, who could not seem to give up stemming for parallel Christies found new inspiration when he acquired his very own race card.

Poor equipment probably discourages more children than anything else. No adult can learn to turn in boots two size that will not slide in the first place.

We should not except miracles from children under these conditions, even though it does seem unreasonably hard to find good equipment for children, even in some reputable ski shops.

Let the child experience putting on skis and taking them of at home, and let him walk around indoors or in the yard on skis. This eases the new experience when he first reaches the snow. Give him poles long enough to permit walking without bending at the waist. Now, when he is ready to try his skis on snow, choose a sunny day. Help him get started walking, but do not encourage downhill running until he wishes it himself. And when he is wet and cold, bring him indoors. Do not force instruction on youngsters. They just are not as coordinated as we bigger folk. At these early ages, children learn by seeing and doing, not by being told what to do. Above all, do not force children to enjoy skiing. They will anyway, soon enough.

To get them in the spirits of things, children love chants, songs, and rhymed teases, and willingly help an instructor to invent new ones. Variations on the theme of "slippery side, slippery sides' may forestall the common four-year-old complaint that "my skis are too-o slippery".

You may decided to undertake the early stages of getting your child started on skis. Sliding the skis back and forth in place is a good beginning for the first session. A little push will get them moving down a barely perceptible slope. Soon they are walking on the flat, taking turns being engine and caboose, busily making trains noises. They learn to run by playing fox and geese. In this first lesson, time can always be taken out for digging an important hole, for making 'angles" in the snow, and for throwing snowballs. For downhill running and them snowplows, use a slope of 10 to 15 degrees, about 15 feet long, flat at the top, and with a long, barely concave run out. Very little ones can be caught in your waiting arms the first few times. Older ones are encouraged to bounce in the knees. "Making a jet" mark is then followed by making a series of snowplows.

Climbing is something of a problems side stepping is difficult and unproductive. Her ringboning works a little better for some reason, and some children take to it naturally. others simple have to live with the difficulty of sidestepping. By the end of their first session, children are ready for the long walk to the rope tow. This walk includes long traverse up and down, perhaps a little sideslipping and sidestepping, much waving to the people on the chair lift, and a grew deal of conversation.

During the second lesson, most children of four and older will begin turning, at least a little, strictly by imitation and correction. Some need more help. The instructor who can ski backward while holding a child in the proper position has a strong advantage. Sometimes it is helpful to put the child between your skis and urge him to push his skis against yours as they turn, open, and close. By the second session, they are all sick of sidestepping, eager for the tow, and ready to go up. After you have up ten or more fore-years-old, you will have learned thirty-six ways in which children can get entangled. You will also have learned thirty six ways in which children can get entangled. You will also those who do not wait for help, who delightedly take hold and zoom up the first time. And there are those who must be chest-carried. Your biceps develop alarmingly, but children love it. An early tow ride gives them a goal to shoot for.

When they can take a slalom set with their poles, it is time teach them real sideslipping, preferably on a steep, icy bump. After that there is a great deal of follow-the-leader and free-for-all down the hill.

Children who nuts attend many classes before they can move in to intermediate groups should get a real break from time to time. A hike through the woods looking for tracks and birds can be a tremendous adventure. Watching a junior races will sometimes open junior novice eyes to saucer dimensions. In this respect, activities designed expressly for children can be of great help. Before any such event, class time is spent boning up on the fine points of egg racing or the problems of the obstacle course. For children it is a great deal of fun.

Children of three and older believe in their hearts that they can fly-they have done so in their dreams. On skis they have a good chance to prove it.

Ten positive rules to follow with children

1. Enjoy yourself, your child, and the snow. This is a recreation, remember?
2. Buy good equipment (not necessarily the most expensive).
3. Dress him sensibly, for ease of movement as well as warmth.
4. Show him how. Do not tell him how to ski. Demonstrate it.

5. Listen. You would be advised to believe it when he say he is cold, tired, hungry.

6. Do it yourself. Parents are the best teachers, competence permitting.

7. But quit while you are ahead. Put him in ski school when you lose patience or he loses faith in you.

8. Help him when the falters. You are a parent, not a drill sergeant.

9. Let him take a chance. Most of us are woefully short on opportunities to dare, to take a calculated risk, and to fall on our own face without being tripped. Let him try the hill, the tow, the competition he yearns for.

10. Have fun! That is what skiing is for.

13 WAYS TO TURN YOUR SKIS

Each winter to bring us to a new ski technique, a final solution of how, given mastery of the parallel Christie, to turn a pair of skis. Each new technique is hailed as a revolution; old techniques are cast to the dust bin. In the 1950's, skiers were told to discard rotation in favor of reverse-shoulder action. In the 1960's, we were told to discard reverse shoulder for anticipation in which the upper torso is turned in the direction of the turn, almost like old-fashioned rotation. For years we were told to get our weight forward. Then we were told to absorb and flex *avalement*.

Where does the truth lie? Does a skier need to keep changing his technique? Are the old turns obsolete? The answer are both "yes" and "no". Yes, a good skier should learn techniques like *avalement* because, quite obviously, they will make him a better skier and enable him to take advantage of the vast improvements in the new boots and skis. No, the old turns are not obsolete: some are essential to learning how to ski; others are especially useful for certain kinds of show and terrain conditions

Watch a top World Cup racer go down a slalom course and you'll see him employ a whole repertoire of turns: step turns, reverse shoulder, anticipation jet turns with *availablement*. He's not making conscious effort to vary his turns—step here, jet there. Rather he has gone to school. He is making optimum use of all the techniques that have been developed to change direction. And so should you.

On this and the following pages, we show 13 ways to turn your skis. Each, based on maneuvers described earlier in this chapter has its use depending on the snow, terrain speed, and your ability. A good skier will master them all.

Whether its snowplow stem or schwupps, this turn remains a cornerstone on which most beginning skiers build technique even GLM skiers do it on shorter skis. The skier puts his weight on the turning ski and uses it to steer his way in a new direction.

The reasons are twofold. First, it is essentially a turn enables the skier to put a tight control on his speed at all times. For the beginner speed equals fear and insecurity. Thus by controlling speed in the steered turn, the learner gets rid of psychological factors that impede learning. Second the steered turn can be done without the difficult timing of unweighting and upper-lower body coordination required in more advanced turns. The skier simply applied his weight to the curved side of the ski and effects a change of direction.

Here, you see the skier doing a wide-track stem Christie in which the outside ski steers the turn and the skis are brought together parallel after the change of direction has been started.

Stop turn

The most director way to change direction on skis is simply to step the skis, a little at a time. Here, the skier is moving at a slow speed down the hill. To turn across the hill, he steps his inside ski then brings the other one alongside. The step is repeated to increase the change of direction.

This kind of turn is so common is usage that it often seems ignored. It can be used to avoid obstacles and other skiers on the hill and to change direction quickly in slalom. It is one of the most common turns in cross country skiing, and it helps many skiers turn in deep, cement-like snow. Stepping is also the normal way to change your direction in a stationary position. For a classic use, watch a skier using it to move ahead stealthily in the liftline.

The simple step, above all is important for developing balance and ambidexterity with both feet.

Rotation

This turn is the mother of them all. Even though it was first seen back in the 1930's, it has lost none of its beauty in the 42 years it's been around.

Here, rotation is executed with a nonclassic down motion to initiate the turn. The essence of the turn is to use a rotational movement of the upper torso to power the change of direction. This power of rotation is transmitted to the legs by a blocking action of the hips. Actually, it's a contraction of the abdominal muscles that acts as a clutch, transferring the upper body's rotation to the legs.

Here the skier feels the rotation of the upper body, led by hand and shoulder, lock to his stomach muscles and act on his legs and feet all the way through the turn. The tricks is to avoid overrotation without block-age, thereby using up the rotary power when the turn is only half complete.

Rotation is still a practical turn for all kinds of deep snow. But best of all, when executed by a good skier, it is an elegant, fluid turn and imparts a wonderful feeling to the whole body. What a relief from those choppy little turns down the fall line.

Reverse or Counterrotation

This is a wonderful theoretical turn with some interesting practical applications built on the third law of the eighteenth century physicist Sir Issac Newton. The law states that for every action there is an equal or opposite reaction. Applied to the reverse-rotation ski turn, it works in this from the skier goes up to unweight his skis from the snow. He rotates his legs and skis downhill to make his change of direction. This rotary action is made possible by an opposing reaction of the shoulders which move the other way.

This kind of turn became popular in the 1950's, a time when ski instruction experts used the analogy of a man standing on a piano stool: if he rotates his feet in one direction his shoulders rotate the other way and vice versa. The reverse-shoulder or counter-rotation theory became the basis for explaining the new Austrian wedeln or "tail-wagging"-a series of short turns down the fall line in which the shoulders are reversed from the direction of the turn. As demonstrated in a pure reverse turn here, the shoulders stay reversed throughout the turn. It gives the skier an extreme comma position with a sharp, biting carve of the skis-somewhat unstable, but interesting to look at and to do.

Because counterrotation turns only work easily where the skis meet little or no resistance to turning from the snow, they are desirable in all kinds of turns that involve extreme up-unweighting or skis in the air. This makes it a good turn for a bouncy, up-and-down flight through the bumps. It's also used for quick-punch turns in slalom, or tight maneuvers, watch a racer making a recovery turn.

In the sequence here, the skier initiates the turn with counterrotation, then completes it with a nice round rotary movement, body square to the skis.

The varied situations in which split-rotation can be used are too numerous to catalogue. Here are a couple of samples. You are rounding out a nice turn across the hill, body square to the skis. Here are a couple of samples. You are rounding out a nice turn across the hill, body square over your skis. All of a sudden you need to make a quick turn to avoid a skier. User quick up-motion, twist the skis under you and reverse your shoulders. Then you round out the turn leisurely, completing it with rotation. Another situation: you're in the middle of a long rotated turn, and suddenly you spot a rock ahead. Quickly, you angular your body, lead with the downhill shoulder, and complete a sharp turn with counterrotation or reverse. Truly, an adaptable turn.

Mambo

Pure playful rhythm, mambo is a series of turns linked together so smoothly it looks like milk pouring from a bottle in slow motion. The challenge of mambo is how well you can defy gravity and get away with it. Here's how it's done.

Start on a relatively gentle slope and gain enough speed to overcome resistance of the snow. From the fall line, the first turn starts with a down and forward motion while the upper body is rotating and leaning slightly in the direction of the first turn. Arms are held shoulder-high and wide for balance. Turn your skis slowly at first, then quickly cross the hill. For a split second, while the skis are turning fine way and the body is initiating a turn the other way, you'll glimpse the classic reverse shoulder position. But it's only a glimpse. Unless you keep moving into the new rotated direction, you'll fall over.

It's simply a continuous twisting and untwisting to a rhythm. Make the rhythm long and you can climb the side of a gully, hang suspended for a moment in reverse gracefully into the finish of the turn back into the gully and up the other side. Make the rhythm short and you can wind through bumps like a snake.

Ruade

Here's a museum piece of a turn that still has its uses. The ruade (literally, "horse kick") was popularized in the late 1940's by the great French technician Emile Allais. Using both poles, the skier stays forward and kicks the tails of the skis in the air from side to side, like a horse kicking his heels, it's good turn to know the next time you find yourself on a steep slope in mashed potatoes ice-crusted snow, or in a narrow uninviting gully that must be skied.

Foot Swivel off a Bump

Here is one of the easiest turns in skiing yet few people stop to practice it. It's used frequently, and almost unawares, by good skiers in mogul fields. But its principal advantage is that it is an ideal way to show beginners and many advanced-intermediate skiers how to learn anticipation thereby putting them on the route to modern ski technique.

An ideal learning turn is one-like the steered or short ski turn-which avoids the need for the skier to overcome a multiplicity of psychological factors and coordinated body movements and allows him to concentrate on just one or two things in the split second a turn occurs. The advantage of a foot swivel off the top of a bump is that it eliminates the immediate need to coordinate unweighting with turning. It puts the tips and tails of the skis in the air and concentrates all of the skier's weight on one pivot point under his feet.

To illustrate this, place a pencil length wise on a tabletop, apply some pressure on it, and note the resistance it creates when you try to turn it. Now take the same pencil and hold it firmly, point down, on the table -top; you can turn it with no effort. This is the equivalent in a ski turn of being atop a bump and getting rid of the snow's resistance to turning.

In this sequence, note the skier's position before he reaches the top of the bump. His head and shoulders are facing downhill anticipating the direction of the turn. There's a lot of coiled energy stored in that body. Why doesn't it cause the skis are on the snow and resist the turning action. But now, in the next figure, the skier is no top of the bump, the tips and tails (although you can't see the latter) are off the snow and the coiled energy through the legs is permitted to twist the skis in the new direction.

And that's anticipation, an integral part of all modern skiing.

The upper body is twisted in the direction of the turn, but the feet-the other end of the wire-resist turning because the skis are solidly planted in the snow by the edge-set. To continue the analogy, release your fingers from the fixed end of the spring wire. It untwists rapidly in the direction in which you had twisted the other end.

You have now illustrated what happens when unweighting releases pressure of the skis on the snow. Their resistance to turning has been alleviated and the feet are permitted to twist in the direction of the turn.

In making the turn, watch for two things. First the way the pole is planted is important. The pole should not be planted by reaching forward but rather by extending the pole laterally down the hill with your hand. Second, you should be able to feel a tendency of the feet to shoot or "jet" forward slightly as the pressure of the skis is released form the snow. As a result, turns of this kind have been christened " jet turns". It is an action skier moves toward the more advanced technique of modern skiing.

Avalement
There's a school of thinking in the sport which says that all skiing is simply a series of controlled changes

of direction down the hill. The operative of word here is "controlled." And the key to control is to keep the skis in contact with the snow. That's what *Avalement* is all about. It is a French word which means "swallowing." The skier swallows up irregularities in the terrain, like bumps, by a folding action of his legs, which act as shock absorbers. In this way, his skis stay in contact with the snow, turns are carved throughout and the upper body travels in the shortest and most efficiency line down the hill.

You see this in the sequence here as the skier executes a turn with anticipation incorporating *avalement* over the top of a bump. As the reaches the bump his legs fold up so that he appears to sit back for an instant. This is the movement of *avalement*. As a result of the leg retraction which swallows up the up-unweighting effect of the bump, the skis are not thrown in the air but remain in contact with the downside of the bump to make the turn.

Racer's Step

The racing step in the functioning turn of giant slalom. Inn this turn the skier's aim is to go directly and on as short a line as possible from one gate to the next. Normally, this does not leave a great deal of room to make a turn. One option is to make an uphill checking turn to get high enough on the gate, but this is a sure way to lose speed. The solution is the step turn which not only gets you up the hill and on a line to make the turn on the outside ski, but the act of pushing off the downhill ski maintains and increases speed.

The sequence here shows how it's done. The skier traverse across the hill, pushes off the downhill ski to accelerate, and steps on the uphill ski. Finally, he puts it on edge and starts the turn. The step turn's value is not limited to racing. For any skier wishing to make a big improvement in his skiing, it's an important turn to learn because it teaches you to "go outside"-that is to get on the outside ski of the turn early and make it carve on the snow.

Banked turn

The most efficient way to ski deep snow is to consider the snow as having the same effect on your skis as water does on a water ski. That is you're dealing with a soft pliable surface that the skis can sink into. A water skier turns by banking. A now skier can do the same in deep snow.

Starting in the fall line, the skier first gathers enough speed to get the skis planning near the surface of the soft snow. The turn is started by simply edging the skis in the direction of the desired turn. As the skis meet the resistance of the snow on the bottoms the skier starts leaning in the turning direction. His weight rests against the bottoms of the skis as the turn progressively increases the resistance of the snow and cause the skis to turn even more sharply.

To start the next turn, the skier releases the pressure of the legs slightly (retracts), causing the resistance against the snow to end momentarily. The knees move laterally to change the edges and simultaneously start leaning or banking with the upper body in the new direction. Banking turns in soft snow is fun, like riding a roller coaster especially at high speed.

Aerial Turn

Most changes of direction on skis involve overcoming

the resistance of the snow to turning. Here's a turn that involves no resistance. Here the skier gets himself airborne off a bump and makes the turn in mid-air, landing on the snow in a new direction. Note how the skier's shoulders are rotated as in anticipation in the direction of the turn before the feet are turned.

The trickiest part of the aerial turn is the landing: it should be delicate and soft, giving you just enough edge bite to hold the turn without catching the snow surface hard and taking a spill. In high-speed skiing through a mogul field, the aerial can be used to avoid which are too difficult to ride out. Aerial turns are excellent for developing body balance. For the pure delight of floating through the air and turning at will the aerial turn is hard to beat.

For one thing most American skiers are quite technique-conscious. They have, whether they realize it or not, considerable concentration on doing things *right*. This is fine. But it can also lead to stiff and unrelaxed skiing. This is where freestyle comes in. The simple introduction of something different, something quite useless in itself something on which nothing depends and which means little if not successful-this is the ideal relaxation.

The skier who tries something even a Reuel (turning with one ski lifted to the side), is likely to find that after a few successful or unsuccessful turns, it does not matter which, he will suddenly start skiing better when the returns to his "standard" turns. This is of course a well-known gambit: one "just for fun" interlude is used in many kinds of teaching particularly in the teaching of physical skills. Something about the complete lack of pressure in attempting a freestyle maneuver-you have never tried it, so do not worry about not making it-is carried over into your next turn.

The is not to say that more specific results cannot be had from freestyle. The very act of attempting to do something a bit out of the ordinary will call forth additional skill at balancing timing, and edge control-the skills which are the "secret" of expert skiers.

The skier could start with something as simple as a mild jump off a bump, or a jump turn of 180 degrees in place or a half tip roll. Or simple skating steps. Beyond that some rhythmical acrobatics like the "Charleston step" or consecutive Reuel Christie turns, are even better for the skier's frame of mind and for his ski skill. Today ski acrobatics also forms part of the equipment of every top racer. Freestyle skiing cultivates balance, agility, and lightning reactions. Anyone who sees international races such as those shown on television will agree that only a truly acrobatic control over skiing technique can give the power to master downhill courses at full speed, to deal with the forest of slalom poles, or to prolong the flight off a ski jump by means of tiny corrections of posture.

In fact, the theory of play as a way of learning is becoming more popular even as related to standard learning routines in ski classes. The attempt is being made, particularly by those interested in the value of freestyle to make the movements of the turns light and playful rather than forceful and rigid. This has been the implication of the wide acceptance of the wedeln turns as a goal of skiers. The wedeln turn in extremely useful in racing and on steep slopes (in the form of "jump wedeln"), but most skiers who wedeln are doing the lazy, light and fun-creating dance down a ballroom slope just for the heck of it. This is perhaps, more than any other facet, the indication that skiers are looking for fun turns just as much as control and direction turns. Freestyle just makes this wide implication into an explicit goal. The whole theory of freestyle is based on the fact that skiers are out to enjoy their own movements on skis as much as enjoying mastering the slope.

Here is how a few of the more popular freestyle maneuvers are accomplished:

Inside Christie. This is a "backward" turn in that the weight is on the inside ski, which is necessary for most freestyle stunts. The inside Christie first will help you to know when your weight is on the inside ski. This means you will be more sensitive to this feeling and be able to eliminate having your weight inside turns. Second the inside Christie will make your "skate up" an effective maneuver. Third, like all freestyle maneuvers, it will improve your balance.

To start the inside Christie, make your first turn from the fall line into the hill. Start down the hill in a straight run on both skis at fair speed; then lift one ski and edge the other. As you edge, lean and turn to the side you are leaning toward. Swing the weightless ski so that it makes a right angle with the turning ski. You will find you have to sit back a bit more in the turn than you usually do. Hold the lean and the edging until you have completed the turn to a stop.

Now, when you have learned the single turn, you connect the inside Christie: Instead of coming to a stop you "change edges," that is forcefully rock your weight to the other ski with a pronounced forward thrust. Make your next inside Christie on this ski. Connected inside Christies are like long skating steps down the hill, an extremely valuable exercise for balance, strength, and for getting you out of a rut.

Knee Wiggles. Acrobatic skiing has many things to teach the average and above-average skier. One of the simplest acrobatic trick maneuvers, the knee wiggle contains a very basic lesson for every skier. In order to get into the proper edging position so the skis will hold when going across the hill, the skier must bend his knees "into the hill". This puts the skis on edge, so they will hold. But many people do not make this "bending-in motion" often enough. They should because it is a fundamental reflex action necessary to stop the skis when they are sideslipping. In order to make the bending-in motion, the knees first have to be bent forward in a "half-kneeling" position. Otherwise, the knees cannot be turned towards the hill at all!

The knee wiggle which builds up this bending-in reflex is done as follows: first traverse slowly across the hill. Push the knees forward (half-kneeling), and push them toward the uphill side or " into the hill." Then, with knees still bent, move them out until they do not bend in toward the hill at all. Repeat this, slowly at first as you ski, and then faster and faster until you have a true knee wiggle. Keep the upper body bent over the lower ski a bit, but keep it as quite as possible. Let the knees do all the moving Lastly, do the knee wiggle on steeper slopes. It will give you "instant edging" when you need it for traversing. Better skiers will use it to carve a nice controlled arc in the last part of a turn.

Javelin Traverse. The all-important traversing position is composed to two bends—first, the bending in of the knee (as in the knee wiggles), and second, the bending in of the hips. Here is an acrobatic trick which will help you develop proper hip bend (or "hips into the hill"). Called a javelin traverse, it consists of picking the uphill ski off the snow and pointing the ski down the hill as if it were a javelin or spear. The perfect comma position when traversing.

To do the javelin traverse, start with a traverse and pick up the upper ski without changing the upper body position. Keep doing this until you can do it comfortably. Then, when you have your balance, pick up the ski and point the tip downhill until it is at right angles to the ski on the snow. The hip is now best properly, and is in the proper "into the hill position. Try to keep the hip in this position as you return the ski to the snow.

For the next move hop the first ski again, and so on. Keep doing this in a very relaxed lazy manner for four or five hops to begin with. To use it as a real strength-builder, work up to ten or fifteen hinge hops. There is an extra great dividend to this hinge hop. The hinging action, whereby the ski tip is pressed into the snow, is the very same action used to "unweight" to take the weight off the skis in a parallel turn. (of course then it is done with both skis at once.) If you already know how to hop and keep the ski tips pressed into the snow, you have a head start on parallel skiing; or if you already ski parallel, you have a good exercise for improving the speed of your unweighting. The hinge hop also teaches you to ride one ski at a time. The best way to get across a small particularly sharp dip or series of ruts is to ride over on one ski. You will have developed the proper reflex for it by training in the hinge hop.

Javelin Turn. You need balance, courage, and most of all proper angulation for a good sharp parallel turn. All these qualities can be built up by a little acrobatic exercise which we call the Javelin turn, but which is really an exaggerated, intentional crossing of the fronts of the skis. There is no other exercise that illustrates so clearly hoe the hip and hip must lead the turn. In the Javelin, or tip-cross turn inside of the body *has* to lead or you will fall.

To practice the Javelin turn, start off as in any parallel turn, and then pick up the inside ski of the turn. As the turn progresses, keep pointing the tip of the lifted ski father and farther to the outside of the turn so that by ski is at right angles to the tracking ski. Make sure to keep the tip of the lifted ski well off the snow.

Two or three javelin turns early in the day will get you set in the correct, powerful "lead with the inside" that is the secret of a really carved parallel turn.

The Sit-back. The thing that every skier has to do to make long successful runs on a mountain (rather than stopping after every two turns) is to build up the thigh and leg muscles so that he can put strain on them without feeling uncomfortable. The sit-back acrobatic trick is the best and quickest way to condition the legs. You can also measure your condition with it. If you are able to get at the way down on the skis and back up you are in excellent shape.

To perform this trick, pick an easy slope, hold the

poles out from your body, bend your knees slightly, and start to sit down slowly. Keep your upper body relaxed and sit back until you feel uncomfortable.

Then come back slowly to the standing position. Try it again. Try to sit back a bit farther. Do this acrobatic trick several times a day and by the end of the season you will be able to sit right down on the skis and come back up. And skiers on the slopes.

The Butterfly turn. The skier must swing the ski up behind in a skating motion. In the final position the ski is cocked with the tip pointing back. The timing of the quick swing from the snow to a position behind and above the skier is crucial.

The Single Ski Christie. In this maneuver, the skier goes down the fall line of a gentle slope. The skier lifts one ski and thrusts it out behind him as far as he can. This straight run can be changed into a Single Ski Christie by leaning to inside while extending the tip of the lifted ski to the outside to maintain balance.

The Crossed Ski Turn: In this maneuver, the ski on the inside of the turn is moved out over the weighted outside ski as the turn progresses. The final right of left turn should be completed with the lifted ski at right angles to the running ski. The upper body stays in a reverse throughout the turn. This exercise puts a skier's flexibility to the final test. If you can make a turn on a single inside ski and on a single outside ski, your flexibility and timing are such that you can go on to the butterfly turn.

Single Swing. The large percentage of skiers who find that their first run is a tough one and that they need two or three runs to get in the groove, ought to consider the single swing as a way of making the early runs count. This is a sure-fire way of getting your important muscles limbered of sharpening your timing sense, and of making you ready to go out and really knock that first run dead.

To do the single swing you start by going straight down an easy slope. Then you lift one ski and swing the ski tip out to the side until it is almost at a right angle to the ski on the snow. In order to do this properly you have to swing your upper body and hands in the opposite direction.

Next, swing the tip in and across the other ski until it points in exactly the opposite direction. At the same time, to balance correctly, the upper body and arms swing in the opposite direction. Do this swing first with one ski, and then with the other. Then start doing it at a higher speed, so that the ski swings in and out like a windshield wiper. Two or three minutes of this and you are ready, relaxed, and willing for that first run.

Reuel Christie. If you are able to "skate" on skis and to maintain your balance well while on one ski, you also can do a Reuel-one-legged-Christie. First, be sure to pick the right terrain-a concave surface (a shallow gully is perfect) with a gentle slope. Skate off in either direction at a fairly slow and comfortable speed, pushing off with the outside ski and then shifting *all* your weight to the inside ski. Do not ski too fast. Now try rotating your body in the direction of the turn. The first few times you try the turn, lift only the tip of the outside ski and let the tail ride on the snow for balance. Later, as you get the feel of the turn, you will find it more comfortable to bend your body sharply forward at the waist. The outside ski then can be lifted high above the snow. However, the general position of the ski will remain the same-the tip must be higher than the tail.

The best way to learn edge control for a Reuel Christies is to practice uphill christies on one ski. Using the right ski practice turning to the right and vice versa. From a traverse, lean your upper body slightly uphill in the direction of the turn, pressing your knee downhill to release the ski's edge in a forward sideslip. Use your leg muscles and foot to steer ski uphill. To improve your balance spread your arms wide to either side. When you gain confidence, increase the steepness of your traverses.

Naturally, linking Reuel Christies is much harder to accomplish. When you have completed one turn, you will find it helpful to plant one pole, or both poles, in the snow as you go into the next turn. Using the poles for balance state off at about a 45-degree angle, trying to shift your weight *forward* into the new turning ski. Again, the same policy holds the tip of the outside ski should be held well above the tail.

The Charleston. The Charleston is a medium-difficult freestyle maneuver, yet it is great and it *looks* hard. In fact, this maneuver will give you a few minutes of good training in rhythm, coordination, and balance to enliven the next dull runout.

Practice first on the flat without moving down the hill. Stand in place, and jump rhythmically from one ski is kicked out to the ride. While the shovel stays on the snow. As soon as you have that rhythm down pat, try doing it while moving down a gentle incline. Shift from one ski to the other, kicking the tails out. Keep the upper body moving straight downhill while the legs dance. There is an almost automatic little turn that occurs, "wedeln on the inside ski," when the Charleston is really done right. You lean uphill a bit on the weighted ski to make the turn come quickly-and it has to come quickly or you lose the rhythm. Next try it on steep slopes. On the steep slopes it is difficult. You will find you have to kick the tail of the ski over the fall line to keep your speed down. But once you have it, you will find your ability to control the edges has increased your enjoyment of each run by 100 per cent.

The Tip Roll. This maneuver is a medium hard freestyle routine which a good skier can master without too much risk if he wants to put in a bit of time at it. It is a great tuner-upper before you start down a hard trail; a couple of tip rolls and you are psychologically ready to tackle anything.

The tip roll should be performed on an almost flat slope. It should be done with very little speed and can be made to either direction left or right. To execute a tip roll changing direction to the right, start forward slowly and plant both poles to the right side of your ski, about a foot behind the tip. Sink down immediately into a comfortable crouch. At the moment the toe of your right boot is close to your poles, spring up, pulling your knees up and at the same time, keeping your tips close together on the snow. Now shift all of your weight completely onto your poles. Keep your arms in a half-bent position and your knees together. Your slight downhill motion, with which you started will automatically cause your tails to swing out to the left as you roll around on your tips to change direction to the right. Sink down into your knees to absorb the shock as you land. For a tip roll to the left, plant your poles on the left side and proceed in the same manner.

When first attempting this turn, in order to build your confidence stand in one place in a stationary position. Plant your poles in the manner described and have someone pick up the tails of your skis and roll you around. This will give you the proper feel of the motion involved and help you to become accustomed to the unusual sensation of the tip roll.

LIFT AND TOW TECHNIQUE

Ski lifts and tows are transportation devices that enable skiers to travel from the bottom of the slopes to the top with varying degrees of comfort and ease. The first lifts were simply animal "skins" attached to the bottom of the skis, and used to "walk" uphill. The next step in the evolution of lifts was the rope tow, which is still very much in evidence today; but it is gradually going out of existence in most areas, except where economy or rapid beginner transportation are necessary for operation.

ROPE TOWS

The rope tow is a system of pulleys over which a rope travels in a long loop, the lower part of which is used by skiers to travel uphill. At each of this type of lift, a protective shack is normally located to keep skiers away from the dangerous "end" pulleys.

When riding the wrist of your outside hand-the hand that is away from the rope. Sidestep into position at the tow rope, and be sure both skis are in the proper tracks and pointed straight up the hill. Using the "inside" hand, grasp the rope gently allowing it to slip through fingers of *gloved* hand. Gradually tighten grip. It helps to walk the skis forward as you tighten grip on the rope. As you move forward, bring outside hand around back and grasp the rope with that hand for additional support. Keep skis running straight in tacks and keep knees flexible.

While riding the tow, keep the skis in the track and the knees relaxed and bent. As bumps are encountered let the bend of skis. The outside hand behind your back will give added support. Keep weight forward to prevent the crossing of skis. When dips or hollows occur in tow track, let the legs straighten into depression but avoid stiffening them. Keep your weight forward on the tips to prevent the skis from wandering and resume your knee bend on upward side of hollow. Resume the normal stance on flat. To slow down, should someone ahead stop, relax your grip on the rope but do not let go. Hold the rope loosely; gradually tighten grasp when the rope resumes motion. For an alternate riding position grasp the rope with both hands in front or with the inside hand behind and outside hand forward, holding the rope at side. That is often by midday, you will find your hands and fingers tiring from using the same position. If you continually change the positioning of your hands during the day, no one hand or arm will become overtired. For instance if you use a one-hand-forward-and-one-hand-behind-the-back position, you should alternately rest the hand behind your back, them move both hands to the front grip, taking the strain off the arm that is usually forward on the rope. Occasionally however, when on a steeper incline, you hand and your rope sliding through your hand and your forward motion slowing to a stop. The remedy: the first unweight your skis with a sudden drop of the knees. This momentarily takes your body weight off your hands, enabling you to get a new and firmer grasp. As you feel your forward progress resuming drop your knees even more and keep them well bent until you are under way again.

As you approach the top of the hill, release back hand (the one with the poles). Then at the top of the hill release the forward hand, being careful to avoid snapping the rope. As you do this, place your outside ski across the fall line, edging it. Then bring your other ski parallel and ski away from the top of the move away immediately from the top of the tow to make room for other skiers following.

THE T-BAR OR J-BAR LIFTS

the T-bar or J-bar lifts are systems using a cable and a series of poles with T- or J- shaped attachments at the end to tow skiers uphill. T-bars normally accommodate two skiers each J-bars one.

When riding a bar lift hold the poles in the outside away from the bar. While waiting for the T-bar, wait until the people ahead have left, and then quickly get into position for the next T-bar unit. As it approaches, the lift operate will grab the unit and bring it forward to a position under the buttocks and in back of the thighs of you and your partner. You *must not sit down* or attempt to take any weight off your skis. The T-bars and J-bars serve to pull skiers uphill and not carry them or otherwise support them. You should also graph the central pole of the T-bar (or the inside pole of the j-bar) with your inside hand as the bar is brought into place by the lift operator.

While riding lean against the bar but to not sit. Keep your knees flexed to absorb terrain variations and let the skis run in the track with inside ski next to partner's inside ski. Relax: avoid pushing against your partner's encountered and let your flexed knees absorb variations naturally. When the track is higher or lower on one side, partners can adjust the balance by one riding slightly behind or ahead. When partner are of unequal height or weight the bar can be tipped to one side to afford better balance for both riders. Further adjustments can be made by one partner riding slightly ahead of the other or by repositioning placement of crossbar.

When the unloading station is reached one partner "tends bar" holding the bar and pulling it down slightly to allow the other to ski away from the lift line. Then the first partner disengages the crossbar by twisting it to a vertical position and gently releasing it. Let the spring carry bar back to hanging position but do not snap it. Swinging bars can be dangerous and can foul in the cable Ski away from lift lines as soon as possible when unloaded *then* replace pole straps on wrists, not before. Others will be unloading right behind you.

Pomalifts

The pomalift, or platter pull as it is sometimes called is a system of poles and a cable with a dishlike disk attached to the base of each pole, and used as a brace (not a seat) by which to pull a skier.

You should approach the pomalift with poles held in the hand away from the lift operator. The operator will hand you a lift unit. Relax and be prepared to hold to the pole of the poma as it accelerates. The lift operator will ask if you are ready, and upon receiving an affirmative reply, will pull a release cable sending your individual unit and you along your way. Your initial reaction should be much like that on the rope tow, with arms straight, knees slightly bent, and general body position relaxed. Shortly after the lift begins to move the spring and sleeve of the unit will extend and there will be a few seconds lapse in speed (usually almost a standstill). At this time, you should push the bar between your legs, so that the dishlifts you squarely in the back of the things and behind your buttocks. You must *not* sit down or try to take any weight off your feet. The pomalift is designed to pull no to lift or carry you. Let it pull you uphill.

Once you are comfortably under way the bar can be held with one hand. Relax and keeping your knees flexed to absorb minor terrain changes, look ahead for bumps or hollows which may occur in the path. Keep the skis parallel. When variations in the terrain do occur, let your knees absorb them as your legs extend and contract over changes.

When preparing to unload, bend your knees and pull down on the bar with both hands. Spread your legs slightly and disengage the disk from between your legs. Hold on to the bar with both hands until the unloading station is reached. When unloading gently release the bar with one hand, letting the spring recoil it toward the cable. Do not snap the bar or let it swing excessively as it is released. Then ski away from the lift line quickly to clear the unloading area for those following behind.

Chair Lifts
A chair lift (single double, triple, or even quadruple) is

a chairlike device supported at the end of a pole and attached by either a single or a double bar to a cable used for transporting skiers uphill. the chair may be capable of carrying one, two, three, or four people, with the double chair being the most popular.

When loading a *double-bar chair lift*, step quickly into the position indicated by markets or by the attendant. Hold the poles in your inside hand and watch for the oncoming chair over your outside shoulder. As the chair approaches grasp the bar with the outside hand and sit down gently.

When loading a *single-bar* chair lift, step quickly into the indicated position as above. Hold the poles in the outside hand and watch for the chair over your inside shoulder. As the chair approaches grasp the bar with your inside hand, and sit down gently as the chair catches you behind your knees.

When comfortably settled on the chair lift, close the safety gate, if there is one by pulling it in or down. If hooks are provided, hang up your poles. Then relax and enjoy the ride. When approaching points where the chair is close to the ground, keep your ski tips up to prevent catching in snow. Approaching the unloading station, open safety gate, hold the poles in your outside hand, and keep the ski tips up until clear of the ramp. If the unloading station is on level ground, stand up at the designated point and with a sliding motion ski quickly away from the chair following the prepared track. Chair partners should depart in opposite directions away from the chair clear unloading track quickly.

If the unloading station is on an inclined ramp, ski

down the ramp, turning in the opposite direction from your partner. Use a snowplow or stop-Christie to stop. Duck down as you ski away to avoid the chair overhead.

Other lifts

There are even more complex lifts which are used in the operation ski areas in and out of this country. For instance cable cars and gondolas provide "mass transportation " by carrying from three to three-score to the top. Although cable cars can become as crowed as sardine especially in Europe, this is luxury transportation. The skis come off and one stands or sits inside, protected from the elements. The small gondola cabins seating two or three persons detach from the cable, permitting loading or unloading inside barn-size buildings. Actually, these more sophisticated uphill transportation methods are quite easy to use and require no special training other than ability to follow the directors of the operators and the safety rules as posted.

Lift lines should be avoided if possible since they mean spending hours standing and waiting. Try to learn the heavy-traffic habits of the area you are skiing and arrange your time during the off hours or on the lesser used lifts at peak hours. (peaks hours at most areas are in the morning when skiers are getting on the mountain.) If one must stand in lift lines, observe good manners. Keep off other people's skis, and do not try to sneak ahead. Also keep in mind these five simple rules which apply to every lift.

1. Carry both ski poles in one hand-the hand away from the lift support, the loading platform your left partner, or the operator.

2. Stay alert and make sure that no part of your equipment or clothing will come in contact with any obstacle.

3. Read carefully any and all instructions posted at the lift loading platform or along the route of the lift.

4. When unloading be sure to get out of the lift tracks as quickly as possible, and watch out for returning chairs, poles etc.

5. If you fall the lift as it starts fall! Never attempt to hang on if you are in anything but the proper riding position. Do not let yourself be dragged; rather let go.

4
■ THE DRILLS AND EXERCISES ■

When learning any new sport there is an initial period of difficulty as your body adapts to the new demands placed upon it. In skiing, first boots are attached to your boots, and suddenly you have a metre or so extension in front of your toes and behind your heel. When you try to turn in the normal manner you find that you step in your skis. Your boots seem heavy and the skis clumsy, and when you stand on a slight gradient, your skis want to slide away from you. All beginners go through this frustrating period so there is no need for under concern. The beginners exercise teach your body to adjust to the fact that yours feet have now 'grown' fore and aft, and that they now have slippery plastic bottoms and sharp metal edges.

At the end of the first morning you will realize that the plastic bottoms allow the skis to slide, and that the metal edges digging in to the snow enable the skis to turn or stop. You will also feel more comfortable on the skis and will be ready to learn more advanced maneuvers.

The exercise which follow are internationally standard exercise used for teaching beginners. We recommend that you practice as many as possible.

1 The basic position on skis

The body should be facing downhill and comfortably balanced over both skis, the knees slightly bent, the skis a little less than hip distance apart, the shins leaning against the fronts of the boots, the back in a normal relaxed position, the head centered, the shoulders relaxed and the arms held in front of the body with the elbows bent as though a tray were being carried. And the ski poles pointing slightly backwards.

2. Walking and gliding on skis-with and without ski poles

keeping the body in the basic position, begin to 'walk' forward by pushing one foot in front of the other. This is accomplished by shuffling one ski forward and then shuffling the other ski forward, shifting your weight alternately from the front foot to the back foot. It is best to try this with the aid of the ski poles for a few strides, by holding the ski poles in the middle and gliding forward without their aid.

3. Turning in position using tails and shovels as pivots

Now that you have taken a few pace forward, it is time to turn around to walk back. This is easily accomplished by taking little steps in a circle, using either the tails (black of the skis) or shovels (fronts of the skis) to pivot about. Let's start with the tail pivot and turn to the right (clockwise).

Keeping your body in the basic position, lean on the left foot so as to reduce the weight on the right foot and, leaving both ski tails in the same place, step the front of the right ski to the right ski, leaving the tails in the same place. Repeat this motion of stepping the front of the right ski to the side, followed by the front of the left ski, leaving the tails of both skin in place. This will result in a 'fan' shape and if you continue around you will outline a circle in the snow. This procedure should then be repeated to the let anti-clockwise again using the tails as a pivot.

The same exercise should be carried out using the shovels of the skis as a pivot. In performing this manoeuvre, the shovel of the ski is kept in place and tails of the skis are walked around to the right anti-clockwise) complicating a circle then to the left (clock wise) completing a circle.

4. Straight schussing down the fall-line

first it is necessary to understand the term 'fall lined. This is the steepest path down the section you are on, and thus the direction in which you would slide if you fell, or the path down which a snowball would roll. The significance of the fall line is that when your skis are pointing down it, they will automatically slide; only when your skis are perpendicular or at right angles to the fall line will you be able to stand still without relying on your ski poles. This exercise is the first time that you will experience the feeling of skiing, in other words, the skis sliding over the snow ideally with you standing on them!

Assume the basic positions again pointing down the fall-line, with your ski poles in the snow preventing you from sliding forwards. So that you do not fall backwards, it is very important to lean against the front if the ski boots as the skis slide and not to lean backwards. Maintain the weight on bath feet, relax, release the ski poles with a title push, and try to keep your balance as you glide down the hill. If you are on a hill with stop automatically as you lose momentum on the uphill slope.

At this point, having successfully made it down the hill, most of my student break out in to their first big happy smile, and the ones that get a particular gleam in their eyes are the ones that we know are hooked on skiing for life.

5. *Sidestepping up the hill*
Having made it down, it would be fun to do it again. To get back up, we sidestep. This is a simple manoeuvre, archived by keeping the skis perpendicular to the fall-line and walking the skis up the hill using the metal edges to bite in to the snow to prevent the skis slipping sideways.

6. *Diagonal sidestepping*
This manoeuvre is similar to the previous one, only this time the ski is stepped slightly forward at the same time as you step it up the hill so that you are climbing on a diagonal course, rather than straight up the hill. The skis, of course, remain perpendicular to the fall-line even as you climb diagonally.

7. *Schussing down the fall line-lifting tails alternately*
Here is a good balance exercise. This manoeuvre is similar to straight schussing down the fall-line. The variation is that you alternate lift the tails of your skis as you schuss down the slope.

Start off in the basic position with your skis facing down the fall-line. Start gliding and, as you pick up speed, lift the tail of one ski (by leaning your weight over the other ski) for a count of two. Place the tail back on the snow, lean in this ski and lift the tail of the other ski for a count of two. Repeat until you automatically stop on the uphill reunite.

8 Schussing down the fall line-picking up gloves

This manoeuvre teaches you how to bend down and to relax. Place a few gloves in the snow, just to the sides of the fall-line. Start in the basic position with your skis pointing down the hill. Hold your ski poles without putting your hands through the straps. Now push off and leave your poles behind. As you side down the hill, bent down and lift each glove as you pass alongside it.

Bending under ski pole arches

In this another fine manoeuvre, and is as good for adults to practice as it is for children-although children tend to beat adults at it! Arrange ski poles in a series of arches by placing one pole horizontally through the straps of two vertical poles planted in the snow a meter or so apart. Stand in the basic position above the ski pole arches and start it slide. As you approach the first arches, flex (bend) our knees, however your heaps and crouch low to the around so that you pass under the horizontal pole. As you pass the arch, then bend again as you pass under the next horizontal pole.

10 Getting up after a fall

Everyone falls, and so everyone must get up. But trying to get up incorrectly can be very exhausting and frustrating. Grating up correctly, while not easy in the beginning, soon becomes a habit and is not tiring or difficult once mastered.

When you fall, it is best to try and fall sideways with the skis parallel, as this is the least likely way to get injured. Naturally it is not always possible for you to falls as you would like, but modern release binding are designed to kick the boot out of the ski in a fall, so it is pretty difficult to injure yourself these days. But it is still preferable to fall sideways if you can.

Having said that, after you fall and are splayed across the snow with legs and arms pointing in all directions, what should you do next? Generally, at the speeds you will be travailing during basic exercise, the skis will remain on when you fall. So the first step is to arrange yourself so that you are sitting with your skis together, perpendicular to the fall-line, and with your body uphill of your skis. Your legs should be bent and your knees tucked up towards your chest. Now, remove your hands from the ski pole grips and place the ski poles in front of your chest with their tips in the snow next to your uphill though. Place one hand on top of the grip and the other just above the basket and you will be in the 'ready' position. The trick to getting up effortlessly is to lean your chest forward the entire time. Now push upward with your lower hand and simultaneously press down on the top of the grip with your upper hand. If you accompany this action by leaning your torso forward so that your knees are bent towards your chest, you should come up very simply.

It is equally important that your top ski is very secure in the snow so that when you put your weight on it, it does not slide forwards or backwards. Once the preparation is completed, the turn can be performed.

Step one: swing (do not lift) the lower ski forward and up, place the ski tail in the snow as far forward as you can and as close to the uphill ski as possible with your knees as straight as well balanced, leaning slightly uphill on the edge of your uphill ski, being supported by the ski poles.

Steps two and three are to be done in tandem, though not hurriedly. Step two; lower the tip of the vertical ski and place it perpendicularly across the fall-line next to the upper ski and in the opposite direction. The tail of the lower ski and should not have moved. The trick to make the step easy is top bend your downhill knees and to lean your torso over the bottom or downhill ski as you place the ski on the snow. People who experience difficult at the point do so because they try to lean backwards rather than forwards. If you lean forwards as suggested, bending the lower knee, it is extremely easy to perform step two and then step three: lean on the lower ski and bringing the uphill ski around and place it parallel and next to the lower ski, completing the kick turn manoeuvre.

To summarize, the kick turn is performed as follows: Preparation; Step1-swing lower leg up and plant ski tail forward and close to uphill ski; step 2-leave tail in place, lower the tip of vertical ski, bend the knee, place the ski alongside uphill ski in the opposite direction, and lean out from the waist over the downhill ski: step 3-bring uphill ski around, followed closely by ski pole.

13 The snowplough stop (wedge)

The snowplough or wedge is a means of slowing down or stopping on a gentle gradient at slow speeds. Though some of the modern ski school no longer teach this movement to beginners, most of the national ski school still do. We personally feel that the snowplough is a very valuable ski manoeuvre for intermediate and advanced skiers, but is potentially dangerous for beginners to perform. It gives them a false sense of confidence, making them believe that they can stop when they lose control and are going too fast. As the knees are in a twisted position in the snowplough, using this movement at high speeds can put too much stress on the legs and knees, and fall can result in spiral leg fractures or ligament tears. Furthermore, when beginners lose control they tend to lean backwards, which further gravities the situation. Consequently, we delay teaching the wedge to those beginners who plan to ski with me for a full five day program until after day three. By carefully choosing the terrain, we avoid placing our students in situations where they need to employ the snowplough to stop. In the afternoon of Day you will learn to stop by stepping the skis towards the hill, which is a graceful movement leading to the more advanced manoeuvres.

However, since this book is designed to help you if are teaching yourself, and as you may find yourself in situations when it would be useful to have such a means of slowing up or stopping, we are including the snowplough (wedge) in the basic exercise. It is very important to remember that this movement should only be performed by beginners on gentle slopes at slow speeds. (should you begin to lose control and start skiing too fast, it is preferable to fall sideways, swing your skis below you, and use the ski edges to bite in to the snow to slow you to a stop).

To perform the snowplough or wedge, choose a smooth, gentle slope with an uphill runout at the end. Face down the fall-line in the basic body position and allow your skis to slide. Be sure to press your shins against the front of your ski boots throughout the entire manoeuvre. As you gain momentum, roll your knees and ankles towards each other and, keeping the ski tips fairly close together, being to lower your hips and push your feet outwards. Try to keep your weight equally distributed over both feet as you press down, with your upper body balanced midway between the skis. Continue pushing outwards until your skis form a 'V' and you stop.

It is advisable to practice the snowplough (wedge) first on the flat, and 'walk' the skis to the side until you are in the wedge position. Keep practicing on the flat until you feel completely comfortable with the final stopping position before trying it on the gentle slopes.

Having successfully completed all these exercise you should now feel much more comfortable on your skis and should now feel much more comfortable on your skis and should be capable of controlling them at slow speeds. Your are now ready to learn the manoeuvres that will allow you to ski in control at higher speeds and on steeper slopes.

EVERY DAY DRILLS AND EXERCISES

First rule: Begin all warm-ups by filling the muscles with energy: oxygen-rich and nutritious blood. Accomplish this by performing activities that increase your heart rate, without excessively stressing or stretching your muscles and tendons before the blood has filled your muscles and joints.

This is a gradual process, taking perhaps 5 to 10 minutes to engorge your muscles and joints. There are safe shortcuts employed by highly trained and conditioned athletes who achieve sufficient engorgement and higher ranges of flexibility sooner because of their greater cardiac output. Even there athletes, however, use the principle of *gradually* working the torso and limbs.

Why warm up?
The intention of a planned warm-up program is threefold: (a) to decrease the risk of injury (ask several injury victims and you'll often find that warm-ups were never a part of their skiing day); (b) to keep your body flexible and ready to adapt to changes in snow conditions, terrain, or other demands you may place on yourself (prestretched muscles respond more quickly to demands than unstretched muscles); and (c) to promote your potential for skiing with the highest level of efficiency. Ask racers and competitive skiers if they warm up; most will admit that they ski better after a high-energy warm-up.

Warm muscles can be gradually stretched to greater ranges of motion than cold muscles, especially important for winter sports. The more flexible you become, the more this may help to minimize the injury you might sustain in a fall, because a flexible (warmed-up) body can better absorb the shock of falls, off-balance compressions, and awkward positions that are all potential aspects of aggressive skiing.

Unfortunately, flexibility is lost as we age, particularly in men, and this loss in seen in the later twenties and on. This is one of the reasons why young people can function on the slopes with little or no warm-up. They play more with the snow and ski less intensively and less aggressively. For over-30 skiers,

Fig 1: Skate on flat terrain

daily stretching is crucial both before and after skiing. Your body's reaction to changes in conditions or surprises in the snow (e.g., skiers darting out of trees, holes, rocks, cliffs, etc.) is tied to the quickness of response of not only your feet, legs, and skis but also your stabilizing upper body: hands, arms, shoulders, head/eyes. Your lower body in particular needs to be limber and quick to respond to signals from the brain. It must be ready to extend and retract; to change the pressure on the ankles, knees, or hips depending on the turn; to set an edge or get off of an edge; to ski onto an edge; to separate the skis and feet; to move the legs independently; to skate and step; and in general, to be very dynamic and versatile.

A series of planned warm-ups to use each time you go skiing will help to maintain your flexibility and versatility throughout the ski season.

Some warm-up ideas

Many skiers we know like to engage in some kind of aerobic activity and at-home stretches before getting to the mountain. Admittedly, others we know dread such a thought. If you share my view, you know how the early morning warm-up acts like a prewarm-up for a more thorough warm-up on the mountain. If you don't do this prewarm-up, there are a host of activities to prepare your body for stretching once you get to the mountain.

After a lifetime of athletics, believe the warm-up is a major contributor to athletic performance. Consider the following in your skiing:

1. Do early morning sit-ups to warm the body. Strong and toned abdominal muscles are one of the greatest allies to centered skiing and a problem-free back.

2. Fill your muscles and joints with blood. Begin stretching after doing something that makes your heart beat faster and large muscles work harder, not excessively, for 5 to 10 minutes. Then stretch: a) the fronts and backs of the legs, b) the inner thighs and groin area, c) the lower back, d) the midsection, waist area, and e) the shoulders and neck. In the process of stretching the inner thigh, groin, and legs, you will also exert proper stretch to the knees and ankles.

3. Use your first chairlift ride to stretch! First work your shoulders by rolling them forward (imagine making small circles at your shoulder joints), then reverse direction and roll them back. Continue rolling slowly until your head is over your left shoulder. Then roll your head back in the other direction, over your chest to your right shoulder. Repeat twice. Third, rework your shoulders by

pressing them down into your upper arms and holding for a five-count. Lift them up toward your ears, holding for a five count. Repeat three times.

If you have room, work your mid-section and lower body by twisting the latter (legs together) to the left, while you twist your upper body (at the mid-section) to the right. Hold for a 7 to 10 count and switch sides, upper body left, lower body right. Repeat as many times as you can, working on your upper and lower body separation: Twist to the extremes and hold a tight separation during the 7 to 10 count. You might even get the sensation of bringing your inside ski up slightly during the exercise to achieve even greater separation. Of course, be careful not to catch your skis on the lift towers.

Work your thighs and knees by lifting your lower legs slowly, your legs out straight, tails of your skis perpendicular to the snow. Lift one leg at a time, or both legs together. Hold for 10 to 20 seconds each time, longer if you can. For safety reasons and effect, do the leg-lift movements slowly and avoid rocking the chair.

4. Casually ski two easy runs doing acquaintance drills, and follow there with some additional stretching. All you want to do with there runs is loosen up and integrate your flexibility stretches with your skiing body. ski the first run very relaxed; the second a bit more aggressively. Do basic wedge turns for a hundred yards; stem (skidded) wedge turns for 50 yards; converging step turns without skidding; matched ski turns without skidding; a series of diverging turns; and some attempt to ski on a single ski, turning it in both directions.

Two helpful stretches with skis on are (a) leaning down and touching or leaning down and touching or leaning as far as you can toward the tips of your skis and (b) standing tall, both poles steadying you, lifting one ski and placing its tail in the snow so it is tall in front of you; slowly lean into the raised knee and stretch the back of your leg.

If you're feeling loose, warm, fit, flexible, and are ready for a more dynamic stretch, try my favorite: the *World Cup stretch*. Straighten out your downhill leg and place your inside ski in an exaggerated diverging step, flat on the snow. The action of the World Cup stretch is to sit down on the inside ski as you turn your upper body to face over your downhill ski, which you have placed on an extreme inside edge. The stretch is completed by holding for a 10-count, allowing a bit of movement in your hips to push them more into the hill. Switch sides and repeat as often as you like for a few minutes. The fullest expression of the stretch is when you thrust your poles, hands, and arms forward over your downhill ski while pushing your hip into the hill.

5. Takes a few minutes to think about how you want to ski this particular day; aggressively, casually, fast, quick, stylishly, efficiently.
6. You're ready to take a "glory run!" Ski the way your body feels like skiing and let your mind take a vacation. This run can set the stage for the rest of the day; why not give it your all? If skiing is sport to you, be an athlete and warm up to glory!

One of the truly frustrating aspects of skiing is becoming stymied, and thereby inhibited, by your inability to do a number of things on skis. We wish we could carve a turn with minimal skidding; get by a certain knoll in a race course; feel relaxed after skiing moguls; execute a rhythmic pole touch for an entire milelong run; stop on the dime; ski for long distances without becoming fatigued; and smoothly link turn after turn in a variety of conditions.

Discovering problems in our skiing is easier than accepting that these problems exist; unless we accept them however, we may forever plant self-destructive bombs in our skiing. The answer is to recognize the problems and challenge yourself to do something about correcting them. Unfortunately, trial and error adjustments made to compensate for any number of our problems lead not to better skiing, but to better survival tactics on the slopes. The result is many hours of frustrating and fatiguing skiing, even though we're supposedly having fun.

In this chapter we've assembled the information gleaned from many on-snow and off-snow sessions with experts, particularly Mike, John, and Brent for drills and exercises. We spent much of the time identifying problem areas common to the recreational skier on his or her way up the high performance ladder. With their assistance and my experimentation in a variety of conditions, field-tested some 50 drills and exercises designed to be corrective for a host of conditions. Following each drill or exercise is a *kinesthetic hint*; that is, a reference to the sensations you ought to feel if you are properly, executing the drill or exercise. These may be muscular, joint-related, or oriented to sense of perspective or general ski-snow awareness.

We asked George Capaul, assistant coach of the U.S. Ski Team (men's slalom and giant slalom), for his impressions of the average recreational skier. Although George is quick to applaud everyone's love for skiing, he is candid about what he sees on the slopes. "Most recreational skiers," he says, "have real technical problems and need a lot of work on basic fundamentals." His fundamentals include being balanced on your skis forward, sideways, longitudinally, and to the rear; being able to respond to all conditions with a proper pole plant, upright stance on skis, and even weight distribution along the entire length of the outside ski while turning; skiing square to the fall line; and keeping your head up and looking ahead or what George calls *high beam* skiing.

It's not until you master these basics, George says, that you're ready to deal with technique.

"A problem modern recreational skiers have is that due to all the grooming, it's easy to go fast, and many equate going fast with intermediate skiing. Still, these skiers go out on groomed trails and say, "Yeah, I can handle this,' but were these skiers skiing at a time when trails were skierpacked, rough and mogully, they might be very beginning skiers. In a way, the groomed trails have hurt ski schools because before, skiers needed instruction to get down steep hills; today, they feel they can handle anything... that's groomed. Ski schools teach basic fundamentals, and lessons are an essential part of high performance skiing."

The key problem areas common among the ranks of recreational skiers are addressed in this chapter. These include overrotating or twisting the upper body while turning; lack of carving (excessive skidding while turning); lack of rhythmic pole use; overall lack of extension/movement in skiing; lack of edge control; lack of speed control (unfinished turns); lack of variety in turning skills and choice of turn radii; and tense and static skiing.

Each problem area is discussed briefly, followed by an explanation of applicable drills and exercises. As you might imagine, a number, and reference is made to this when applicable. Sometimes these multipurpose drills and exercises are presented with adaptations according to the particular problem. Similarly, some drills and exercises are designed to accomplish much more than has been indicated in this chapter; these are presented only for their specific application to the problem under discussion.

A perspective on drills and exercises
Think of the drills as narrowly focused opportunities to learn by doing. Don't regard them as a critique of your skiing. They are sensory as well as mechanical experiences. Think of the exercises as broadly focused opportunities to draw your skills together while concentrating on the task of the exercise.

When doing either drills or exercises, proceed with an eye toward allowing change to creep into your skiing. Admittedly, some drills and exercises will seem complicated and impossible, whereas some may strike you as infantile to your level of skiing. These are not reasons to avoid them. In fact, the more effort you have to put into doing a drill as prescribed, the greater the technical benefit to your skiing. This continues up to the point at which you can perform the drills effortlessly as a means of warming up before more aggressive skiing.

You may be thinking about the embarrassment you'll experience while falling all over the mountain trying to do a basic or advanced drill and about how silly you'll look performing drills on beginner slopes when you consider yourself an advanced skier. These egoistic thoughts get in the way of high performance skiing. The drills are necessary for you to become a better skier. A five-year member of the U.S. Ski Team, Mark Tache encourages drills and instruction that require you to focus on the fundamentals of different aspects of skiing. Without drilling and training, Mark says, "A lot of would-be performance skiers will spend a lot of skiing time practicing bad habits over and over again. Without direction, they'll tend to stay at the same level in their skiing. Some choose to get to a point where they're comfortable on their skis, bad habits and all, and these skiers will likely never be motivated to ski better. It takes an annual commitment to getting better to really improve. That's what is so unique about this sport: You never reach a point where you say, 'I know how to ski.' It's always a challenge; you're always learning."

Pete Patterson, another former U.S. Ski Team member and medalist in the downhill, highlights the importance of practicing the basics to develop high performance skills. "Learning to ski by picking up the ability to negotiate different terrain in a year's time shows a skier is working real hard on his or her skiing. But, even though this skier appears to be rapidly progressing, you can see the real inexperience in the more subtle aspects of their skiing. It takes years of experience to be able to ski efficiently."

Commenting on the plight of many weekend-only

skiers, Pete adds, "Unfortunately, they don't have the opportunity to ski as much as they might like, and they may find it difficult to get to the level at which they feel good. They must be patient, though, because there's just no other way to develop high performance skills without practice and time.

"What you've got to realize is you always need practice, coaching, or instruction. The best skiers in the world go out, work with a coach, and discover things about their skiing that they're not doing as well as they were a couple of weeks earlier. The coach lets them know; it's really a never-ending process even at the World Cup level. You can always use, and probably forever need, the fine tuning of a coach, instructor, whomever."

Five Easy Rules for Drills and Exercises

1. Understand what the drill or exercise is designed to accomplish.

2. Be aware of which condition is most appropriate to the drill or exercise, for example, groomed slope, slight bumps, firm snow, soft snow, bumpy, or steep. Also, know the slope rating for the intended drill or exercise: beginning, intermediate, advanced, and expert.

3. Know how to perform the drill. If it's performed incorrectly it may enhance errors. Further, you won't get that kinesthetic appreciation of what you've accomplished: a ski feeling that can accelerate a refinement in your skiing when you use it to guide your increasingly more subtle and proper adjustments for skiing in the high performance mode.

If you know what it feels like to "hold an edge" or "angulate your hip" into the turn, you can use this kinesthetic knowledge to prompt you to replicate this feeling at certain times during your skiing when you must subtly adjust to get more hip into the hill, more completely finish a turn in the bumps or steeps, or ride your turning ski a little longer in the recreational race course.

4. Commit yourself to a block of skiing time and, unless you're already familiar with the drill or exercise, do it several times to work out the bugs before using an entire run for it. You will find some drills immediately frustrating, especially single ski skiing and turning, hopping drills, and a number of angulation drills; this is to be expected. These cases will require more than a few attempts to perfect. If so, try them again each time out, until you learn them!

5. Don't take the easy way out by avoiding difficult or embarrassing drills that cause you to fall down. By doing so, you're likely to ignore an aspect of your skiing that's undeveloped. Achieving this development through more difficult drills will boost your confidence and enhance your skills acquisition.

If you have the opportunity to rehearse any drills at home by thinking through their mechanics and/or physically arranging yourself (without skis) in the positions called for by the drills, do it!

In the drills-exercise format of the following section as well as for the remainder of the chapter, there is reference to conditions and slope rating. Unless otherwise noted, conditions are smooth, groomed, firm snow; slope rating is intermediate to advanced. These are referred to as standard in the text. The environment created by these conditions and slope rating is ideal for learning to do drills. As a rule, when you are able to perform drills efficiently, take them to more challenging terrain and variable conditions.

Reference is made to assuming the drills position when performing the drills. Always assume the drills position when doing drills, unless otherwise noted. The position: skis parallel, hip-width apart; knees slightly bent (flexed); upper body relaxed, head up, chest tall; hands and arms forward about waist high, poles extended out behind you on or off the snow, and back straight.

The following terms appear throughout the drills and exercises. To flex is to press down and forward. To flex the legs is to press the ankles and knees forward. To rotate is to twist. To counter-rotate is to move your lower body (legs, boots, and skis) one way, while twisting your upper body (arms, shoulders, head, chest, and upper abdomen) the other, at least as far as facing down the fall line; the place about which all the counterrotating takes place is your waist (upper hips and lower abdomen). To touch a pole is to tap it in the snow. To plant a pole is to decisively push the tip into the snow.

To traverse is to go across the fall line in the #1 position; a slight traverse is to go across the fall line in the #2 position; a slight traverse to pick up speed is to go across the fall line in the #3 position.

A comfortable turn rhythm and slope is something

you define for yourself, but it implies that you feel absolutely no intimidation from the kinds of turns you must do or from the slope upon which you're going to perform the drill or exercise.

To steer your skis is to use all of the turning moves you make, including gross or subtle foot/boot and lower leg/knee movements and the rotation of your femur (thigh bone) in its hip socket, to guide your skis in either the predetermined direction or in the direction they naturally seek because of the angles you've created with your ankles, knees, hips, and shoulders. Angles are created when you collapse any of the foregoing body parts into your center of mass and thus break the vertical axis of your body. Your center of mass is the abdominal region around your navel, between and above your hips, as differentiated from the center of gravity, which can be outside of mass.

Weight transfer is moving the weight of your body from one ski to the other. Usually, this transfer occurs from your downhill (outside, working, or turning) ski to your uphill (inside, resting, or inrigger) ski in preparation for your next turn. The weight transfer occurs after the turn has begun, however, with the White Pass turn popularized by the Mahres and with a converging step turn. As soon as the transfer takes place, the skis switch roles.

Your skis are referred to in many ways: Basically, the ski that's doing most of the edging, has the most pressure applied to it, and is closest to the bottom of the hill is downhill, outside, working, and turning. The ski that's doing the least amount of edging, has very little pressure applied to it (although it's actively turning), and is closest to the top of the hill is uphill, inside, resting, and an inrigger.

Lack of Speed Control

This may not only be the most common problem among skiers but also one of the most dangerous. Add uncontrolled speed to your skiing and your increase the risk of serious injury. Add controlled speed to your skiing and you increase the potential for safer risk taking. Consider the following drills and exercises to learn to subtly control your speed while skiing all out or as slow as you like; think of acquiring speed control to add versatility to your skiing without having to rely on dramatic braking measures and skidding to slow you down. In fact, learning to slow down in stride is also a wonderful way to learn how to accelerate at will.

Speed control can be achieved by learning to finish your turns and to use platforms and preturns in your skiing. When you learn to finish your turns, you learn how to carve the inside edge of your turning ski as well, and stop the excessive skidding of both the turning and the inside skis.

Steering up to a preturn platform

Purpose: To control speed by momentary steering of your skis away from the fall line to effect a smooth decrease in speed, which allows you to set up for your next turn with a rhythmic dip up and into the hill. This is especially useful for setting up your first turn in the steeps when you've had to traverse to the place where you're going to drop in and ski the steeps with commitment. The degree to which your edges are engaged while steering up and away from the fall line determines the rate of deceleration of your skis and the distance they travel up the slope. This movement is actually a preturn in which you steer your skis and the distance they travel up the slope. This movement is actually a preturn in which you steer your skis up the slope an instant before turning them down the slope. The distance you travel in the preturn varies, but is measured in feet, not yards.

Conditions: Standard; once you've got this down, take it to the steeps, bumps, and skiable ice.

Slope rating: Standard; truly advanced skiers should take this to an expert slope.

Performing the Drill. Begin in drills position, FLEP #2. Keep a definite pressure on the inside edge of your downhill ski while lightly maintaining contact with the snow on your inside ski. Midway through your traverse (you're not moving that fast), begin to steer your feet and lower legs/knees up. As you do so, allow your upper body to stay square with its original direction. Follow your skis until you stop just to get the feeling of steering up. Turn around and repeat in the other direction. The inside edge of your downhill ski will naturally increase its angle of edging as you steer your legs away from the fall line. Repeat side to side until you can control the steering up motion of your skis.

Next, do the same procedure at FLEP 3 or 4, only shorten the distance traveled across the slope and, instead of stopping when your skis turn up the hill, use their movement to initiate your next turn down the hill. It's easy, but you've got to trust yourself. As your skis start up the hill, you touch your pole and throw or lean your body down the hill in the direction of your pole touch. Concentrate on only this and you will begin to get the feel of steering up to a preturn. To smooth it out requires a number of subtle skills, not the least of which is active inside-ski steering. Do the drill and learn to steer up; the other pieces to the puzzle will emerge in other drills.

Kinesthetic Hint. During the steering-up phase, you should feel your lower body pulling away from your stable upper body. As you refine the preturn, you'll use a corresponding dip up with your upper body to propel you into your turn. Muscularly, you'll feel the most pressure in the middle of the front of your downhill quadricep (thigh); with corresponding knee angulation, the pressure is felt more to the outside of the thing. For a change of pace, hold your thigh with your hand as you do the exercise to feel the pressure while gradually steering up. The thigh feeling is more intense and short-lived when steering into the out of the preturn.

Diverging turns
Purpose: To control speed by getting you to ski away from the fall line, yet allowing you to fluidly link turn after turn by making subtle adjustments in your speed. This is more dynamic than steering up because, in part, you're transferring your weight early to your new turning ski. The quicker you get your weight to your new turning ski, the sooner you can turn, the more quickly you can establish speed control.

Conditions: Standard

Slope rating: Standard

Performing the Drill. In drills position ski across the slope in FLEP #3, but instead of steering up at the end of your traverse, push (don't step or lift) your uphill ski/boot, lower leg/knee up the hill away from the fall line and in the direction of your outside ski. As you diverge your inside ski away from your outside ski, let your body follow the direction and pull of your inside ski. As soon as you put your weight on this diverging ski, your outside ski, which is madly edging in response to the diverged ski, will correspondingly lighten the be easier to steer up the hill, in part because it is attached to the body and in part because the momentum of your turn is away from the downhill ski. Do this until you stop. Practice to both sides until it feels comfortable.

Next to make this drill more dynamic instead of stopping after you've diverged your inside ski, use the same movement as the last drill to turn down the fall line. Unlike steering up to a preturn in which both skis are steered up, with diverging turns you are relying on one ski to make a quick and subtle diverging move to check your speed. So long as you have not yet transferred weight, this maneuver will make your turning ski carve in the snow and move in the direction of the diverged ski. When the diverged ski is stepped into its position at high speeds it becomes a very dynamic form of skiing, used routinely in racing and at times in bumps.

Kinesthetic hint. Muscularly, you'll feel pressure in the lower thing and on the inside of the knee of the diverging leg. The outside of the thigh and knee of your downhill leg will feel increasing amounts of pressure as your downhill ski edges in response to the divergence of your other ski.

Wedge hoppers

Purpose: To establish quick on and off edge-speed control for skiing very steep and bumpy terrain

Conditions: Standard

Slope rating: Standard

Performing the Drill. Hold yourself in a comfortable wedge at the start of your run. FLEP #6. Keep your upper body upright and flex your knees and ankles, favoring one side by making it your downhill ski and putting most of your weight on it. Spring off this ski (assume it's your right ski), extend up, and hop to the left ski, making it the downhill ski. Each time you spring to a new ski that ski is always wedged toward you. Hop back and forth, ski to ski, maintaining the wedge. Try to land softly, keeping your center of mass facing downhill while your lower body hops side to side Incorporate a natural pole plant rhythm, planting your poles out in front of you toward the tip portion, not the sides of your skis.

Kinesthetic Hint. A tremendous feeling of frustration is usual for not being able to do it right away or even after a while. The trick is in the positioning of the lower body and the non-working ski, the amount of edge angle on the working ski, and the relationship of the ski to the fall line. The nonworking side of your body should feel like it's coiling or crunching in on the working ski. You should experience a feeling of control and heavy breathing!

Discovering platforms

Purpose: To control speed at a specific point in time or specific spot on the slope; to learn to establish the positioning on your skis for initiating a preturn; and to gradually or abruptly check your speed just before you reach the point of turn initiation at which you know you've started to physically influence the turning of your skis in the other direction. According to Brent Boblitt, "Platforms allow you to slow down or speed up in accord with the rhythm of you skiing and direction of your descent. If you're able to make a good platform, you can utilise an effective pole plant. With a proper platform, you're stable and you can make offensive and defensive moves. Offensively, you use the rebound set up by the platform to project yourself down the hill with more speed and authority. Defensively, you use the platform to check your speed by absorbing the rebound with your body and using only a minimum amount of rebound to help redirect your skis down the fall line.

Conditions: Standard

Slope rating: Standard; the steeper the better as your become more comfortable with platforms.

Performing the Drill. You've got to be creative. First, put your skis in a platform by standing on the side of a hill in parallel position, perpendicular to the fall line; hold yourself there. Now, bounce up and down until your skis come off of the snow, ready to land again in another platform to keep your from sliding away. Be more aggressive: Hop high, land on your skis, and plant your downhill pole on the downhill side of your boot, forming a platform with your skis and pole. Ski around the mountain and whenever you get a chance form check platforms and propulsion platforms. Have fun with them; they add versatility to your skiing and help you in the steeps. Using a gentle slope, try to hop up and turn your skis 180 degrees, ending up with a platform in which your former uphill ski becomes your new downhill ski.

Kinesthetic Hint: When you hit a check platform with pole plant, you feel the pressure on the balls of your feet (i.e., pressure forward). If you feel the pressure of your lower legs against the fronts of your boot, it may mean that you're too far forward. You may feel pressure on your downhill knee and your uphill thigh as well. Your uphill ski is slightly ahead of your downhill ski. In a very exaggerated check platform on steep terrain, your downhill hip is pinched and your uphill is stretched. As Tony notes, "The proper place to feel the pinch is the iliac crest at the top of the pelvis."

In a propulsion platform, your heels set quickly and you experience a brief but distinctive flex at your knees and a quick propulsion/extension out of this flex as you project yourself into the next turn. There's a very definite feeling of floating or weight-lessness at this moment of propulsion.

Exercises

The following exercises are designed for standard conditions and all slope ratings. Although the first exercise lends itself to bump skiing and power, it's very important to have your speed control skills in check before taking off on someone's heels in the bumps or on fast icy terrain. Generally, it's not a good idea to follow skiers into very big bumps, in steeps, and in powder. Following a skier in spring slush and crud can be a good learning experience, but be sure to leave plenty of room between you and the skier in front of you so you can react to unexpected turns or falls.

These exercises help you not only to use more speed control tactics in your skiing but also to be more reactional in your skiing, to look ahead, to anticipate, to experiment with different rhythms, to add timing to your skiing, and in general, to be more versatile.

Following Someone's Tracks. Ski right behind another skier. This adds discipline to your skiing and forces you to make subtle speed control adaptations to keep you from crashing into the skier you're following. If you're crowding the skier ahead of you, it's not because you're a great or superior skier, but because you haven't refined your speed control skills.

Lack of Carving and Excessive Skidding
Although most skiers who lack speed control end up skidding excessively at the end of their turns, not all skiers who skid excessively lack speed control. These skiers are skidding their tails not to brake but to steer their skis: It's easier for them to turn a flat ski rather than an edged ski. The first group of skidders usually rides medium-length and long skis on more advanced terrain; the latter group of "skidders" usually rides shorter skis.

Whatever the length of ski, Tony notes, "Any radius of turn of under approximately 90 feet will have some displacement of the ski (exceptions: skiing in crud and Mark Girardelli)." This is true for even the mythical perfectly carved turn. Indeed, there are times when we intentionally skid our skis, as in short-swing turns, to make a descent while sideslipping, to maneuver through tight areas, to react to unexpected obstacles (accompanied by quick foot movements), to perform stem christies in the crud, bumps, or slushy conditions, and to stabilize oneself in the bumps.

I don't want you to throw skidding out the window; I do want to provide you with a series of drills designed to help you finish your turns and learn the skills that will give you the choice of whether, when, and just how much you want to skid your skis.

Wedge progression

Purpose: To develop finished turns through the use of subtle and more obvious angles

Conditions: Standard

Slope rating: Standard

Performing the Drill. Begin in a comfortable wedge with the insides of your boots at about shoulder's width, the tips of your skis approximately your to six inches apart, assuming FLEP #2. Traverse the hill at all times maintaining the wedge with the rest of your body in drills position. As you pick up speed, allow only the downhill ankle to tip into the hill toward your uphill ski. This is a very slight tipping: Your knee should barely move at this stage of the drill.

You'll notice that your downhill ski will begin to edge more decisively; this is due to the angulation of your ankle. Now it's time to add knee angulation by gradually tipping your knee into the hill after you've tipped your ankle. As you do, you'll feel the downhill ski solidly edging and carving through the snow. The greater the pressure created by your angles and the more you tip ankle and knee into the hill (at least in this drill), the more your skis will turn up the hill to their eventual stop.

As soon as you become acquainted with this drill move to FLEP 3 or 4. Remember, the most difficult part of this drill may be in maintaining a wedge throughout the carving of your downhill ski (you must do this to better isolate the subtle control you can exert on your skis through the use of these two angles). Go across the hill and angulate until you come to a stop: Continue this all the way down the run. Give yourself plenty of room.

It takes discipline to hold a wedge while traversing

Next phase in the progression: Pick a comfortable line down the mountain. Maintaining the wedge and drills position, practice the same ankle and knee-ankle pressure, but instead of coming to an uphill stop, transfer your weight to your uphill ski at the instant your skis feel they're beginning to slow down (i.e., when they begin turning up the hill). As you move your weight to your wedged or stemmed uphill ski, it becomes your new turning ski. Therefore, if you want to turn easily without resistance, you simply have to lighten that old downhill ski, but still keep it wedged.

Assuming you've held the wedge position with both skis, as soon as you transfer your weight to that uphill ski (new turning ski), it will turn. In its wedged position, the ski is technically converged in the direction of your next turn; as soon as it feels the pressure of your weight and the force of your momentum, its ski mechanics will project it down the fall line.

Repeat this over and over again, each time exploring the use of your ankle and knee in creating angles. if you begin to skid through your turn, first apply a little ankle angulation, then knee angulation and see if this helps to lessen the skidding. Again, in this progression maintain a wedge at all times. As a rule, persistent skidding suggests that you're abandoning your edges too soon or not using them with much conviction. Use this drill for learning how to patiently ride your edged downhill ski all the way through a turn until you've transferred your weight to the other ski.

Kinesthetic Hint. When angulating the ankle, you only feel pressure against the inside of your downhill boot. When adding the knee, you feel the added pressures on the inside of the down-hill knee as well as the inside portion of your lower thigh (the gracilis and sartorius muscles as well as the inner portion of the quadricep). Isolate the pressures and relax the rest of the body to realize the precise value of this drill. Tony adds, "When I combine steering and knee angulation, and the resistance to the resultant pressures increases, I feel the muscles on the outside of my quads near the knee."

Foot pedals

Purpose: To develop the balance and independent use of your legs in order to use each ski more effectively relative to terrain changes, the action of the other ski, and changes in conditions.

Conditions: Standard

Slope ratings: Standard

Performing the Drill. Ski parallel across the hill at FLEP #2 to #4. Actively pick up one foot/ski and set it down; pick up the other foot/ski and set it down; continue across the hill, turn, and continue back the other way. Do this as rapidly as you can as if you were pedaling a bicycle. At all times keep your hands in drills position.

Kinesthetic Hint. You experience a feeling of momentary weightlessness when each ski is lifted off the snow, especially when the downhill ski is elevated. To stay in balance, you must keep the upper body quiet and relaxed and let your legs do the work from a stable pelvis.

Ankle flex

Purpose: To finish your turns by the use of subtle ankle angulation and active foot steering throughout the complete arc of your turns

Conditions: Standard

Slope rating: Standard

Performing the Drill. At first, use FLEP #2 or #3 and drills position to get accustomed to the mechanics of this drill. As you cross the hill, tip your ankle into the hill, then relax it; tip-relax tip-relax, all the way across the hill. (Recall in an earlier drill that when you tipped your ankle into the hill you were in a wedge and were supposed to hold the angulation constant.) See how much control you can have on the movement of your skis with these subtle tips into the hill. You'll find that there is quite a bit.

Now, make this more challenging by steering your feet up the hill when you're ready to end your traverse. Coordinate your ankle tipping with your foot steering by turning your downhill foot/boot up the hill at the same time you tip your ankle. Simultaneously lighten your uphill ski and steer it up. (Lighten doesn't mean lift; rather, it means leaving your uphill ski in contact with the snow, but exerting no pressure on it to drive it through the snow, or push it against the snow.)

Turn or steer your downhill boot up the hill as you guide your uphill ankle up the hill

Ignore any awkwardness you may feel at first and, when you're ready to turn, concentrate on transferring your weight to your uphill ski as soon as you start to steer up. If your direct your upper body and center of mass down the fall line as soon as you've transferred the weight, you'll add rhythm and the sensation of smoothness to your turns with less skidding. You don't necessarily need a huge angulating movement to control a skid; ski with edge control by learning to use your ankles more subtly.

Kinesthetic Hint. You feel distinct pressure against the inside of your downhill boot with twinges of pressure radiating up to the inside of your knee. After doing this consistently across the slope, your downhill leg feels wobbly on both sides f your knee. Your uphill leg is very quietly steered, feeling little or no pressure.

Diverging step turns

Purpose: To use your uphill ski to prevent your downhill ski from skidding by learning to pressure and steer your skis to a more aggressive edge while not losing the ability to hold the downhill ski. By steering the inside ski away from the working ski, you help to tip the working ski to an edge by simultaneously increasing knee and ankle angulation. By steeping the diverging uphill ski away without this angulation you are moving your mass away from the working edge and decreasing its effectiveness.

Conditions: Standard

Slope rating: Standard

Performing the Drill. Refer back to the discussion of diverging turns in the section on lack of speed control; instead of pushing the diverging ski away from the downhill ski, step it away by lifting its tip slightly off the snow and stepping it into a diverged position.

In this version of the diverging turn, you make your step very soon after crossing the fall line and thereby cut way down on your traverse across the hill. You get into the rhythm of diverging, getting tall (extending), and turning rather than the previous drill's rhythm of diverging, getting tall, turning, and gliding. In this way, you can learn to more quickly round your turns and shorten their radius.

Kinesthetic Hint. If you exaggerate the drill (in this case a good idea), you may experience a pronounced pinching in the downhill hip/waist area similar to the feeling of an extreme side bend.

Short-Swing Turn

Short-swing turns have definite platforms at their start and finish, but very little pressure in the middle. In fact, it's one abrupt platform to another, turn to turn. There's a lot of quick swiveling; in a sense, the middle of the turn occurs off the snow.

People often think of a short-swing turn as a short distance turn; however, when i perform a short-swing turn at a high speed, making one very quick edge set to the next edge set, I travel perhaps 20 feet between turns. At a very slow speed, I can do the same move and travel only four feet. Besides the mechanics of the short-swing turn its distinguishing characteristic is not in the distance traveled but in the signature it leaves on the hill.

When you look at a series of short-swing turns etched in the snow, you clearly see where the edge set occurred to begin a turn, as well as where the edge set ended and initiated the next turn. These two edge sets look like railroad tracks set across the fall line at the particular angle you skied. Between the tracks the snow has been brushed away, creating a windshield-wiper effect; the snow always brushed off to the side of the fall line.

In sum, the short-swing turn has extreme pressure at the edge set in the beginning of the turn, no pressure in the middle (the windshield wiping phase), and extreme pressure at the finish (the new beginning). Understand that the short-swing turn is nothing more than a very dynamic short-radius turn and one that's an essential part of high performance skiing.

Converging Turns
Unfortunately, covering turns are associated with snow plows and stem christies, things that people generally want to out grow. The stem christies is quite valuable; on a very steep hill, it is sometimes your most effective turn. I like to use the stem christie on the race course at times when I want to hang on to the speed of my outside ski, yet still be set up for the next turn. What I do is keep my weight on the outside ski coming out of the turn and allow by center of mass to fall down the hill. Just as I'm about to catch the outside edge of my outside ski, I step onto the converged (or stemmed) inside ski, making it the new turning ski, and I ride it through the next gate.

A converged ski shoots you directly down the slope to where you want it to go and at a quicker pace. You are taking a force that is aimed in one direction and decelerating it very quickly; this creates forces, mass, and acceleration (M-A). Mass is constant; yet whenever you put a ski across a resultant force line, you create resistance. If you can deal with the result of that resistance, you will execute dynamically balanced turning; if you can't, you're going to crash. We are, however, at the mercy of gravity as we go down the hill. In a turn, I cannot accelerate when I'm turning, I can just decelerate less (you accelerate when you turn into the fall line).

One of the differences between a skilled skier and one who is less skilled is that the former decelerates less than the latter when turning. Done correctly, a converging turn can give you a measure of acceleration at the very beginning of a turn Sometimes you want this in your skiing, whether it be in a race course, mogul field, or free-skiing, whether it be in a race course, mogul field, or free-skiing, the latter of which requires you to make dramatic changes of direction to avoid obstacles or other skiers.

The Round-Finished Turn

The whole trick to a rounded turn is to allow your center of mass to get down the hill before your skis so that the skis will follow you, rather than the opposite. As your skis follow you, they will form the letter's in the snow. Generally, skiers who keep their center of mass up the hill from their skis tend to make a very quick, choppy initiation of the turn; they ski straight ahead for a while and then make a rather abrupt, sloppy finish to the turn because they are not steering the skis to finish the turn. These skiers are being steered by their skis. You want to lead the action rather than follow it and let your skis catch up with your body.

Lack of Edge Control

Though it's possible to ski without using your edges,

going straight down a hill can be very boring. Most recreational skiing consciously uses the inside edge of the downhill ski and the outside edge of the uphill ski, even though in actuality both edges of both skis work in subtle ways as you work your way down a slope. High performance skiing consciously incorporates both edges of both skis whenever they're needed. So, when we refer to edge control we refer to the ability to use both edges of both skis whenever the conditions and situation call for it. The following drills are designed to help you explore the possibilities of edge control from many different perspectives.

Sideslipping
Purpose: To increase your sensitivity of your edges relative to the movements of your feet/boots, with respect to the influence of your angles, your position on your skis, and the position of your skis relative to the fall line.

Conditions: All kinds

Slope rating: Intermediate through expert

Performing the Drill: In each of the following sideslipping drills, you're most often riding flat skis; that is, skis that are not gripping an edge and that glide or drift down the slope over the snow, sometimes brushing away the snow. Sideslipping is slipping in balance sideways. It is guided by the influence you give the skis with the weight of your body and by the subtle manipulation of the edges with your feet. As a rule, sideslip in the drills position but with your skis a little bit closer together and your center of mass and upper body facing down the fall line.

Stand at a 90 degree angle to the fall line, edges set, with your uphill ski slightly ahead of your downhill ski. Tip both of your boots down the fall line, just enough to allow the edges of your skis to release. If you keep your legs together, you allow your downhill ski to slip completely free of any edge pressure, using a subtle feathering or edging of the outside edge of your uphill ski to give you stability and control your speed.

On steeper terrain use the subtle edging and feathering of the uphill edges of both skis to control speed. Sideslipping is an excellent drill to do on very steep terrain or ice where it really tests your edge control skills.

To sideslip straight down the fall line, keep your weight centered right over your boots. If you want to move forward while sideslipping, anticipate the change by directing your weight slightly ahead with a forward flex on your boots, initiated with a slight flexing in the ankles. If you want to move back while sideslipping, direct your weight slightly behind with a comparable flex in your heels.

These subtle weight transfers in anticipation of the directional change, along with slight knee flexions and ankle movements that change edge pressure, influence the appropriate directional shifts of the tails and tips of your skis. Don't think too much about executing subtle ankle movements; instead, constantly keep your downhill ski running free or sideways. Learning the subtle control of your edges comes with practice of sideslipping in varied conditions.

Play with the following variations of sideslipping,

realizing that you'll likely have a strong side and weak side for slipping. Work on both.

Basic Sideslip. Sideslip straight down the fall line; on an angle down the fall line with the tips of your skis leading the way; and on an angle down the fall line with your tails leading the way.

Repetitive Sideslip to Hockey Stop. Sideslip to a point where you make a hockey stop: Simultaneously set the uphill edges of both skis by flexing at the knees and tipping your boots into the hill. To complete the hockey stop, flex and tip simultaneously, planting your pole down the hill from your boots to square your upper body down the fall line for balance; angle your knees into the hill to keep your skis from slipping. The platform developed by this hockey stop drill resembles the kind of platform you would use to ski the steeps.

Continue the drill by standing tall, releasing your edges, and sideslipping to another hockey stop. Repeat in a straight line all the way down the hill, switching sides and experimenting with different speeds. If you want to vary this, make half-hockey stops by flexing and tipping to a stop without using the pole plant, though still facing your upper body down the hill.

Expect to feel pressure against the inside ankle, outside knee, and outer portion of the thigh of your downhill leg; also expect to feel pressure against the outside ankle and hip of your uphill leg.

Falling Leaf: Sideslip like a leaf falling from a tree; first, slip the tips forward and then slightly uphill so that the skis almost stop second slip the tails back down the hill and then slightly uphill so that the skis almost stop. Continue down the hill, alternating the sideslip of the tips and tails. You can accomplish this by incorporating the directional changes of the preceding drill and by keeping your upper body relaxed rather than moving it to try to move your skis. The movements are very subtle. Continue to allow your downhill ski to run free by not pressuring its edges during these adjustments; feather the uphill ski by subtly applying on-and-off edge pressure to control direction and speed.

Directed Sideslip. Pick a target down the hill and sideslip to it; make this a moving target and sideslip to follow it.

Turn-Traverse Sideslip: Traverse-Turn Sideslip. Make a comfortable turn at slow speed traverse for 20 to 30 feet, then let your skis sideslip down the fall line for another 20 to 30 feet. Traverse diagonally across the hill, turn, and at the end of your turn let your skis sideslip. You can do this by skidding, but concentrate on sideslipping.

Pole Push Sideslip. Assume a sideslip position, flexed low so that you can place your poles to your sides and in the snow up the hill behind you; your center of mass is facing directly down the fall line. Release your edges and, pushing off with your poles, propel your slippage down the hill. Push easy and push hard; work with staying in balance over your skis. Employ your subtle foot action to keep you going straight and skiing a flat ski.

Sideslip Sprint. Just for fun and to get loose, sideslip as fast as you can down a slope. You experience being in balance and relaxed with effortless motion as if your boots were hooked with hinges to your lower legs; your upper body stays quiet while the hinges allow for subtle foot movements. You have to concentrate to feel your knees moving.

Single ski traverse
Purpose: To develop balance and pressure-edge control.
Conditions: Standard
Slope rating: Standard

Performing the Drill. In drills position, stand only on your downhill ski and traverse the hill at FLEP #1 or #2. Lift your uphill ski completely off the snow. Repeat in the other direction; go back and forth several times. Next, ski across the hill, each way, standing on only your uphill ski, holding your downhill ski completely off the snow.

Kinesthetic Hint. When skiing on your downhill ski, you feel pressure in your downhill knee and quadricep muscle; when skiing on your uphill ski, you feel a balancing tension in the inside of the uphill knee and inner thigh (gracilis and sartorius muscles, as well as the lower quadricep). Overall, you experience a feeling of balance in your hips. During the most awkward part of the drill, skiing only on the uphill ski, counterbalance with the downhill ski by holding it off of the snow, slightly converged toward the uphill ski.

Hot wedges
Purpose: To develop greater responsiveness to dynamic edge pressure, which is especially important in sleep terrain and greater quickness with on-and-off pressure, which is especially important in icy conditions.
Conditions: Standard and varied

Slope rating: Advanced and expert

Performing the Drill. From a wedge position, use exaggerated ankle and knee angulation to tip your skis on edge, one at a time making quick dynamic turns straight down the fall line. Hold your angles long and hard for deep carving; hold them briefly for quick on- and—off edge sets. When skiing longer edged turns, let the inside wedged ski float in a slight wedge to avoid resistance. When skiing quick on-and-off edge sets, keep the non-turning ski in contact with the snow in its wedged and ready position.

To make your wedges "hotter," add aggressive extension and flexion movements of your legs and an active pole touch rhythm. Vary the angles as much as possible and be very active with this wedge. Next, take it into moguls.

Kinesthetic Hint. You feel persistent pressure on the insides of your knees and lower thighs when holding the hot wedge. Repeated on-and-off wedges produce a lot of pressure on the insides of the ankles; if you don't feel it, you're not edging enough. In either case, you breathe a lot when performing hot wedges, yet your upper body is very quiet.

Chase skating

Purpose: According to Brent: To develop mobility in your skiing, flexibility in your moves, and better independent leg control, weight transfer, and edge-control

Conditions: Standard

Slope rating: Standard

Performing the Drill: This drill requires a lead skater and a chaser, but is predominantly for the chaser. The lead skater takes off across the fall line at FLEP #2 or #3. Skating at all times, even when turning, the chaser takes off after the lead skater and tries to catch him or her by using the same tracks as the lead skater. If you pick a skater who's a little faster than you, this is an excellent drill. If you're faster, give the lead skater a head start before you take off in pursuit.

Kinesthetic Hint: There's a very active pushing off of your downhill ski with each skating step. As you push off, simultaneously extend your uphill arm up and forward (elbow bent about 20 degrees) and thrust the elbow of your downhill arm in to your waist (elbow bent at 45 degrees). Very active are the key words in this drill!

Long leg, short leg

Purpose: To acquire versatility on skis and learn both how and when to use your edges; specifically, transferring your weight with subtlety when turning, riding a flat ski, getting your hip into the hill, and facing your center of mass down the fall line and your upper body over your turning ski.

Conditions: Standard

Slope rating: Standard

Performing the Drill. Assuming a wedge, ski across the slope at FLEP #2 to get used to the drill. Your task is to really ride the inside edge of your downhill ski, which is extended as far as possible away from your body. To make it straight and more on edge tip your upper body out over the downhill ski. When you do this, extend your short leg somewhat to stay in balance. Your wedged or converged inside ski should ride flat on the snow with your knee up under your chest, your boot under your hip.

As you do this, allow the inside ski to be very light, in contact with the snow, but exerting little or no force. Just ride the downhill ski until you're ready to turn and use the finish of the carving/turning to initiate your transfer of weight to the weight-less inside ski. At this point of weight transfer, simply extend this new turning ski (your long leg) while retracting the other ski as it becomes your new inside ski (your short leg). Repeat this all the way down the hill, getting the maximum extension out of your long legs and the maximum quiet and flat-riding out of your short legs.

Kinesthetic Hint: If you feel a pressure in the downhill hop when you're doing this drill, you're performing at a basic level. If you feel a definite pinch with the pressure in the waist and hip area, you're getting more extension out of your long leg and working at an advanced level; as a result, you're getting more of your hip into the hill: the giant slalom racer's goal. In either case, your inside leg feels like it's doing very little; it's as if you had to lift your inside knee up to shorten the leg and get it out of the way in order to fully extend your long leg.

High speed stem christies
Purpose: To develop a sense of sequential leg rotation or, more simply, the use of both of your legs independently to effect a more dynamic turn. In that christies were designed to include some skidding, the edging of the downhill ski is gradual; but in this drill,

the gradual edging is more like quickly graduated skidding, which allows your lightened inside ski to smoothly match the down-hill ski. In a way, when the drill works you are matching the inside ski with the stepped ski at approximately the same time the latter stops skidding

Conditions: Standard; can be variable

Slope rating: Advanced and expert

Performing the Drill. First, you must think of the words dynamic and refinement. At slower speeds, this drill is used to teach skiers to match their skis while turning. We're going to rev it up for the advanced skier's acquisition of more refined edging skills. Start in drills position, FLEP #4. Ski comfortably but a bit more aggressively down the hill. When you're ready to turn, actively step your uphill ski out and down the hill ahead of your present downhill ski, pointing the tip of your ski in the direction your want to go. As soon as this stepped ski makes contact with the snow, it will be flat and skid, becoming your new turning ski. Stand tall for a moment and then flex at the ankles to make the edges of your ski seek to stop skidding as you move your new inside ski to a parallel position. If you do this at a high speed and in control you'll learn a great deal about the tiny movements your edges make with the help of your feet-to propel you down the mountain. At first, be very obvious with this drill and use a lot of exaggerated movement; even make it playful! Step side to side all the way down the run.

Kinesthetic Hint. You should feel yourself becoming very extended and tall when making the step, until the ski begins to skid. When you begin to skid you sense a momentary loss of speed, which is not regained until you match the other ski with your flexing movement.

Swiveling

Purpose: To develop greater edge sensitivvity and control as well as balance and confidence.

Conditions: Standard

Slope rating: Beginner and low intermediate

Performing the Drill. Part One: Just as in the dance, the twist, you swivel both skis together with little edge pressure or angles. Move to a run where there is plenty of room and swivel away. Move the two relatively flat skis in unison to the beat of your twisting at the waist. This involves counterrotation: While the upper body twists right the skis twist left; upper body left, skis right. If you need to add directional force to the drill to avoid obstacles, feather the inside edge of your downhill ski as you swivel.

Part Two: Swivel as above, but this time travel across the fall line while swiveling. Gradually bend your upper body at the waist into the hill while swiveling, moving from a slight to an exaggerated bend. Your skis will react by edging with each bend of your upper body because you've created angles. Many high performance skiers consider the relationship between the hips and edges one of the most important in skiing If you add ankle flex with this bending you can exert even more directional control over your swiveling. Again, it's all a matter of edge control and subtle angles.

Kinesthetic Hint. In part one you sense that you are twisting madly, yet if your skis are not flat, you'll catch an outside edge and fall. While keeping your skis flat, you feel the focus in your feet. In part two, while executing the exercise across the fall line, the movement of your hips is abrupt and forceful; the sensation of your skis edging in quick and definite.

OVERROTATION OF UPPER BODY

Problems arise when you use the weight and force of your upper body to make your lower body turn the skis. The obvious problems are skidding turns, edging without precision, falling back on your skis, skiing out of balance, becoming fatigued easily, and looking and feeling as awkward as a child taking his or her first steps.

These problems won't necessarily disappear if you stop over-rotating your upper body. This is because controlling your upper body is only one aspect of the remedy. Fortunately, overrotation has such a major impact on your skiing that learning to control it will take you a long way in overcoming these problems.

Imagine trying to walk if you were always throwing your body forward when you stepped forward. Your body's natural reaction would be to coil back to restore balance. The same force operate in skiing. Your arms complicate matters: When you overrotate your upper body by swinging your arms around like helicopter blades, one arm ends up down the fall line (which is okay) and the other arm ends up pointing up the hill behind you (which is not okay). Quickly, you adapt by swinging back the other way and, subsequently, throw yourself out of balance. Back and forth down the mountain, you ski out of balance out of control, out of sync, falling back, falling forward, skidding, slipping, losing direction, and following your skis.

This description of the consequences of overrotation should make it clear that skiing in the high performance mode involves getting the most out of the rotational balance between upper and lower body. To quote Dr. George Twardokens:

> The standard source of turning force in advanced skiing is rotation of the lower limbs turning against a relatively stable upper body. The mass of the upper body is composed of the head, chest, upper extremities and the ski poles. The lower body mass includes lower limbs, skis, boots and bindings. The pelvic region sometimes rotates together with the lower limbs, and at other times it provides resistance for the lower limbs together with the upper body.

In the most basic language, overrotating your upper body excludes the opportunity to make precise turns; that is, turns that are free of the problems noted earlier, and turns that do not lead to muscular fatigue. Try the following drills and exercises to work on stabilizing your upper body relative to lower body rotation.

Pole feeler; Poles in front
Purpose: To develop a quiet, stable upper body that is square with the fall line and not used as a force to make your skis change directions.

Conditions: Standard; mild bumpy terrain with good snow

Slope rating: Standard

Performing the Drill. For the pole feeler, find a comfortable turn rhythm and slope. Instead of using your poles to initiate turns, grip your handles as if they were swords. Extend your arms and poles to your sides forming a human cross; then assume a lower then normal skiing stance, allowing the tips of your poles a touch the snow. Your ski poles are now your antennae. Ski down the run, using your lower body to make the turns, at all times keeping your poles to your sides and in contact with the snow. If your poles come off the snow, or drift in front of or behind you, stop. Begin again in the starting position, and resume the drill, skiing the entire run doing pole feelers.

If you have problems with thus drill, you may be guilty of some or all of the following: twisting too much at the waist/upper body; dragging your arms behind you while turning; not moving your knees; not working your skis independently; and not using subtle foot/boot pressure, steering, or banking.

5
THE TOOLS

CLOTHING

Several years ago, while teaching a group of skiers, it became clear that after the first couple of runs that all but one were good parallel skiers. She was just inconsistent; the occasional skilful turn mixed in with a number of hesitant turns resulted in a rather disappointing performance. Her skiing ability, plus a mixture of very dated and drab clothing made her very self-conscious, which did not help. We persisted for a couple of days, but with no real improvements. One evening we all went to a bar and on the way passed a ski shop, in the window of which was an attractive one-piece ski suit.

We are not suggesting that you all go out and buy a new outfit every time your skiing hits a plateau, and it does sound rather superficial to say that the way we look should to say that the way we look should affect our performance, but believe that it an important factor. An average skier's time down a slalom course might well be bettered if he wore racing pants and a racing jumper. The reasons for this are complex, but relate to a technique that will be discussing later known as visualisation. Many of you will probably protest vehemently that this does not apply to you, and it may not. We know a number of skiers who need to dress down to feel comfortable. The point is that you must feel good about what you are wearing both mentally and physically, and it must be appropriate for the task.

On the practical side there are a number of important points about clothing which will affect your performance. You are operating in a very hostile environment, and as you well know, it is not all sunny days and clear blue skies. The temperature can easily drop to minus 20°C (-4°F); add to this any wind and the wind-chill factor will reduce it still further. Your body must be protected from these extremes of temperature so that it can perform the highly skilful tasks asked of it in safety.

At the same time the clothing must not restrict movement, and this is the first dilemma that the designer has to face up to. All warm clothing relies on trapping dead air, as this offers the highest degree of insulation. If the clothing is too loose, you will move this dead air as you move around, thus destroying some of its insulative value. Conversely, if it is too tight it will restrict your circulation which in turn will make your extremities cold.

For this reason, ideal clothing system is based on the principle that it must be well tailored. It will fit closely around the main body, usually with a belt or elastic waistband. The arms, shoulders and legs will allow a full range of movement without disturbing the main bodice and the air trapped inside it.

When you try on clothing make sure that you try on the whole system and put it through the complete range of movements you are likely to make when skiing. For example, if you are buying a separate jacket and pants, try them both on at the same time. There is nothing worse than finding that when you bend over the small of your back is bared. It is very important to keep this area protected as it is the place where your kidneys, which carry a lot of blood, are closest to the surface. In fact, some motor cyclists wear a kidney belt which is a broad band of extra insulation around their midriffs. Whether such a device could be designed for the skier who is obviously more mobile, Perhaps a scarf tied around the waist would be as good.

A one-piece suit tends to solve this problem, but whether it is better than a combination is a difficult question. Providing you can unzip the front you can regulate the temperature quite well, and the value of a one-piecer in the powder speaks for itself. Having said that does get down your neck will have to travel the whole length of your body before it can escape, by which time it is cold water.

Basic Design Features

Whether you adopt a one-or two-piece system there are some basic design features to look for. The collar should be large enough to allow your head to be encased up to the level of your mouth and perhaps as far as your nose. We always found this feature far more satisfactory than a scarf, although many people do use scarves, particularly the silk ones which the snow does not stick to. We do not favour hoods that we cannot detach, because when we fall over it fills up with snow and then it seems impossible to empty it without it going down your neck. The system we prefer is a thin windproof nylon hood which is stored within the collar of the garment. We then suggest to wear a normal ski hat, and in the same compartment as the hood we store a motor cyclist's silk Balaclava for when the temperature are really cold.

Moving on down the body, we would like to see someone design an integrated glove system where the glove and the sleeve could be joined together. Cold hands can make you feel miserable even when everything else is marvellous. There are two main reasons for cold hands: the first is that the gloves are often too tight hampering circulation, and the second is that they do not adequately protect the wrist, where the blood supply is closest to the surface. An integrated system would not only help the second point but would also prevent area after a fall. Mitts are unquestionably warmer than gloves, but personally prefer the dexterity offered by gloves unless, it is very cold. Whichever you decide upon ensure that they are big enough and that they cover the wrist. We often sew a Velcro band around the wrist and on the inside of sleeves to make own integrated system. Whenever you have to take your gloves off in cold conditions put them inside your jacket rather than on the ground or on the top of your ski pole, and just before putting them back on blow into them a couple of times it is like putting on toasted gloves!

Any zips should have good covering flaps to prevent snow sticking to them and the wind blowing through them. We like to have a number of pockets in which to store things, and we find the large cargo style pockets, out of harm's way on the legs, especially useful. These pockets must have adequate zips and coves otherwise they just become collectors of snow.

Velcro has limited uses as a fastening system on ski clothing because it very easily becomes clogged with snow; for this reason it should not be the only method employed.

Extra padding on the knees is very much appreciated on long chair-lift rides where the knees can become very stiff with the cold. Additional waterproofing on the seat is also welcomed on those little pockets that used to appear on the arms that we could keep our lift passes in? We hate having the thing dangling around neck, threatening to strangle as it spins in the wind, and don't feel confident about the security of the plastic pouches that you can slip over the arm. A lost lift ticket can cause enormous problems. There are a number of different systems to be found at the bottom of the trouser legs, which as long as they are robust, keep out the snow, fit over the top of the boot and do not restrict leg movement when they are in place, should be fine.

If we were wearing a combination of jacket and trousers then we always prefer salopettes. They help to eliminate any chilling around the kidney area and avoid the problem of separation between the jacket and the trousers. Personally, we don't like racing plants as we find them too cold in many conditions and a little restrictive; on the other hand they do give a lot of sensory feedback about what the legs are doing which some people like. If you like them and are warm enough in them, then wear them.

Materials

Of all the insulative materials available, the best is still natural down. The problem is that it is very expensive and if it gets wet it becomes a soggy mass with little insulative value. Many of the synthetic equivalents are close to down in performance, and since a new one appears every season we can only suggest that you compare the clo values. A clo is a unit representing the insulative value of a material.

For the outer skin we can choose between cottons, nylons and the revolutionary breathable waterproof fabrics. We have found the latter to be excellent at their best and at their worst no worse than anything else. It is important not to expect too much from them and to remember that they need careful handling. When they become dirty they will not work so well, and in some cold conditions any condensation will freeze thereby blocking the pores through which the water vapour would normally pass. If you do sweat in them, it is probably because you are wearing too many clothes; if the body is too hot it will sweat in order to lose some of this excessively heat. Remember, they do not prevent you from sweating, they just allow the water vapour to escape thus reducing the build-up of condensation. If you do choose a garment made of one of these breathable waterproof fabrics be sure that all the seams are taped, otherwise they will leak annoyingly. Many manufacturers have started to use cotton fabrics again, but generally they are no cheaper and do not appear to have any great advantages over other materials. Bearing in mind these criteria, the rest is up to you and the designer's imagination.

Underwear has also undergone some radical changes; string vests and itchy woollen long johns are things of the past. The new breed of underwear will draw the sweat away from the skin, reducing that clammy feeling. These new polypropylene-based materials are certainly an improvement and most people find them very comfortable. However, wool is' still one of the best insulators, and if you really suffer from the cold, you can buy woollen vests and long johns which are much improved from the itchy of the past.

Glasses and goggles

Before moving on to the hardware of boots, binding and skis, let us first say a word about glasses and goggles. They are essential items and should be worn at all times on the mountains. Too many people do not wear them, presumably for reasons of vanity. Even when there are clouds about the dangerous ultraviolet rays are still getting through and the damage they do is permanent. Whether you wear glasses or goggles is up to you. We tend to wear glasses until the weather is very bad, and then we find goggles better.

Double lenses do not seem to mist up as badly, as single ones, and a useful tip is to carry a piece of lint on to which you have sprinkled a small amount of washing-up liquid. Periodically wipe the lens, inside and out, and this should prevent any further misting. Some goggles sport different coloured lenses that are supposed to enhance visibility when it is bad, and some certainly seem to do so.

Boots

Downhill Boots

Downhill ski boots come in two designs: front entry and rear entry. The pros and cons for each are numerous and tend to be very personal, so let us first outline some basics which hold true regardless of the design.

Comfort should be your biggest priority when choosing a boot. Uncomfortable feet can ruin an otherwise perfect day, not to mention the detrimental effect they will have on your skiing. A bad workman blames his tools the old saying goes, but if it is painful for the master craftsman even to hold his chisel then how can he possibly carve accurately with it? The same applies to skiing : sensitivity in your feet leads to sensitivity in your skiing. Feet that are constantly in discomfort cannot concentrate on giving you the feedback you require to ski well.

With most modern boots it is only necessary to wear one pair of socks and on very cold days these can be supplemented by very thin polypropylene inner socks. The boot should fit firmly around the heel and ankle, but be loose enough round the toes to allow them to wriggle about. This is important in order that the circulation is not impaired thus causing cold feet. When you try on a pair of boots the following may help you choose the correct fitting:

1. Do the boot up completely and stand in them as through you were skiing, with your shin bones resting against the tongues of the boot. This ensures that your heel slides to the back of the boot, and if you don't do this the boot will often appear to be too small and be cramping the toes.
2. In the warmth of the shop your feet will probably have swollen more than they would when skiing, so try the boots on with either a very thin pair of socks or no socks at all.
3. Put on a pair of skis if possible and go through the motions of skiing for several minutes. This should

highlight and likely painful spots. It will also entertain the other customers, but at least you will be sure of the comfort of your boots.

Ski shops the world over have improved dramatically in the last few years on the quality of the service they offer, and most will do an excellent job of ensuring your comfort. A good ski boot will have very little flex laterally or backwards, but should flex forwards. This forward flex is absolutely vital. Jump up and down a few times trying to land as softly as possible, noticing how the ankle bends. Now try the same thing with your ankles stiff. Several years ago a major boot manufacturer produced a model that was, because of its comfort, very popular. Gradually, however, ski-instructors began to notice that these boots caused the user's skiing to be noticeably wooden, simply because the boots were too stiff. Even racers were cutting the boots about to improve the forward flex. Fortunately, the company has redesigned the boot, incorporating a good forward flex system.

Boots that have a variable flex system are good, because in the warmth of the shop the plastic will be soft but it will probably have a different flex pattern when used in the sub-zero temperatures on snow. Some skiers will also want to change the flex pattern according to the type of skiing they are doing.

A modern boot has a number of other adjustments. The forward lean angle of the boot can often be adjusted and this is quite different to the forward flex. When we bend our ankles forward, moving our shin bones towards our toes, we make the whole of our foot more stable laterally, and this can be advantage when we are trying to control an edged ski.

The boot can help by allowing some forward flexing, but also by having a degree of permanent lean built into the design. The amount you use is a matter of personal preference, but we would try to use as little as possible providing you can flex your boot easily- what feels right probably is right. There are some notable ski teachers who argue that we should have very little forward lean in order to allow a much looser style to develop. This is certainly true of the ski racer who often has to glide on a flat ski to maintain speed, but for the skier of real snow it only applies to what are known as surf turns.

The other major adjustment is what Jean-Claude Killy, one of the most successful ski racers of all time, called the 'secret weapon': Canting. For many years, arguing that when skiing our legs are never static and that they would adapt to slight misalignments. Then we brought a pair of boots with a canting facility and, without checking, we put them on and walked at to meet ski class. Even while walking out we realised that something was wrong and as soon as we started to ski we felt in total sympathy with class of beginners. How do we control these planks on the ends of our legs? On inspection we discovered that boots had been canted, so at the first opportunity rapidly adjusted them to a neutral position. If canting can work negatively in this way, it follows that it can also work positively for those who need it. The amount of canting is quite difficult to assess, even with the aid of a canting machine. We suggest you use such a machine as a starting point and then adjust your boots until you find the position with which you are happiest. Your ski-instructor should also be able to give you good advice.

When we buy expensive boots, we are paying not only for the aforementioned facilities but also for the ability to customise the boot to our foot. This is usually achieved through some sort of foaming system and the facility for customisation is a major breakthrough in boot comfort.

Another major breakthrough is in the type of footbeds available. Most ski shops are able to supply custom-made footbeds for your boots through a variety of systems, and we believe the extra expense is well worthwhile. For many years has been an argument on the merits of rear versus front entry boots. To mind the major difficulty with the rear entry design has been in coping with the problems of different forefoot shapes. If the boots did not fit your foot shape there was very little facility to change the profile. The latest ranges of rear entry boots are much better in this respect, however, and with modern advancements is design these boots should gain in popularity. The main advantage in front entry boots is their ability to be adjusted throughout the boot's length. Rear entry boots do have one major or advantage however, if you undo the back of the boot it is much more comfortable to walk in. Many ski tourers have started to use them, especially those who go in search of good skiing rather than good climbing.

Ski Touring boot
Most touring boots are a compromise between a ski boot and a mountaineering boot, and like so many compromises, it is rare to get the best of both words and more common to get the worst. Despite this, there have been a number of recent models that have been very good. As ski touring has gained in popularity so

more time and energy has been spent on giving us, the customers, what we ant: a ski boot that is also good foe climbing or a climbing boot that can be used for skiing. There are several new boots on the market that sport all the adjustment facilities the downhill boots, and we think it is only a matter of time before we see a rear entry downhill boot with a Vibram Climbing sole. Whichever boot you choose the major this time it must be for both going downhill and uphill.

Skis

Choosing Your skis

It is important to have the right ski for a particular type of skiing and the criteria for choosing an off-piste ski are as varied as those for a piste ski. A ski that is good in light powder, for example, will not be very good on hard, neve. Generally, however, the majority of off-piste conditions do favour a softer flexing ski. This tends to be more forgiving in the varied conditions met away from the prepared runs, and a soft shovel can be a help in allowing the tip of the ski to float to the surface in deeper snows. If you aspire to ski steep terrain the superior holding power of a stiffer ski will be a definite advantage. This ski will also have a similar advantage on hard icy surfaces where the soft ski will be very unnerving. Shorter than normal skis are certainly easier to turn in difficult snows, but can put you at a serious disadvantage if there are long schusses involved. Several years ago we were invited to observe the French Guides undergo their ski touring training at the Ecloe Nationale de Ski et Alpinism in Chamonix.

Since most of you will be skiing on-piste as well as in real snow we would recommend that you do not buy a specialised powder ski but stick initially to the skis you enjoy using on the prepared snow; you will be able to handle them off-piste as well. Our own preference is for one of the high performance recreational skis which seem to be good all-round performers. They usually have a softer tip and tail, a good stiff mid-section to help the ski grip the ice and a lively feel to them. The side cut will lie somewhere between that of the slalom ski and giant slalom ski and they should be skied at about 10 to 15cm (4 to 6 inches) above head height. When deciding on the length of a ski look at the manufacturer's recommendations; it will be designed to be skied at a particular length relative to your ability, style and body size, and nothing will be gained by skiing it any shorter.

When choosing skis for touring you are faced not only with hundreds of downhill skis but also with a selection of specialist touring skis as well. These often have broader shovels to help the ski plane to the surface and a hole in the tip, which we always assumed was for clipping a karabiner into in times of need. We are now in doubt about this as the only time we have been in such need we found the hole too small. The skis are usually built robustly, although many piste skis nowadays also sport the tougher P-tex 20000 bases. At the tail you will often find a small botch, which has been cut there to help hold certain skin systems in place. This is easy to file out yourself if your skis do not have such a feature. Finally, the top surface is usually brightly coloured to help you find your ski when it comes off in the deep snow. We wonder how long it will be before a device is on the market which can be fixed on to the ski and used with our avalanche transceivers to aid the ski's recovery in powder.

To make this awkward choice you must first decide whether your interest will be with traditional touring where the main concern is to use the ski to travel in the high mountains, or with the slightly more recent idea of using touring skills to reach better skiing. If it is the former you will want to choose a ski that is slightly shorter and therefore easier to carry, whereas if it is the latter you will need a ski capable of performing well.

Whichever skis you have, they are looked after in the same way, Repairing maintaining your own skis is not a difficult task, and it is very important that you make any necessary repairs swiftly and efficiently. If you put a hole in the base of your skis that goes through to the material underneath the P-tex, it is essential that you seal this hole before water can enter. If water does enter it might freeze, delaminating the sole in the process. You an temporarily plug the hole in two ways. Firstly you can rub wax into the gap; this is very temporary but will at least keep the water out for a while. Secondly, and more permanently, using a lighted P-tex candle drip molten P-tex into the hole. It may be necessary to clean the hole is very big, to build the repair up in layers. This repair will be quite messy and full of dirty-looking carbon deposits, but you can always do a more professional repair when you return home. Keep an eye on the repair; sometimes usually because the sole is full of wax, the repair does not stick. IF the happens you will have to clean the sole with a de-waxer first and then do the repair again. Let the repair cool completely, then, using a metal scraper, level the P-tex down to the ski base. At the end of the season you can clean out all these messy repairs, de-wax the sole and renew the P-tex repair. The cleanest way of doing this is to use a P-tex gun or a very hot iron to melt the P-tex you can also buy it in thinner strip-form which is easier to melt. Having melted it in, continue as before. If the hole is very large it may be necessary to glue a slab of P-tex into place using Araldite or a similar adhesive and then fill in the gaps with melted P-tex.

Keeping your edges sharp is as important to the off-piste skier as it is to the piste skier. Obviously the edges will make no difference in powder, but no hardpack and ice sharp edges are essential. We blunt the edges for about 20cm (8inches) from either end on the inside and a little further on the outside edge. This makes the skis left-and right-footed, so remember to mark them as such. The exact amount to blunt them can only really be determined by trial and error. The purpose of blunting the edges is to stop the front hooking into the turns and to prevent the back from catching at the end of a turn.

Take the trouble to buy a good quality file and a file card to clean it with. Any single cross-cut file will do, but look at the end of the file to check it is not twisted -cheap ones often are. Only file on the forward stroke lifting the file clear as you return to the start; this will prolong the life of your file considerably, as it is only designed to cut on the forward stroke. Steel has a grain similar to that in wood, and you will achieve a much better result if you stroke with the grain. To determine which way the grain goes, file in both directions: one should feel smoother and produce a cleaner-looking surface although much will depend upon the quality of the metal used. If you can't tell don't worry just sharpen the edges from the tip to the tail.

The base of the ski must be flat-filed to ensure that the ski is not railed in other words that the edges are not proud of the base. Ideally you should do one edge at a time stroking from the centre of the ski outwards, thus stopping any of the swarf (the metal shavings) from becoming embedded in the base. This, however, is quite difficult, so alternatively just make sure that you brush the swarf away frequently. Check the flatness with a straight edge; your metal scraper should suffice.

Having flat-filed the base, turn the ski on to its side and sharpen the edges. You can buy a number of devices that will help you to ensure that the edges are sharpened at 90 degrees. When you have finished sharping them, use a stone to run along the edges just to take away any burrs that are present. To check whether the edge is sharp enough. We scrape the top surface of nail across the edge and if a thin silver is left on the metal then we know it is right. We now use some low-grade wet and dry (emery cloth-wrapped around a block to rub down the sole, which prepares it for waxing.

There are basically two types of wax: hot wax which as its name implies, is applied in a molten form, and cold rub-on waxes. The latter come in a variety of colours which indicate the temperatures at which they should be used and they are simply rubbed on to the running surface of the ski. The former also comes suited to different temperatures, but for most uses the universal grade seems to be adequate. For many years we used to argue that we went quite fast enough without having to resort to waxes to gain speed. The point that we missed was that wax not only allows the skis to glide downhill more easily but also to glide downhill more easily, and we spend most of our time trying to ski round corners.

The waxing system we use is a universal hot wax supplemented with an appropriate rub-on wax when the temperature reaches either of the extremes and the skis begin to stick. The P-tex base is a porous surface and as such will absorb quite a lot of wax. Using an old domestic iron we melt the wax on to the surface of the ski and then literally born it in, adding more wax if the base absorbs all that is present. You must never let the iron rest in one spot, but keep it moving gradually over the surface. The base will get quite hot and the ski will take on reverse camber, but providing you keep the iron moving you should not do nay damage to the ski. When the P-tex will absorb no more wax, let the ski cool.

Once the wax has cooled you can start scraping it. Using the plastic scraper, clear way all the surface wax, especially the wax that has dripped on to the edges. Then, buff up the surface with a cork to get a really good finish and the ski will be ready to use. In soft snow conditions this type of hot-waxing can last up to a week. Providing you scrape the base thoroughly you can wax your touring skis in the same way; the skins will still stick.

At the end of the season hot-wax your skis and store them without scraping them down, making sure that the wax covers the edges so that they will not rust.

Bindings

The advice for normal piste bindings is simple: buy the best you can afford. The top models of every range are all very good, and are probably as safe as each other. Each has a slightly different functional capability-one design will release better with one type of fall, whilst another will be best in a different type of situation; but what type of fall causes the most injuries off-piste we do not know. Whichever model you choose, it must be correctly adjusted according to the manufacturer's recommendations. If you are hiring remember that the shop will generally only adjust what is known as the pre-tension. In other words, they will fit your boot to the binding but they will not adjust the tension to suit you that is your responsibility. There are a couple of quick and easy tests that you can do that will at least tell you whether the binding will release in the event of a fall;

1. *The toe-piece* Check that when the boot is in position there is sufficient space to be able to slide a credit card between the sole of the boot and the anti-friction pad (which must also be in good condition). If you cannot do this, raise the toe-piece by rotating the large screw on top until you can. Remove the boot and see if you can rotate the toe-piece using one hand. Your wrist strength is proportional to your ankle strength so if you cannot do this the binding is set too tightly. To adjust it, rotate the large screw at the end of the binding; this will move the cursor, inside the window on top of the binding. The higher the number, the tighter the binding, so adjust it until you can only just release it. If you have the setting too low, the binding will pre-release and you will fall unnecessarily. This

part of the binding can easily freeze up overnight or even over an extended lunch-break, so it is a good idea to acquire the habit of giving it a quick twist with your hand to ensure that it is working freely before skiing. The heel piece will free itself by the action of stepping into it.

2. *The heel-piece* To check that this part is correctly adjusted, step into your binding with your boot fastened as it would be if you were skiing. Let's say the ski is on your right leg: step the left foot forward and then vigorously push your right knee towards the tip of the ski; the binding should just release. If it is set too lightly it will pre-release. This manoeuvre may need a couple of attempts before you get it just right and it might help to have someone standing on the tail of the ski. The heel-piece has a similar window to the toe unit and it is adjusted in the same way, using a screw this time at the rear of the binding.

If your binding bears no relation to description or if you do not feel confident about making the adjustments, ask the ski mechanic or your ski-instructor to show you how. They are unlikely to be insured to actually make the adjustments themselves, but they should be able to show you how to make them for yourself.

These tests are by no means foolproof, but in the absence of manufacturer's guidelines they should at least prevent you from skiing on bindings that are too tight for you. If the bindings do come off too easily tighten them up about half a division at a time until they only release in a bad fall. Many very good skiers believe that if you ski properly you can ski on very light settings, but we think that this can be just as dangerous as you then run the considerable risk of them pre-releasing at the slightest error in judgement, resulting in upper limb injuries as bad as broken leg. Furthermore, some of the techniques in real snow involve considerable rotational forces to be applied to the binding which, if it is set too lightly, will cause it to come off. All modern binding have a ski brake and it is vital that this works correctly; a loose ski quickly picks up speeds of 60m.p.h. or more and at this speed it could be lethal to someone who has fallen over below you. Unfortunately, as most of you will be aware, ski brakes do not work very well in deep snows. We have all seen the sorry soul digging forlornly in the hope that he will find his ski that has so mysteriously disappeared without trace.

The alternative is to wear powder leashes, but you then run the risk of being hit by the ski in the event of a fall. However, most falls in deep snow, although spectacular because of the explosion of snow, do not normally involve you in the tumbling action that is a real danger with leashes. Another option is to have leashes that are about two metres (2 yards) in length. Store them inside the snow gaiter at the bottom of your ski pants (but these could be even more dangerous). Similar lengths of cord with a floater on the end have been successfully used; the floater rises to the surface making it easier to locate the lost ski.

If you do not want to use leashes and you do lose your ski, the following hints may help you to find it. Mark the spot where you landed with your ski pole and start to search about two to three metres (2 to 3 yards) higher up the slope. It is important that you do not poke around aimlessly; use the tail of your other ski or a partner's ski and slice down the slope at about 25cm (10inch) intervals. The more you walk over the area, the more likely you are to tread the lost ski deeper into the snow. By being methodical about our searching we have never lost a ski and usually manage to find it quite quickly.

It is not quite so easy to deal with touring bindings because they have to perform many different functions and no binding, in our opinion, does them all perfectly. Let us go through these various functions and decide upon some priorities. The first is that, as nearly as possible, the binding should release as well as a downhill model. This presents no problem for the heel unit, but it is quite difficult to include a downhill toe unit. It is may feeling that whichever units are used they should be capable of being released whether the binding is in the uphill or downhill mode. The reason's that people do fall over going uphill and also on short downhill sections where it would take too long to change the mode.

Whether you have to remove the boot in order to alter the mode of the binding is not of great importance, because you always have to take the ski off in order to fix the skins in place. Whatever, system is employed to fix the binding in the downhill position. It must allow for the easy removal of any build-up of ice. Also, because of the added friction caused by a vibram sole, the toe unit must have a compensatory mechanism. The unit should have a climber, which is a simple device allowing the user to climb uphill more easily, and it should be possible to employ this feature without stepping out of the binding.

Bindings need very little maintenance; all do is slacken the tension springs at the end of the season. If the internal workings look a little dry, re-grease them. Be sure to use a grease which is recommended by the manufacturer; some greases may not perform correctly at the low temperatures we encounter when skiing.

Poles

There are two types of hand grip available ; the traditional strap and the sword grip. If you use a strap ensure that it is correctly adjusted and preferably of the variety that will release in the event of the pole getting caught. The choice of grip is entirely personal, but if you are touring we would suggest that the strap is more versatile. Paul Rammer, an American who has designed a complete touring system, advocates a grip which incorporates a handle similar to an ice-axe head that can be used to help stop a serious fall.

Some poles have a shaft that can be shortened, but in experience this is just one more thing to go wrong. They are designed specifically for touring, when carrying the poles on your sack can be awkward. Different length poles can also be useful when climbing on your skis. To overcome the problem of having to hold the poles at half-height we bind a length of string around the staff for about 20cm (8 inches) below the handle. Some touring poles can be screwed together to make an avalanche probe, which although quite thick and therefore difficult tc use, is better than nothing.

There are many different designs of basket. The bigger ones are quite good in the powder, while those which swivel about their centres are best for steep skiing where a stiff basket may pole planting difficult.

Shovel

The main criteria are that it should be strong and light, so most of the good ones are made of aluminium and have a curved blade to give added strength. With the advances in modern plastics there are a few shovels that are made of this materials, but we have had no experience of them. The remaining items of equipment are only likely to be used by the ski tourer.

Skins

These are synthetic strips of bristly material that are fixed to the base of the ski and allow the skier to go uphill-they will slide forwards but not backwards. There are numerous systems by which they are fixed to the ski base, the most popular of which is by gluing. The glue remains on the skin and may need replenishing at times. After a while it may form into small globules, and it is then time to remove the old glue and recondition the skin with new glue. The old glue can be removed with a solvent but this is very messy; it is better to use a hot air gun to melt the glue and then scrape if off with a metal scraper. On tour it is wise to carry a small piece of rag with which to wipe away any excess moisture as this will impair the sticking action. The system that we use, and which we have always found very satisfactory, has a small hook on the back of the skin which fastens over the heel of the ski and an elasticated hook for the front.

To store the skins fold the back half on to itself and do the same with the front half, so that all of the sticky surface is covered. The advantage of this method is that when you come to fit the skin you can do it one half at a time, thereby preventing snow sticking to the rest of the skin. If the skins get too cold their ability to stick will be affected. Some tourers actually wrap them around their bodies when not in use to keep them warm, but we have always found it sufficient to store them in sack.

Ice-axe

All you need for touring is a good strong walking axe which will normally be about 60cm (2 feet) in length, anything longer will be unwieldy. There is one type of axe which has a spike that can be extended to form a ski pole, and this might be quite useful if you go in for steep touring. An axe with some from of plastic or rubberised handle is a good choice as it will not feel so cold to handle. It is vital that you keep both the pick and the adze sharp, which can be easily done with a file by simply maintaining the bevels as they exist on the axe already.

Crampons

For ski touring you will generally only need a lightweight pair of ten point crampons, but if you intend using them for any sort of climbing as well you should get the twelve point variety that also have front points. They can be attached to your foot either with straps or with a step-in arrangement similar to some of the old step-in bindings. Whichever system you buy, ensure that it secures the crampon firmly in place and will not fall apart midway through the tour. Again the crampons must be kept sharp if they are to be effective.

Rucksacks

You will need something to carry all this equipment in and the range available is enormous, so here are some criteria to help you to choose. It must be capable of carrying all of your gear and this will mean a capacity of at least 55 litres for most tours, possibly even bigger. On the sides you will need some system by which you can attach the skis. Be wary of some of the purpose-built systems for this function which we have found to be both weak and the wrong size; simple straps are probably the best.

6
SKIING THE STEEPS

Indeed, there are refinements in the application of basic skills to different conditions, but the basic mechanics of skiing change little from condition to condition. What changes is our interpretation of the conditions, and the application of our skier sense to changes in terrain, snow texture, wind, temperature, wet, other skiers, and ourselves. With this in mind, let's ski the steeps.

Situation: Very steep chute with 45-degree drop

Conditions: Snow is wind-blown pack with 3 to 6 inches of loose, good snow covering the chute. No obstacles; it is cool and calm, and the lighting is good.

According to Mike, if you're intimidated by this situation, it's inevitable that you'll have to deal with your fear to be able to ski a steep chute with confidence. Although overcoming your emotional fear is highly individualized, most skiers find that a necessary ingredient to successfully overcoming fear is developing skills most suited to skiing the condition that troubles them. In very steep terrain, these skills include a solid pole plant, sound edging and angulating skills, good upper and lower body separation, extension and flexion, the active steering or guiding of your skis, and the ability to rhythmically link your turns.

Figure 1: First, practice establishing a platform on intermediate terrain

You need a solid pole plant to stabilize your body and thus to momentarily block plant to movement (momentum) downhill across the path of your skis. Blocking your upper body with a pole plant accomplishes another very important goal-getting your upper body in a *countered* or anticipated position as shown in Figure 1. Once established, this countered position allows you to control all other movements necessary to safely and confidently ski the steeps.

From a countered position, it is easy to form a platform in the snow beneath your skis that gives you a measure of stability and edge control. Specifically, you want to create a platform by standing over the center of your downhill ski and outside edge of your uphill ski set firmly in the snow. We call this instant of edging control an *edge set*. When accompanied by a blocking pole, plant the edge set creates the *three-point platform* crucial to skiing the steeps. In fact, in steep corridors or chutes, you must think platform after platform, turn after turn.

When you ski into this chute, look down the hill and seek the fall line, but do not attempt to pick up speed and then turn. As soon as you get into the chute, make a *preturn* with a slight uphill steering of your skis in combination with your pole plant to establish your first platform. The critical factor here is commitment: You must make a commitment to follow the lead of your first turn and continue to look down the hill and *make turn after turn you get to the bottom*. This commitment to a series of three-point platforms will help to ensure consistent upper and lower body separation-your upper body stays countered down the fall line in an anticipated position. This position prepares your body to use its natural skiing resources to execute a quick, smooth change of direction once you release the pressure on your skis and pole.

Take a look at some of your natural skiing resources useful in the steeps: Coiling and uncoiling of muscles; extension, flexion, and rotation in the joints; kinesthetic awareness; balance, and a sense of *integrated rotation* of all appropriate turning/steering forces needed to execute a turn without the overrotation of any of these. Applied to the steeps, you extend your legs (knees, ankles, and hip joints) as an expression of the uncoiling of your countered upper and lower body, and you use a rebound-type pushing off your pole to help direct your body mass into and down the fall line. Simultaneously, you actively steer or guide your skis into the new turn, and you use the flexion of your knees and ankles to make an edge set platform that controls and serves to complete your turn, leaving you in an anticipated position for the next turn.

Figure 2: Head down the fall line

Your Pole Plant

Although in mush of skiing we use the *pole touch* as a timing device to add rhythm, as an additional terrain, as a condition and balance sensor to the brain, and so a *signal* indicating the transfer of weight from the old turning ski to the new, in the steeps we rely especially on a blocking pole plant, often referred to as a defensive pole plant. While aids your rhythm in the steeps, the solid planting of your pole downhill momentarily blocks your upper body from moving into the new turn before your legs have uncoiled, adds stability to your platform and helps keep your upper body facing down the fall line in a countered or anticipated position figure 1.

Edging/Angulation

When in the steeps, you want to ski the edges of both skis effectively, keeping the majority of your weight on the inside edge of the downhill ski as it firmly grips the snow. Your outside hip and knee are *angled* into the hill (some refer to this as angling into the turn). The uphill ski is edged on its outside edge with just enough pressure to give you balance and control over both of your skis. The risks of not using angulation and a countered upper body are (a) *inclining* or leaning into the hill, with the likelihood of having your his break loose and slip down the hill out of control; (b) lack of balance; (c) lack of versatility and poor turning power, and (d) lack of speed control.

Rotation in the Steeps

In the very beginning or preparation of the turn, you are in a flexed and coiled position with your ankles and knees bent forward, your skis together and edged in the snow. As you uncoil, your legs extend (straighten) and your body projects down the fall line, creating a feeling of free-falling down the mountain in the direction of your pole plant. To effectively ski the steeps, you must learn to trust this extension outward and down the fall line with each turn. Use what the conditions give you, and in the steeps constantly allow your momentum to travel downhill. Turns in the steeps have a dramatic preparation (the platform), a short initiation (during extension) where the skis are very light and follow the body around, a very brief control phase where the skis are steered with both feet (beginning flexion), and an abrupt finish (maximum flexion), which leads to new turn preparation.

Your uphill leg is a short until you extend. As you extend and change direction (i.e., steer), your former uphill leg becomes your downhill leg and becomes very long and braced against the edged ski. Use the rhythmic sequence discussed here when skiing the steeps, and work to avoid the sings of static skiing: being timid, leaning back, locking the knees and hips, and using the poles little or not at all.

Figure 3 illustrates something fun to try. Stand about a foot from a secure counter or wall and imagine you're sitting on a bicycle that's parallel to it. Think about the position of your feet and legs when pedaling this bicycle: one foot and leg are up (an uphill ski), while the other foot and leg are extended down (a downhill ski), Now extend your right foot, and bring your left foot up as if pedaling the bicycle. The counter is about a foot away from you on your left. Imagine letting your bicycle fall against your left leg. What's your natural reaction? To seek balance.

Figure 3: Feel the angles, as if in the steeps

To seek balance, you throw your arms and upper body over your right hip (down the fall line). In real life, your bicycle leans to the left as you shift weight to the right. In this example, you fall into the counter with your left hip and fully rotate your upper body over your right hip, arms extended as you settle your left hip into the counter (steep terrain), just like you'd do in the steeps, coiled and all. Your right leg is longer than your left, and you've just set a platform for a right turn.

Turn yourself around and do the same with your right foot up; set a platform for a left turn in the steeps. Ever wonder about angles in your skiing? Take a look at yourself with your hip planted against the counter, your feet parallel to the counter and your arms and upper body facing away from the counter. Look at the angles formed by your hips, knees, and ankles.

Machine-Groomed Steeps

Situation: Steep run that's been machine groomed, offering plenty of room and plenty of thrills and challenges for skiers in search of high performance.

Conditions: It's cold and crisp, not a cloud in the sky, and the snow is freshly groomed and firm. No wind or flat lighting.

According to Mike, these are some of the most invigorating ski conditions there are. Above and beyond powder, crud, and moguls, a groomed steeps is a type of slope on which you can really draw on and engineer all the skill concepts you have. The best type of turn for you to use in these conditions will vary depending on your skiing ability and interest, but if you'll follow my lead for a moment, the turn to do this slope for getting the thrill of acceleration is the medium-radius turn.

With the medium-radium turn you are able to ski in a more up-right position on your skis for longer periods between turns than with the short-radius or short-swing turns. And even though your period of relaxation between turns (i.e., the time you are skiing upright) is not as long as in long-radius turns, medium radius turns allow you to ski longer in these conditions without having to confront the issue of fatigue.

In the medium-radius turn predominantly ride your down-hill or outside ski, applying foot and ankle pressure through the angles created by your ankle, knee, and hip as they are pressed or flexed forward and into the mountain (into the turn). Thus, in the medium-radius turn, you flex and pressure the downhill ski gradually until the end of the turn, where there is a brief point at which you become compact (a point of maximum pressure/flexion to your skis and in your legs). Once the ski is released, or relaxed, you will feel yourself being deflected or slightly rebounded in the direction of the next turn from the energy that had built up in the skis.

The momentum of your upper body mass travels directly over the end of the old turn to the center of the new turn. The key here is to work independently from foot to foot, leg to leg, just like the bicycle: As one foot increases pressure, the other relaxes until it must apply pressure (pedal), at which time the foot that was previously working decreases its pressure (relaxes).

As you use one leg more predominantly than the other moment to moment, so too are you using one ski more predominantly than the other, *steering each to an edge*. Skis have several technical characteristics built into them that enable you to ski them independently and with different pressures applied throughout turning. Of particular importance here is a ski's camber, which is put on the ski to equally distribute the skier's weight (pressures) over the entire length of the ski, giving it sensitivity at its ends for turning, stability, and holding. Your skis have the built-in ability to flex in several different directions. In the medium-radius turn, you can really sense what ski design is all about.

Using Your Angles
One thing to think about when you are working with

your skis on this type of terrain is to first *focus* on your upper body and then transmit a portion of this focus to your skis, think of it like this: Your upper body *seeks* the new turn, your skis follow its lead. For example, in a long-radius turn, you angle your out-side hip into the mountain to get things started, then angle your outside hip into the turn to increase the amount of edging on your downhill ski, and finally, angle your ankle subtly into the turn to complete the edging of your turning ski. This sequence of angles adds precision to the shape of your turn. If you want to shorten the radius of the turn, instead of moving the hip in first, move your knee in first; in this way, you can steer your ski to edge more quickly. When on edge, skis insist on turning!

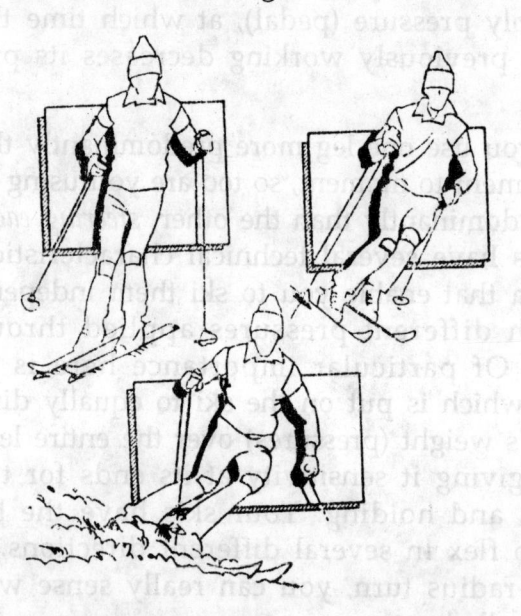

Figure 4: Use hip, knee and ankle angulation to effect dynamic turning

Try this exercise on groomed terrain. If you're already comfortable in the steeps, use this terrain for the exercise, but be forewarned that some aspects of this exercise may produce very fast speeds. You may want to go to a gentler slope. Ski down to a place where you can safety stop, out of the way of other skiers, yet still on the slope. Pick up some speed and make three turns being sure to first angle your hip, then knee, then ankle. STOP! Next make three turns being sure to first angle your knee, then ankle. STOP! Do you feel the difference? Its huge, because angling in your hip alone is not enough to get your turning ski into its edge without the aid of distance. On the other hand, angling the knee will quickly set your turning ski on edge, and in a much shorter distance. Now take the same, run and without stopping, make a series of turns in which you go from hip angle, to knee angle, to ankle angle, back to knee angle, then hip angle.

Which angles would you want to use in the steeps if you felt you were traveling a bit too fast? Knee and ankle, of course. As a rule knee angulation (knee-in) creates sharper turns; hip angulation (hip-in) creates turns a longer radius. To tighten a medium-radius turn, check your speed or move to a shorter radius or short-swing turn, get on the edges very quickly, and angle the knee. In actuality, you use many angles both of turn and to subtly change aspects of the turns. Use the rule on knee and hip angulation only as a guide.

When you create a long-radius turn, all the processes of a medium-radius turn are slowed down. The hip goes in much slower and gradually. You progressively tip the ski onto its edge. For tighter turns in the steeps, your knee is angled in. To radically create angles for extremely tight turns in the steeps, however, you want to get your hip as close to the hillside as possible with your uphill leg very short and your downhill leg fully extended and long, with your ski edged in the snow.

In the earlier example of the steep chute, we explained the technique of the blocking pole plant. When the turn is necessarily tight, requiring you to use the pole to block your body from crossing too far over your skis, the pole plant should be used because it's a far more forceful and dynamic way to keep your momentum under control. When using this pole plant, the blocking of your body's momentum may lead to a rebounding of your skis off the snow. Use this, but control it; on the groomed steep slope, you want to keep the skis in contact with the snow as much as possible.

For most of your skiing, however, the more rhythmic and less abrupt offensive *pole touch* serve as a recontact with, or sensor point, the snow and accentuates the perpetual turning of your skis. Overall, it enables your body to move across the skis while you're turning them, creating new angles that help you transfer your weight from one ski to the other without losing ski-snow contact. Use the pole touch to establish and maintain rhythm and timing in your skiing. As the pole is touched on the snow, move from the old downhill ski and ski the new downhill or turning ski. This pole touch rhythm eventually becomes an internal rhythm.

Situation: On the edge of a cornice with a 3 to 6 foot drop

Conditions: Celestial: Snow has firm base with a 3 to 4 inch give; very steep for the first 50 feet after your landing, graduating out for 100 yards of challenging terrain.

According to Mike, here we are atop a cornice that's quite pronounced though tame many standards. For you it's a first, but your friends are all here ad you feel like it's time to take the leap. Let's imagine we're all rookies and establish safe habits for taking this and other leaps. Foremost, the way to approach this is *not to jump off* the particular cornice area where you're standing but to position yourself to *ski off*. You want to be able to ski off the cornice to ease yourself into this new situation and be able to adjust more comfortably to the slope conditions. Further, you get the feeling of actually falling and reuniting with the snow below you.

For your first times off, the angle you choose in leaving the cornice should be one that doesn't put you directly down the fall line. Think of skiing off the cornice in a *fan progression*, which plots your progress in getting to know the cornice and ensuring terrain and represents the different angles at which you have skied off the cornice. Think of every higher angle of descent as represented by the rib of a fan, your goal being to ultimately ski the middle portion of the fan where the rib is straight; the fall line. The repetition of the fan progression builds confidence as you learn to control your speed on the steep terrain below the cornice.

Start by taking the shallowest line and then decrease its angle until you are skiing in the fall line. In other words if you still aren't comfortable about skiing down something steep, traverse across it first to get accustomed to the texture of he snow and the look and pitch of the slope. This will help you determine the kind of line in which you'd ski down this hill. Then ski the hill at progressively steeper angles, or at least the steep part of the cornice area, until you can point your skis straight down the hill and make turns to the bottom. Although this is a method of getting comfortable with the steeps, it also cuts up the slopes for others who'd rather just point their skis and go. Use a bit of sensitivity when in the steeps. If you really want to ski off cornices, but are unsure of yourself, don't hesitate to use the fan progression.

Unquestionably the most difficult aspect of cornice skiing is standing on top and making that decision to go off and make a first turn. If you aren't familiar with the terrain or snow conditions this is doubly complicated. To be safe, you should always know the kind of snow you'll be turning in once you land; to this end, some sampling of the conditions is advised.

If the direct approach to take off (i.e., skiing straight ahead for maximum air-time) is foreboding, you have two basic options for getting down: (a) Ski off the cornice at an angle so that when you land you're already edging (you must be strong to control this and have good independent leg skills); (b) use a fan progression and ski off the side of the cornice getting progressively closer to a more direct takeoff.

Let's consider the second option: First you want to get the feeling of what it's to got off, so take the cornice where there's a shorter drop-off, move right up to the edge, and slide off. Next time, go off a little higher point of the cornice and follow that leap with even higher places. These are basic fan progression tactics.

Consider adding an accelerated dimension to your fan progression: a more aggressive takeoff. Once you're comfortable with going off the cornice, move further back and pick up more speed before getting to the edge. Do this repeatedly until you sense a little spring in your legs and feel/ boots when you leap off the cornice. The *spring action* prevents the tails of your skis from dragging over the cornice. Once you've added spring to your leap from the cornice and feel comfortable with the conditions in which you land, will fully experience the exhilaration of cornice skiing.

After you leap off and land, the first turn will be out of the fall line to check your speed and establish a platform, followed by a series of rhythmic platforms and turns (recall the steep chute discussion). Remember also that the fan progression takes time and some cornice take more than a few minutes to get to (many require hiking). Plan to spend a day at it, especially the first time around.

SPECIAL SITUATON SKIING

One of the wonderful things about skiing is the variety of conditions and circumstances it offers. Few other sports offer such a range of challenges that may vary from minute to minute, hour to hour, day to day, slope to slope, or mood to mood. Versatility is no fool's goal in skiing; it's the spice of the sport. Come with us and ski a number of conditions, again, to broaden your versatility and sharpen your skills for high performance skiing. If you haven't given it much thought in the past, pay special attention to our discussion of a high performance way to approach your first day out this season; it comes just one a year!

Situation: The first day of the season!

Conditions: The snow is just right and you and your equipment are ready to get started with the ski season

According to Mike, make this a high performance first day of the season! First, go to the very basics. Take an easy hill and go through *exercise lines*, a progression of exercises, that take you up a staircase to the level of skiing you had achieved by the end of the previous season. Rediscover what it feels like to be on the snow; find the center of your skis. Relax and don't muscle your skis around.

Instead of tipping your skis on edge right away, go out and do wedge turns for a half hour or so. Regrettably, a common fault of first day skiers is to be overanxious to get their skiing back to the level they left last season. On the first day out there's a greater risk of injury if you don't take it easy.

Do wedge turns; start out statically, then slowly add the active steering of your turning ski. Next, and movement by extending your legs to begin your turns and flexing your knees and ankles to complete your turns. Next ad a more active transfer of your weight, foot to foot, leg to leg. Progress to an intentional lightening of one inside ski, then the other. Speed up and change the terrain until the lightened ski starts to match the other. At this point, you will begin to experience the inside or uphill ski becoming involved with steering.

Let the skis skid to make the turns very round and slow; it's almost like manipulating your skis to drag out these turns. You want to get a complete feel of the skis on the snow. These are patient turns allowing you to gradually adjust to the conditions rather than rushing movement patterns to suit your fantasies of last season.

The ill-result of not slowly reacquainting yourself with skiing the first day out is that you miss the opportunity to make subtle corrections in your skiing NOW. The way you approach a wedge turn, extension and flexion, pole action, independent foot-leg action, and steering with your inside ski can be subtly corrected early in the season before last year's old habits reappear.

Time spend sharpening these skills by using very basic slow-speed exercise lines will automatically incorporate them into your skiing. Importantly, don't rush things; take some time to allow your natural movements to re-emerge. Don't start at the top on the first day. This is a process of going through your basic skills and recalling those higher performance skills that got you to where you left off last season.

Situation: Everything looks flat (i.e., the lighting is such that it's difficult to discern contours in the snow, angles, ridges, etc.). Everything looks the same and the light is institutionally drab.

Conditions: The snow is wonderful, if only you could see it! It's firmly packed, with a few bumps and ridges. You're faced with cold air, slight breez, and cloudy skies.

According to Mike, these may be frightening conditions, especially when the light changes rather suddenly. In poor lighting, you're denied the all important and customary visual inputs that help your body to make balancing adjustments while skiing in motion. To counteract this loss, it's critical to accentuate the inputs received through your feet, hands, and ears, for example. The first recommendation for skiing in poorly lit conditions is to reduce your speed. This doesn't mean your turns are shorter in radius; rather, ski medium-radius turns. Ski centered over your skis and taller so that you can make subtle adjustments to the terrain you can't see, which might include rolls, bumps, ridges, or characteristics in the slope that resemble both concave and convex formations of the snow.

Skiing centered over your skis, standing tall, and relaxing makes it easier to quickly adjust to varying conditions. By standing tall you establish the sufficient *range of motion* needed to make the subtle adjustments in your skiing. By skiing more slowly, you feel the direction and character of the slope. If you're skiing fast in this poor lighting, you may find a tendency to lean back or into the hill, which may throw you off balance when the terrain changes abruptly.

In addition to slowing down and staying tall (a) open your stance, which will give you a stabler base of support (balance); (b) ski within the range of trees or obstacles that provide a focal point. Use there shadowed areas near trees, large rocks, and other objects as visual aids to maintain balance, because with them you can *read* the terrain, how it slopes or falls away; and (c) look ahead, as this will establish a horizon and aid in balancing.

At the outset, when skiing in poorly lit conditions listen to what your skis tell you about the conditions via the tactile sensations transmitted through your feet to your brain as well as sounds transmitted through your ears. Listen, feel, sense, adapt, and be guided in poorly lit conditions. Remember, ski slowly, stand tall, and be in control. Trees and other obstacles will help you immensely.

Try a pole-sensing exercise
Select a turn with which you feel comfortable; for example, a medium-radius turn. Open your stance and look for obstacles to establish your bearings. Lightly drag your poles and feel what they tell you about the snow, slope, and terrain. This will also help you to keep centered. As the pitch of the hill changes, the feel of your poles change accordingly; that is, is the hill slopes to the left, you'll feel your left pole dropping away from you. In this way, your poles serve as additional sensors to your feet. The more information you can acquire about the particular skiing conditions, the more you will be able to ski them in a high performance mode.

According to Mike, skiing in the crud is another one of the more exciting challenges of skiing. To be truly versatile and high performance skiers we must learn to ski crud. Crud skiing is one of the least predictable conditions to ski; it can occur anytime during the season. To enjoy skiing crud and difficult snow, you must incorporate aggressiveness, a high degree of ski-snow sensitivity, a blocking pole plant, the active extension and retraction (pushing out and pulling in) of your legs, balance, and strong rotary and steering skills. Lacking all or any of these, crud may seem foreboding, but by approaching the condition with some preparation and the basic *guide and ride* technique, you can learn to make crud an enjoyable part of your skiing. But first, consider what not to d when skiing crud.

1. Don't try to ski curd on flat to moderate terrain—the lack of momentum you'll generate will lead to a lack of turning power.
2. Don't try to ski curd until you're psychologically ready to go for it—a tentative attitude leads to a lack of aggressiveness.
3. Don't try to aggressively ski crud until you're confident making parallel turns or up-stem type christie turns (i.e., skidded turns initiated by the brushing out of your outside or downhill ski) on groomed slopes.
4. Don't try to ski crud until you've developed a sense of pole use in your skiing.
5. Don't try to ski curd until you've gained some confidence in moguls and steeper terrain.
6. Don't ski crud in closed areas.

You might also want to avoid long-radius turns because they present too many chances for your skis to get into *railroad tracks* (the impressions made by other skiers). In a long-radius turns there's a much longer gliding phase that's accompanied by little steering. The risk in crud is getting caught in these tracks at the point in your long-radius turn where you're not steering. In medium-radius turns, you apply stronger rotary skills and steering and are more able to brush away the snow in these railroad tracks. Nevertheless, muscling your skis around with abrupt movements might just trip you up. If the slope is quite steep, don't hesitate to use the more aggressive, sometimes more abrupt, short-radius turn.

In most crud conditions, be more *compact* on your skis; in other words, become shorter. It is possible to become stronger in this position (Mike claims to be) and better able to deal with unexpected changes in the conditions and terrain. If you stand too tall, you are more vulnerable to being rocked backward or thrown off balance. In the lower position, you are stronger and have better control in putting pressure on the skis as needed because of the shorter angles that are created.

Guide and ride

Foremost, use gravity. The steeper the terrain, the greater your momentum, and the easier it is to *guide* or steer your skis into each new turn. Knowing you have gravity on your side, makes it easier to maintain an aggressive, "I can ski this," attitude. Here's a game plan for beginning crud skiing.

1. Generally, ski with a friend just in case either of you need help in the event of an untimely tumble.
2. Sample the crud by standing, walking, hopping, and pushing your skis around in it.
3. Summarize the run you intend to take, and identify suitable exits you can make if the crud's too unfriendly.
4. Start into the terrain with an aggressive attitude, carrying good speed into your early turns. If the conditions call for it, you can decrease your speed. When you start off slowly, however, it's not easy to accelerate.

5. Try a few medium-radius turns to a planned exit, and see how the crud feels. As a beginner, you may need or want to rotate your whole body to get your skis into each new turn. Do this relative to the turn dynamics discussed later, and continue to practice it until you develop the confidence to keep it up for an entire run. In time, you'll begin to slow the rotary movements of your upper body while actively extending and retracting your legs as you leap out of one turn and into another. (In heavy crud, 90% of your turn is done during the leaping phase in which your legs are retracted and your feet are steered or *guided* in the direction of your new turn.)

6. Use your pole plant as an additional sensor for your feet and to momentarily block your upper body from moving down the hill while your legs are pulled out of the snow, *guided* into the new turn, and extended back into the snow. The extension and bending of your skis against the snow actually pushes the snow downhill, creating a platform against which you momentarily *ride* your skis and off of which your skis are deflected as you retract your legs and *guide* your skis into your new turn.

7. Go into crud knowing at first that the crud will probably get the better of you, but that after repeated exposure you'll have your day too. Try not to be discouraged by unexpected tumbles. If, as toddlers, we gave up after unexpected tumbles, we'd never have learned to walk. And let's face it: no walking, no running.

8. Ski crud like a kangaroo, using the strength of your legs to bound in and out of the snow. If you can master difficult snow, your lightness and ski-snow sensitivity in powder and other snow conditions are bound to excel.

Heavier crud

If you're less aggressive skier, you might find simultaneous leg-foot rotation works well for you because you're moving the skis as a single force against stubborn snow. Aggressive skiers often use this approach in heavily chewed-up, deeper crud.

Figure: Keep your feet light, toes off the snow.

210 • Skiing

Along with simultaneous leg-foot rotation, this kind of conditions is best handled by skiing with a compact stance and by keeping your skis on top of the snow. To accomplish the former, use retraction (i.e., bringing your knees up toward your chest); to accomplish the latter, lighten the pressure of your skis on the snow by keeping your toes up off the snow. Surprisingly, the focus on keeping your toes off the snow will help your skis ride atop the snow.

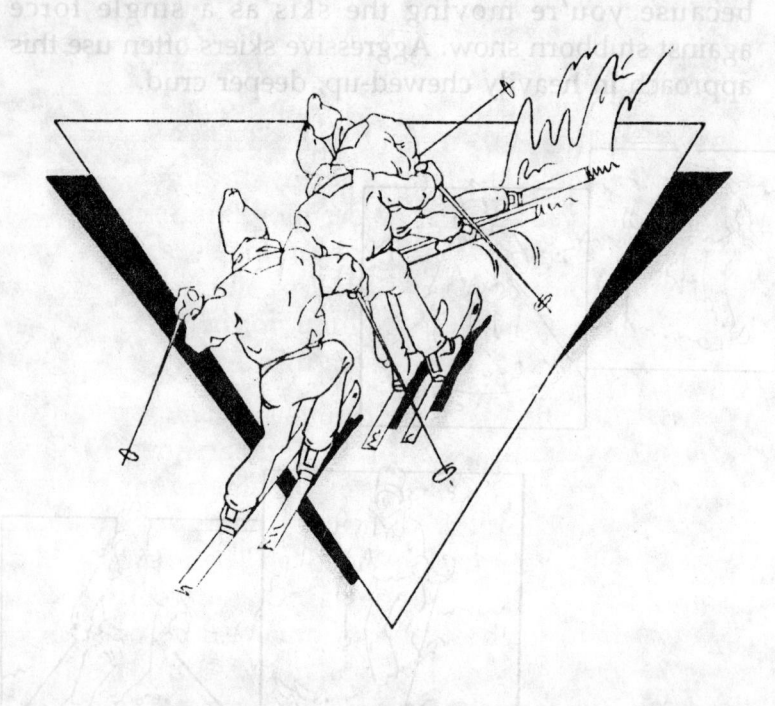

Figure: In heavier crud, independent legs can began and simultaneous legs can finish your turns

Be versatile

As a few general rules for crud skiing, try to use a combination of independent and simultaneous foot—

leg action and go into these conditions with an aggressive attitude. It's usually much easier to "roll back" an aggressive attitude to suit less demanding conditions than it is to muster an aggressive attitude in more difficult crud.

Use independent foot-leg action to guide or steer your skies into your turns, then engage simultaneous action into ride your skis through the belly and finish of your turns. The independent foot-leg action is highly instrumental in achieving proficiency and aggressiveness in the crud; the simultaneous foot-leg action helps to stabilize the completion of your turns.

Want to learn to ski crud? Request a ski school lesson, private or group, that's oriented to these conditions. Don't hesitate to investigate this possibility; if enough students request such a class, one will likely be scheduled. Expect crud to be a bit of work at first but later you'll probably ski it for fun!

According to Mike, spring skiing in the slush is another one of those interesting, often intimidating, conditions we need to add to our high performance versatility. Although soft spring snow that turns to wet, sticky slush is not always attractive to many hearty winter skiers, there conditions can be used to help strengthen your appropriate use of rotary skills, edge pressure, fore and aft leverage, and balance, as well as providing a marvelous opportunity to expose yourself to a variety of otherwise foreboding terrains.

More good news about spring's warm days and cold nights is the production of "corn snow" conditions—little ball-bearing or "kernals" of snow that develop from the overnight freezing and early morning thawing of surface snow. For high performance skiers, *corn snow* offers wonderful opportunities and adventures, especially those unique skiing conditions in wide open terrain and the exploration of hidden, inbounds, tree-lined corridors that receive early morning sun at just the right time. Foremost, think of this corn snow as an opportunity to be mentally aggressive yet physically subtle in your skiing. You go into the condition with a tough, "I'm going to get the most out of this condition," attitude, yet seek to ski lightly, even artistically—you and the ski and the snow are one in motion.

As the day goes on and more and more people ski the corn, the once-inviting snow changes to slush. The warmer the weather gets, the deeper and water the snow becomes. Still, few complain about the sunny days, short sleeve shirts, lightweight pants, and attractive tans. The problems arise when the natural dirt, pine tar, exhaust from grooming machines, dust, oil, and other manmade and natural debris build up on the bases of your skis and cause additional drag and poor ski and skier performance.

To prevent these conditions from ruining your spring skiing, you should take care of your skis and consider the following techniques and strategies. For example, (a) keep the bases of your skis as clean as possible; (b) avoid skiing across the fall line on any terrain where the slush is wet and deep—the added drag in the slush will quell your momentum, and in such snow you want to keep up the momentum; (c) keep your skis light on the snow; and (d) do not completed your turns as much as you would in firmer snow conditions. Too complete a turn will lead to additional drag and a loss of momentum.

Use the conditions

Once you get on steeper, more demanding terrain, you may want to use the slowing effect of spring snow to control your speed. it's also advantageous to use the natural resistance in the snow and he shape of the terrain in which you're skiing to create turning adventures. Part of the art of skiing spring snow is using its characteristics to avail yourself of a variety of terrain challenges that you might have otherwise not skied had they arisen in more firm-packed conditions. Some of these challenges include steeper bump runs that encourage the development of your pole plants and areas in the trees alongside or in between marked runs. *Remember: Closed areas are off limits!*

Use your tacks

Spring conditions develop skier confidence when you take advantage of the many challenges you're afforded. Corn snow, for example, offers a great opportunity to review your skiing through an examination of your tracks. Go out and try a series of medium-and short-radius turns. Critique your tracks in the "corn." Are they symmetrical, rounded, S-shaped, Z-shaped? Next, take a close look at your tacks and see how you make your turns. Are you skidding early in the turn or late; are you riding predominantly one ski or two; are you carving through the snow; are you skiing a parallel or wedge-type turn?

Float (Lighten) your inside ski

One of the tricks you might want to try in your spring skiing is *floating* or lightening your inside ski. Simply don't put much weight on your inside or uphill ski while turning. You should actually lighten it early in your turn, and leave it lightened as you steer it through the turn. Let your inside ski ride along the top of the snow while the outside or downhill ski is working or being guided or steered through the turn. Even if your outside ski is slowed by the slush, your inside ski will not be bogged down if it's kept *light* on the snow. Additionally, by keeping your inside ski *light*, it's ready to take over the responsibilities of the turning ski as soon as you transfer your weight from your outside ski to your inside ski. It's like walking or running down the slope through the slush and it helps to minimize the drag or friction that develops on the base of your skis.

In the morning there is soft snow where the sun has been baking the slope. Ski here first and as the day progresses, follow the sun around the mountain, skiing the snow just softened; avoid staying in any one place after the snow is too slushy. On a really hot day, ski the first run once or twice. As soon as it softens, seek the shady areas that are just beginning to receive sun. The warmth of the day will have begun to soften the snow in there areas, and the direct sun will make the skiing great. Follow the sun, and you'll add two or three more hours of top spring skiing to your day.

Later in the afternoon, assuming you're well rested, you might want to revisit the slopes you skied earlier in the day. By then, the runs may have firmed up. If there's a large enough swing in daytime temperatures (there often is) you may find a little of that early morning corn of these late afternoon slopes. If you're interested and the corn isn't too chopped up, this can be enjoyable skiing.

In addition to the warm weather, glowing tan, possible first-and second-degree sunburns when sunblock isn't used, crudded ski bases, and the wise application of a strategy to skiing slush, there is another aspect of spring skiing that you must address: *fatigue*. Our advice: Ski early and stop early. If you plan to ski aggressively over varied terrain, you might want to start early in the day (taking rest breaks as needed and drinking plenty of fluids), ski through lunch, and then call it a day. You will enjoy your spring skiing experience much longer.

According to Mike, this *washboard effect* is a condition in which the snow becomes rippled and hard. It can occur in soft snow conditions, where continuous skier traffic has caused the snow to become "skied-out." The signs of this are ripples in the snow and characteristic rolling of the terrain. For various reasons, skiers get thrown off balance when skiing on these runs and their skis may skid and bounce, each time creating little bumps and ridges in the snow that lead to the *washboard effect*.

How do you handle these somewhat irritating conditions? First, lower your stance and try to be as loose as possible; open your stance as well. In some cases, use a very slight wedge to create more drag on the snow so you can check your speed. If the slope traffic is sparse, you can view these conditions as another opportunity for developing your skills. Ski in this condition repeatedly. The more familiar you are with these conditions, the more you will derive from them for increasing your versatility and improving your high performance skiing.

Learn how to walk or run through these ripples. Find an area where there ripples dominate. begin from a standing wedge position, then move slowly through these ripples. Your task is to step over each ridge into its accompanying trough. Left foot, right foot; left foot, right foot; as if you were trying to walk downhill. As your pace quickens, imagine that you're running downhill.

The drill accents your independent leg movements and teaches you independent leg retraction for various terrain changes. As you encounter the same situation again, try to do this faster and more quickly. Stand on your skis very loosely and pedal your feet as you go.

7
THE COUNTER TURN

On a steep slope or on a slope with moguls, a very useful manoeuvre for controlling your speed without losing your smooth rhythm is the counter-turn ('S'-turn)-the French call it the contre virage or virage GT. In this movement you use your knees and ankles to steery your skis up the hill just prior to executing a downhill turn. By turning your skis up the hill, you slow them down. Since the skis are continually turning on their edges, this is a smooth way of controlling your speed without resorting to hard edge-set checks or sideslipping. Also, by twisting and untwisting your skis you use the torsional resistance of the ski to aid the turn.

On a mogul field you can control your speed by doing counter-turns around the moguls, losing your speed on the plateau before the mogul and turning in the trough around the mogul.

1. Demonstration of a counter-turn
Before practising the exercises that teach the counter-turn, it would probably be useful to study picture sequence 67 which shows me performing a counter-turn prior to making a downhill turn to the right.

Special tips

When you are driving your skis up the hill, as in picture 67b, it is very important to keep your upper body facing downhill so that your outside hip (right hip in picture) does not swing too far around in the direction of the turn, in order to prevent the backs of the skis from sliding away. (In this manoeuvre the backs of the skis should follow the fronts of the skis up the hill-not sideslip down the hill.) As you lower your hips at the end of the turn, be sure to keep your weight over the instep of your downhill ski boot (or over the middle of both boots if you have your weight on both feet). Try to time the pole plant so that you are planting your ski pole as you reach the lowest point of your flexion movement.

Be sure to roll your ankles and drive your knees towards the hill as you end the turn, so that the skis are well edged and can carve into the snow rather than slip around as they turn.

Since the 'downhill turn' part of this manoeuvre is essentially the same as the downhill turns you have been making during the previous ski manoeuvres, it is advisable to start off practising the 'counter' part of the counter-turn and then, when this feels comfortable, practise combining the two parts.

2. Learning the 'counter' movement of the counter-turn
Choose a moderate pitch on an easy intermediate slope and perform the manoeuvre. (In this sequence the weight is on both skis).

Start by transversing and then begin to lower your hips with the weight over the middle of both ski boots and drive the fronts of your skis up the hill by steering with your knees. Continue flexing/lowering your hips and steering your skis up the hill. Bring your downhill ski pole forward and plant it as you reach the lowest point of your flexion and then stop, making sure that your skis do not sideslide down the hill. Note how, the upper body remains still and facing down the fall-line. This prevents the outside hip from overswinging and therefore keeps the backs of the skis carving in the snow. Practise this movement on both sides.

3. *The counter-turn on smooth slopes*
When you feel confident performing the counter-turn uphill on both sides with a well co-ordinated pole plant, you should practise making the downhill turn from the 'counter' movement.

Practise at first on easy intermediate slopes and when you feel comfortable making smooth, controlled counter-turns, perform this manoeuvre on advanced intermediate slopes.

4. *Practice on a mogul*
When you feel confident making counter-turns on smooth slopes practise them on a mogul field on an easy intermediate slope.

Choose a small mogul and ski towards it. As you approach the mogul start to drive your skis up the hill on the plateau just before the mogul in a counter movement. As you reach the lowest part of your flexion, plant your ski pole on the top of the mogul, and then extend up and around your ski pole. Turn in the trough around the mogul, finishing your turn in a good traverse position, and aim for the next mogul.

5. Practice on steeper slopes with moguls
After making a series of slow-speed counter-turns around moguls on the easy intermediate slopes, you should practise these same turns on an advanced intermediate slope, turning around larger moguls.

SHORTSWING TURNS

The same successful learning formula used for the International Parallel Technique is applied to the learning sequence for the shortswing turn. The basic body movements of the shortswing are first practised on very easy slopes without speed, in order to learn the rhythm and weight shifting without having to worry about skiing out of control. Once these are understood, the shortswing is performed on increasingly steeper slopes at increasingly higher speeds. At first the Shortswing is down with the skis kept very wide apart and with exaggerated flexion-extension-flexion unweighting movements, and then as you become more ate case with the manoeuvre, the skis are brought together and the amount of flexion-extension-flexion is substantially reduced.

After practising the seven interlocking exercises in order, you should be able to ski graceful, controlled shortswing turns on advanced intermediate slopes.

1. Learning the shortswing rhythm and weight shifting (without speed)
Stand with your skis approximately hip distance apart. Your upper body should be upright and relaxed, your head centered, your arms in the 'tray holing' position and the ski poles held vertical, with the tips just out of the snow. Lean your shins against the fronts of the ski boots for support, and relax your knees.

Now roll both knees towards each other so that you are standing on the inner edges of both skis. (During this entire exercise you should keep both knees rolled inwards towards each other.) Lower your hips and lean all your weight over one ski. Since your knee is rolled inwards, your weight will be over the inner edge of this ski. From this position, fully extend upwards and then again lowering your weight will come down over the inner edge of the other ski.

Special tips
Try to keep your torso straight without bending from the waist.

Be sure that you don't 'swing' your hips from side to side as you would do in a 'twist' dace, but instead move your hips and torso up as a unit, over to the side, and down.

Repeat this motion, so that you now push off the inner edge of the right ski and your hips and torso move up, over, and down again on the inner edge of the left ski. Continue to repeat this motion a number of times. Once you can feel that you are doing it correctly you can sing or hum 'Tea-for-two' and co-ordinate the down and up movements with the down and up beasts of the song so that the down movements take longer and the up movement is more rapid. Co-ordinating with he words of the song. 'Tea' is the down movement; 'For' is the rapid up movement; 'Two' is the down movement (with the weight transferring to the opposite ski); 'And' is the rapid up movement; 'Tea' is the down movement, with the weight again transferring to the opposite ski.

Since you are holding the ski poles vertically, if you keep your shoulder, elbow and wrist locked as you lower your hip over the inner edge of the ski, the corresponding ski pole will automatically be planted in the snow. Now that you can do this on the flat you should have no trouble performing it while riding on a gentle slope.

2 *Learning the shortswing rhythm and weight shifting while schussing the fall-line*
Start by facing down the fall-line with your skis approximately hip distance apart and your body as it was in the previous exercise. Push off with your ski poles, and then hold them in the 'tray holding' position, but pointed vertically downwards as you gain momentum. Keep your knees rolled towards each other and, while gliding slowly, perform exactly the same movements as you did while standing still in the previous exercise, singing or humming 'Tea-for-two' and co-ordination the up the down movements with the up and down beats of the song.

Special tips
As you shift weight from side to side your skis may have a tendency to turn off the fall-line. For this exercise you should try to maintain your skis pointing straight down the fall-line while you do the down-up-down weight shifting movements.

Since you do not want to gain much speed, choose a section of the gentle slope that is just steep enough to allow the skis to glide and one that runs down the fall-line.

3 *Wide-track shortswing turn using exaggerated flexion-extension-flexion*
Once you can correctly co-ordinate the rhythm and the

down-up-down movements so that your weight comes down on the inner edge of the ski, you are ready to start to turn your skis across the fall-line. At this early stage of learning the shortswing turn to not be concerned about how expert you look; in fact, we often refer to this as 'sloppy shortswing'. The emphasis is to be on rhythm and learning to shift your weight from inner edge, with up-unweighting while the skis turn from side to side.

Start with your skis on a steep traverse and push off with your ski poles to gain speed. Hold your poles ready to be planted. As you are gliding, lower your hips so that your weight is over the inside edge of your downhill ski. As you reach the lowest point of the flexion movement your ski pole will automatically be planted in the snow and you should begin to push up off that edge as you start your extension movement. Keep your upper body facing down the fall-line and concentrate only on thinking about the 'Tea-for-two' rhythm and transferring your weight to the opposite inner edge while you lower your hip during the following flexion and you did in the previous exercises. The skis will turn seemingly of their own accord, the important point being that you do not have to force your skis around. As you reach the lowest point of the flexion, push up again off the ski edge and, transferring your weigh, allow your skis to turn across the fall-line. Continue singing 'Tea-for-two' as you shortswing down the run.

When you want to stop, instead of making another extension continue lowering your hips and pressing down on the inner edge of the ski and your skis will continue turning uphill, coming to a smooth stop.

It is best not to intellectualize the act of turning the skis, as it can be very confusing while skiing to think about all the movements necessary to turn your skis. The Tea-for-two Ski Dance is an approach to learn to make shortswing turns using rhythm and weight shifting, but the actual turning of the skis is performed exactly as you have already done when making large-radius turns. Therefore, having made large-radius turns your body knows what it must do to turn the skis.

A series of shortswing turns is nothing more than a series of large-radius turns with the traverse the neutral body position eliminated between turns. During large-radius turns there is a separate ending to each turn and a separate start to the next turn. In a short-radius turn the end of one turn *is* the beginning of the next turn.

4 Wide-track shortswing practice on a gentle slope

Having learnt to perform the shortswing manoeuvre during the previous exercise, it is a good idea to practise making shortswing turns down a smooth, easy slope so that the movements start to feel natural and comfortable. Still keeping your skis about hip distance apart, continue on the first few runs to exaggerate the down-up-down unweighting, as not only will this exaggeration help you to perform the shortswing turn, but also knowing how to exaggerate will be very useful when you start to ski in deep powder. After a few runs, you can begin to moderate the down-up-down movements and gradually bring your skis closer together.

5 Shortswing turns with weight on both feet

When the skis are kept a distance apart, a good skier has the option of skiing with his or her weight on one ski at a time, or on both skis. But whenever the skis are brought very close together it is best to ski with your weight distribute evenly on both feet and to think of the two skis as a single wide ski with a joint in the middle. This is because when your skis are together, in order to keep all your weight on the inside edge of the downhill ski, it is necessary to assume an extremely angled body position ('comma' position), leaning your torso out over the downhill ski while your knees are rolled uphill. Although this was the way we were taught to ski years ago and is very stylish, we have since found out how much easier and more comfortable it is to ski with the upper body in a more upright and relaxed position. Having your weight on both feet when your skis are close together allows you to keep your upper body in this upright relaxed position. The following exercise lead to making shortswing turns with your weight on both feet.

A Starting the turn with separated skis and finishing with skis together

Perform your flexion and extension with your feet wide apart. After your skis have crossed the fall-line and you are starting your next flexion movement, bring your top ski alongside the downhill ski and continue your flexion movement with your weight coming down over both skis and then, pressing down on both feet, continue turning your skis until they stop. Repeat this movement on the opposite side.

B Linking turns with the skis close together

Repeat the previous exercise, but instead of stopping when your skis cross the fall-line and your weight is on both skis, push up off the edges of both skis and make the next shortswing turn. Keep your skis close together and your weigh over both skis and, flexing and extending, make a series of three or four shortswing turns.

C Practice shortswing turns with the skis close together

On the same gentle slope used for exercise 4, start skiing with your skis apart and your weight over one ski using exaggerated flexion and extension movement. As you are completing the first turn, bring your skis together and place your weight over both feet and continue skiing down the slope with your skis held close together and your weight over both skis, making a series of linked shortswing turns. As these turns start to feel comfortable, gradually reduce the amount of flexion and extension until you are skiing with only a trace of down-up-down movements.

Once you feel comfortable with the shortswing turns on gentle slopes and can ski equally well with your weight on one ski at a time or on both skis, you are ready to apply this turn to more difficult slopes and conditions. The basic movement will always remain the same. On steeper slopes, on mogulled slopes and on ice, more precise control of the edges will be required. On ice and on steeper slopes, controlling the downhill ski is very important and you will probably want to ski is very important and you will probably want to ski with more of your weight on the downhill ski, while on easy slopes and in powder snow it is preferable to ski with your weight evenly over both feet.

6 Shortswing turns on easy intermediate slopes with moguls

The best way to ski shortswing turns on a mogulled slope is to turn around the moguls rather than turning on their tops.

On an easy intermediate slope choose a ski path that runs straight down the fall-line through the moguls. Start off building a good rhythm by linking a series of shortswing turns on the smooth section of the slope above the moguls, and then ski through the mogul field maintaining the same rhythm, planting your poles on the front flank of the mogul near the summit and turning your skis in the troughs between the moguls as shown in.

7 Shortswing turns on advanced intermediate slopes

An important point to remember while making shortswing turns is that you must always face your upper body down the fall-line. This is very important when skiing on steeper slopes. It is also a good idea to exaggerate the down movement of the down-up-down unweighting in order to control your speed, by turning the skis further from the fall-line as you complete each turn. Furthermore, when first practising skiing on an advanced intermediate slope, you should ski as slowly as you can, concentrating on maintaining good control of your skis at all times.

Choose a smooth advanced intermediate slope and practise making a series of linked shortswing turns. As recommended above, exaggerate you down movements and transfer your weight from ski to ski. When you feel confident making these turns, seek out some moguls on these advanced intermediate slopes and shortswing through the moguls.

8 Skiing on very narrow ski runs

Many ski areas have ski runs that are in fact snow-covered roads and consequently very narrow. In the European ski areas there types of runs often have a wall of earth or rock on one side and a drop-off on the other. As these ski runs are usually the way back to town or to the ski area and are not steep, all grades of skiers can be found on them at the end of the day. Beginners generally snowplough down the middle of the run and the experts schuss or 'wedel' (make quick shortswing turns along the edge. Intermediate skiers, not being as surefooted as the experts, usually get caught up behind the beginners. However, once you can ski the shortswing turn, you can combine this with large-radius turns and swing your way down the narrow run, making turns around the beginners.

It is useful to imagine a line running down the centre of the narrow run, and to call this the 'pole-planting line'. Each time you approach this line you should flex (lower) your hips and plant your ski pole on the line.

To learn to ski on a narrow ski run, choose one that isn't crowded. Start in a traverse position with your body facing down the run, as in picture 61a, and traverse across the ski run. As you approach the imaginary line running down the centre of the run, lower your hips and start to plant your ski pole on the 'line'. Extend up and around your ski pole and swing a large-radius turn, keeping your upper body facing down the run in the basic advanced skiing position. Now complete the large-radius turn and again begin to flex for the next turn as you approach the centre of the ski run.

8

POWDER SKIING

There is something wonderful about skiing in snow where you cannot see your skis, boots, or even legs. The dream if skiing effortlessly through light, new-fallen powder, like most dreams, omits the reality of what you must do on your skis to accomplish this. Skiing powder skiing is momentum skiing down the fall line. If you're undaunted and want to realize your dream of skiing powder like the rest of those skiers in the trees, come along with us on our powder adventure.

Situation: Deep, new-fallen powder on steep, very skiable, tree-covered terrain.

Conditions: Two to three feet of very light snow feel overnight. It's chilly, and the skies are sunny and clear. Now wind and excellent lighting.

According to Mike, skiers without powder skills shouldn't go in to the trees, especially when it's deep. A lot of good yet inexperienced skiers find the deep stuff very intimidating. You've really go to think of new-fallen snow as a fresh element of the conditions with neither tracks in it nor direction to it. If you've got powder skills, however, the opportunity to inscribe your feelings and abilities, your skiing signature, in to new fallen snow is most appealing!

You can approach powder skiing from at least three different perspectives: beginning, more advanced, and expert. Here's an outline of what each embraces.

Beginning
Set up series of tasks four yourself in 5-to 10-inch deep powder. First, ski down a gentle slope, skis together, just to get the feeling of the following four characteristics of powder: (a) texture; (b) depth; (c) resistance against your skis; and (d) balance point. (i.e., where you stand on your skis). Try to center yourself over both skis, balancing yourself as much as possible. Be very deliberate about this so that you're moving along in balance with your skis, the snow, and the terrain.

Figure 1: Get a feel for the characteristics of the day's powder

Now, add retraction-extension movements to your skiing; at first make these rapid movements, then slow them down and make them more subtle. When you look back at your tracks in the snow they may show compressions from your extension and higher areas from your retraction. Repeat this several times until you becomes so used to the powder's characteristics that you feel relaxed in this condition.

Start to feel the skis retracted and extended down, the down motion of your legs and the snow (you are skis) do the work together; retraction-extension in balance. As you consciously retract your skis, the snow will project them up toward the surface where they will have less resistance and be easier to turn.

Figure 2: Ridge and continue to guide both skis through the turn as you extend your legs.

Second, you're ready to added some basic rotary movements (i.e., the simultaneous pivoting of both skis). At this point, you're comfortable with the characteristic of the powder and ready to that looks open. Begin retraction-extension movements, adding a rotary movements as you retract your legs and pivot both skis together, turning them in the direction of your next turn. As you extend your leg continue steering both feet through the completion of turn, letting your momentum counter the resistance the snow retract will exert against your boots and ski at this point. Then you retract again with a new turn accomplished through rotary movements.

Third, you're ready to add pole rhythm. ski as usual, only add an exaggerated pole touch at the end of your retraction (and beginning of your new turn) and follow the pole touch with your retracted legs. When you've put all three together you'll be producing slow vigorous extended movements accompanied by light retracted rotary movements. Your pole is used not as a brace upon which to lean but as a prop that provides rhythm to your turns as well as some deflection and balance in more aggressive powder skiing.

More advanced

Apply the beginning principles but rev them up by adding the following adaptations. First, during your retraction movements, add more emphasis to your outside ski's rising and dipping, thereby allowing your inside ski to actually be lighter in the powder. in doing this, you will be more aware of the weight, pressure, and steering action of your outside ski, independent of your inside ski, in the powder. This is definitely more dynamic approach to powder.

Second, consciously lighten your feet at the end of your down movement. As you flex down, let your feet come slightly toward you; Let them float up. Although deliberate at first, these movements will soon becomes subtle aspects of your powder skiing.

Third, along with the rotary movements of your feet as you come up, project your hip to realign your body to the fall line (i.e., left turn, right hip, right turn, left turn). Do so by thrusting your hip to the outside and forward, allowing your body to fall diagonally down the fall line and into your next turn. (This technique is particularly important on steeper runs with deeper snow).

Expert

The expert skier skis outrageous powder: steep, difficult, chopped, heavy, or light. There are four characteristics this skier must possess: (a) strength and physical conditioning; (b) well developed technique; (c) condition exposure, plenty of experience in these kinds of condition; (d) an aggressively and committed attitude.

Figure 3: Ski the powder as if there are moguls beneath you

The development of export powder skiing involve taking the skill of the beginning and more advanced powder skiers and isolating them as if one were skiing big, steep, and difficult moguls! It's a matter of skiing powder aggressively and effortlessly.

At the expert level of powder skiing, the legs are dynamically moving up and down while the upper body remains relatively still: the upper body is not twisting around to help turn the body but riding atop a very active lower body. At the same time, the center of mass remains relative square with the fall line while moving laterally side to side to accommodate the tuning action of the legs. While the lower levels of powder skiing require you to ski over your skis, expert powder skiers move the skis out from under side it side to side, turn to turn like a pendulum. This is very exciting skiing!

Some professionals advocate the use of the upper body to help turning in powder. Is the upper body being used this way?

According to Mike, there are a number of skiers who use their upper bodies to help them turn in powder. What are doing is creating rotational force. Although rotation is the primary turning powder in skiing deep powder, it's not necessary to use the upper body to provide rotation. You can, however, practice using the upper body to assist rotation by swinging your arm in to the turn to help rotate your body around.

As you are extending to compete a right turn, touch the left pole; as you retract to turn left, thrust your right arm down the fall line to create greater national force. After thrusting forward (downhill), the right arm/pole swings through, and as your legs extend to complete the left turn, your right pole is placed in the snow to initiate your next right turn. As you spend more time in the powder, you will become more familiar with the function and necessity of rotation, you will ski with the necessary rotation without having to cream it by overusing your upper body. Rotating will follow naturally when you learn to ski with your upper body separated from your lower body.

Figure 4: Project your hip forward

Guide and ride
While there are many approaches to powder technique, guide and ride is a naturally evolution of sound parallel skiing. The latter is based on independent leg action led by active inside ski steering.

The key to powder is hinging the knees to the motion of the lower body. This can apply to both the more vertical reaction and extension of the legs in beginning and advanced powder skiing or to the lateral retraction and extension seen in the elite powder skier. Keeping your knees "hinged" or as close together as possible while retrieving your skis out of the snow during retraction allows you a more the simultaneous guiding of your skis in the direction you want to go.

As you continue in to our turn, your focus changes to riding your skies as they bend, arc, or plane through the loose snow until a platform is formed from the compression of the snow beneath the base of your skis. In active powder skiing with slight to more overt independent leg action, there are actually two interrelated platforms formed beneath the snow. This is true even as the knees are held close together, moving up and down to correspond to the independence of your legs.

Whether one or two platforms are formed, the critical matter of guide and ride is to continue to guide or steer your skis throughout the turn as long as your legs are extended-particularly through (and against) the powder that's above your boots. It's helpful to visualize turns in powder as continuous maneuvers that begin as you guide your skis in to a first turn, ride them momentarily as they platform in the snow, and then continue to ride and guide your skis to the completion of this first turn and in to the initiation of your second turn. In effect, in powder as in pack, to link your turns and maintain ultimate control of speed and to ensure maneuverability, you guide in to a new turn by guiding out of an old turn.

Common Mistakes
Skiers make at lest four classic mistakes in powder. First, they carry too much speed in to snow with their

leg (and knees) falling; the resistance built up on the skis when they're compressed against the snow to use the design of the ski to ride and guide through the turn. Third, when skis get "locked" in the snow, instead of changing technique, skiers rely on forcing their and aching things and calves and their skiers will find their mass traveling in one direction and their skis in the other, with no sense of control.

Finally, the fourth mistake actually compounds the first. It's simply forgetting to continue to guide the ski after riding them to a platform. In many ways, this is the same kind of mistakes that skiers with poor parallel turning skills make-they turn their skis fine, but they forget to ride and guide their skis through the completition of the parallel turn. Coincidently, the better your parallel skill on packed and groomed slopes, the easier it is to learn skill on powder.

According to Mike, heavy and wet conditions are probably the most difficult for any skier regardless of skiing ability. Unlike dry powder and groomed slopes, the consistency of heavy, wet snow presents challenges to all levels of skiers. When most recreational skiers encounter these conditions, they seek areas where there has-been a lot off traffic. In these areas it is as if the skiers them selves have groomed the slopes: This is called skier pack conditions. You know these areas: those channels created by constant use, which after a while are [prone to develop bumps and ridges. Yet, these channels offer many skiers the only way in which they feel comfortable getting down the mountain.

Why does this situation occur? Because a good many recreational skiers are intimidated by heavy, wet powder and would rather ski something with a firm look to it.

Venture out in these conditions. Don't spend an entire day in these conditions, but go out and play a while. You have to be a bit more aggressive in these conditions because your ability to turn, move use, or press the snow out of the way of your turning ski is going to be more difficult; wet snow offers a great deal more resistance. In order to overcome this added and unusual resistance, you can activity steer your knees in to the hill (uphill) with each retraction movement, or you can use leap and land turns which are quite vigorous. You begin with slight retraction and extension movements and advance to more vigorous movements. Next, on the up side of the bounce, simultaneously turn both feet and skis to create a hopping turn. Doing this several times creates a degree of fatigue. In order to use this and other exercise functionally in heavy, wet snow, you must have sufficiently functionally steep to provide less resistance against your skis and greater momentum for turning.

Acquaint yourself with the resistance you will experience on a slope. In other words, first traverse the slope at different angles to feel where you are on your skis and feel the characteristics of the snow. In this way, you develop a kinesthetic appreciation of the elements you are working with or against in heavy, wet snow. Once the feeling of the characteristics becomes ingrained you can assume a very aggressive attitude.

If you take a positive and aggressive attitude about heavy, wet snow and use it to become proficient in this condition, you'll add to your overall skiing ability by building greater confidence and skill. For versatility, go out and ski these conditions, leaving a signature in the untracked snow.

Look for opportunities to experiment with different kind of turns. Try leap and land-like hop turns. Extend off the platform beneath your skis and leap out of the snow, retracting your legs and rotating your skis in the direction of the intended turn. Use your landing to complete that particular turn by extending your legs. As you gain proficiency you'll find that it's just like skiing in higher powder; you take the raggedness out of your exaggerated movements and let your legs do the movement up and out of the snow with a still upper body.

The primary goal of perfecting this hop turn exercise is to retract your legs to lesson the resistance of the snow and use the greater strength in your legs to press or bend skis through the snow in to the completion of the turn. This is an active retraction extension turn; one you achieve than begin with. One rule: when your retract, retract both legs and feet with the same amount of force.

Another turn that works well in heavy, wet snow that's not too deep is the uphill stem christie, a very functional one is these conditions. The uphill stem christie is actually a skidded turn where your turning ski sets the arc of the turn would work in difficult, hard-to-move snow. You push the turning ski out, stand on it, release the pressure from the uphill ski, and match it to the turning ski it create a turn in heavy, wet snow. Once you again confidence in this, you will begin to understand the importance of starting your early to establish a good base and completing the turn throughout to maintain rhythm and control in these conditions.

Figure 5: Sometimes a stem christie type turn in crud is effective

According to Mike, these are great conditions in which to be come acquainted with powder skiing. The main reason is that there are no technical nuances that you need to apply assuming you're skiing confidently and efficiently already. The significant change occurs in your mind. Go out on to your favorite slope early. Ski as you normally do right down the center of the slope. If you feel that you are having some difficulty, look back at the tracks you have created and see if they are rounded like a series of the letters or sharp like a series of the letter.

If they are rounded you're skiing better than you think. If they are sharp you are not doing at least one thing that you probably omit in your every day skiing; finishing your turns. If the z is apparent, return to the slope and try lengthening your turns. Ski a long-to medium-radius turn. Steer your skis through five or six turns, making them as rounded as you can (i.e., gradual pressure through the arc of the turn).

Look at your new tracks. If they are rounder than before, continue to ski rounded shorter-radius turns and pick up the cadence of your skiing. Make shorter-radius by increasing the tempo of your pole touch. Don't sit back and don't lean forward; stay more on your downhill ski. Touch with your poles as you usually do.

Most importantly, enjoy this kind of snow when you can. The elements of powder that make skiing more difficult are wetness, pitch, and depth. Ego fluff offers a tremendous opportunity for beginning powder skiers to practice, even if packed-snow skiers.

If you're having difficulties with the ego fluff, it is possible that it is too wet or that there is too little pitch to the slope, causing far too much drag against your skis. (At this point, the ego fluff is crud.) Another cause of trouble skiing any powder is that it is psychologically foreign and intimidating. This reason is, in most case, a small part of the real problem of turning ability. if you can't create a rounded turn on packed slopes, either short or medium-radius, then work on your technical skills out of the powder. The problems you encounter in this kind of powder are just an exaggeration of the problems you have skiing on any groomed slope. If you have technical problems with basic skiing skills, they will show up more dramatically in these conditions. Prefect your skiing on packed or groomed slopes; ego fluff will be the greatest introduction to powder skiing.

General Tips for Powder skiing

1. Your power in the powder comes from momentum: Always carry the momentum of your body down the fall line. Versatility in powder comes from your manipulation of this momentum with ankle flexion, knee steering, and hip projections by which you direct your outside hip down the fall line. Rely on your lower body to rotate while compact or retracted and continue this rotation all the way through the extension and completion of your turn.

2. Go in to powder with the attitude that you're in charge and take command of the conditions. If you go in to the powder feeling intimidated, you'll ski in a cautions and tentative manner. You can't derive flowing rhythmic movements from a muscularly tentative body. To be in charge, you dictate the radii of the turns and ski with the attitude that you're lighter than the powder. Feeling light in powder will allow you to ski close to the surface because of the buoyancy of your skis.

3. The complementary perspective to tip 2, above, is the attitude and sensation of letting go in the powder. Let go and experience effortlessness. This is not an easy proposition when you're intimidated by the fluffy stuff; rather, it's impossible. So, let go;

once you've worked on your powder skills, go out into the powder and ski loose. This will help you to go and as you allow your body and mind to ski without restrictions, your skiing will become effortless. Momentum and attitude will find a perfect balance.

4. The essence of deep, light powder, beyond the sheer ecstasy of skiing untracked snow in the trees, through open bowls, and down chutes, is the quality of its expression as dynamic skiing in slow motion. For a moment, consider skiing a groomed skiing in slow motion. For a moment consider skiing a groomed run very smoothly and effortlessly. Your turns are crisp, rhythmic, rounded, and well-sequenced. Now, imagine that same perfect feeling in the powder, only is slow motion; nothing abrupt, nothing aggressive; you're truly flowing with the powder.

5. Not all powder is slow-motion powder. Recall how the heavier and deeper powder require more aggressiveness and determination. Still, the sense of your skiing has a very subtle and quite component. For example, as you ski more aggressively you must exaggerate your pole rhythm, extension-retraction, rotary steering, and hip projection. The subtlety comes into play when you float between turns from the down/extended position to the up/retracted position. During this flotation your skis cross under over the path of your skis; actually your skis cross under your stable upper body. This interaction takes the harshness out of skiing powder.

6. A powder skier is a centered skier. The powder skier skis over the center of the skis, not the tails as you often hear. You don't need to ski on your tails because your silk is built to bend up against the force of the snow. Skiing quite fatiguing. Some good powder skiers appear to be sitting back at times, when they are actually standing upright, square with the fall line, their skis beneath them poised, and ready to move in their direction.

A revealing centering exercise on smooth terrain so to ski with your boots unbuckled. If you don't stay centered over your skis, you will neither be able to turn as well nor subtly control the speed of your skis.

7. Overall, powder skiing demands absolute commitment to the first few turns, pole rhythm, projection down the hill, continuous movement, looking ahead, being in charge, staying light, letting go, and staying in the powder and exploring the mountain. A helpful exercise for building commitments is to decided that you will make a certain number as discussed with regard to bump skiing, progress to 20. ski around the mountain and hunt up new powder adventures.

8. Finally, hinge your knees together. Doing this will help focus the attention of your feet/skis on turning as one unit.

9
RECREATIONAL RACING

The first step is to get access to practice gates. For the average recreation racer the availability of gates depends on the resorts that you frequent. Although most resorts have regularly scheduled races, if you're looking for practice gates you have to find pay-as-you-go practice courses or coin operated courses (usually a dollar a run). Also, most resorts have recreational racing clinics that provide experts coaching and practice gates.

Many would-be recreational racers are obsessed with the drive to get in the gates. This is true despite advice from the pros that it's far more beneficial for recreational racers to free-ski and do training exercises and racing-related drills on the mountain than to rely on banging gates on a practice course, or running as many races as you can on a public course to learn racing techniques. You must run gates some of the time, however, so it's good to assess the two kinds of course available; the practice course (coin-op courses); and the race course (standard races, league races, resort races, tour citizen races, etc.) Both practice and race courses are set by experienced course setters; most cover intermediate slopes and are friendly to ski.

Practice course allow you to perform drills and

experiment with different techniques at your own pace for as long as you'd like. When the course gets too rutted, you continue to ski it for techniques or pull the poles and set up another less-rutted course nearby. Race courses are far more restricted, providing you limited exposure to the gates, and usually operate on a pay-per-run basis. Although coin-operated race course can be used for practice, most people allow technique to take a back seat to ego by racing as fast as they can.

Of course, fast doesn't always mean velocity. In racing fast involves "skiing smart": skiing the fastest line, using proper technique, making effective recoveries, and concentrating on the course. I'm sure you'll find that the advice and coaching smart in a race course and provide you with useful insights and practical advice on how to make recreational racing an important part of your skiing.

VALUE OF FREE-SKIING

Like learning to ski bumps, you don't learn to ski gates by running gates. Instead, you work on basic technique while free skiing, drilling, or exercising. According to George Capaul, the amount of time spent racing versus actual time free-skiing and training is very small. Speaking of the academy at Waterville Valley, New Hampshire, where he was Program Director and head coach for 10 years, he said. "We trained approximately 400 hours on the snow. Out of this, skiers raced approximately 50 minutes of total time for the whole winter. You figure it out: you practice 400 hours for one hour of racing".

Of course, practice includes running gates, racing drills and exercises, and plenty of free-skiing. Dirk Haas, who in addition to coaching for Northstar-at-

Tahoe's junior race team, conducts summer racing campus in Oregon, advice: "Recreational racers should spend a good 60% of their time free-skiing with purpose: the is, with certain tasks in mind and a generous amount of pure "get-out-there-and-shred" driving them down the hill; 30% of their time on specific racing drills (including practice courses and gates); and only 10% of their time racing".

Only 10% for racing doesn't seem like much until you follow this prescription and discover that all of your purposeful free-skiing to become a better racer is making you a better overall skier. As you begin to have better racing times while experiencing once-difficult runs as easier and fun to ski, racing and free-skiing becomes more complementary. Your time spent on the race course helps you to understand what you need to do in your free-skiing; your accomplishments in your free-skiing give you the confidence to take something new into the race course. Successes in either can build on the other; seeing failure in either can have the opposite effect.

Mark Teach is adamant about the importance of free-skiing for racers, especially newcomers. "Too often when people start getting in to gates, they go overboard. All they want to do is run gates. They think free-skiing won't accomplish anything, but this is where you build your base. Free-skins is where you work on correcting your technical problems, then when you're in the gates, you ski more naturally. If you try to correct technical problems in the gates, it's disastrous".

So, what about preseason skiing? Mark insists people spend 100% of their time free-skiing during the preseason. "I don't think you should touch a pole until you've free-skied a couple of weeks." To this christen adds, "Think of free-skiing as training also".

To keep this in perspective, take a look at what the U.S. Ski Team slalom and giant slalom racers do on an average, early season, pre-World Cup, training day. According to George, "We take five to seven training course runs maximum in the morning when everyone's fresh and reflexes sharp. We shouldn't ski more than 300 slalom gates, and 250 giant slalom gates, but these would be skied very intensely at high speed. After lunch, we go out and free-ski for 1-2 hours, or as long as the snow is good. Then, we usually go in and play a game of basketball".

It is late November, well in to the ski season for many skiers, yet these racers are just beginning their racing season. In fact, if you're intrigued with figures, consider this: George estimates his racers run approximately 12,000 gates before they start racing. Broken down, this represents 6, 000 slalom, 4,000 giant slalom, and 2,000 super-G gates. This is what they've done and will continue to do in preparation for the 1988 Olympics. Says George, "Yes, about 12,000 gates; then we feel that we're ready for the season".

Fritz Vallant, former coach of the U.S. Women's team, and presently head coach at Stratton Mountain School, Vermont, says European racers ski 400 gates a day before the World Cup season. It's not at all uncommon to get in over 10,000 practice gates before their first race. The World Cup season is the culmination of months of practice courses, drilling, and free-skiing.

Mike related a story to me about a discussion he had with Jean Claude Killy concerning the differences between European and U.S. racing programs. Mike asked Killy to identity the most important factor that helped him gain prominence in the world of king. Filly's response; "I first learned how to ski by skiing with a group of kids for years. We skied all over the mountain in all kinds of conditions. After this, we raced".

George related a similar story about his early development as a racer during his childhood in Chur, Switzerland. "We, all the boys in town, always skied in the same place even before we had a lift. As soon as the first snow fell, we packed the hill and continued to ski it all season. Just before we were tanagers, we had volunteer teachers who came out with us every Saturday run, sideslip in every direction, pole plants, different turns, and so on. They set up obstacle courses and drills for us. There were seven or eight maneuvers we had to master, and for which we were graded. If you did the maneuver perfectly, you earned a '4' and a red patch to put on the sleeve of your jacket. What distinguished the good skiers were not points earned in races, but patches earned for mastering basic skills.

"When we started training for racing, we went out in the forest and cut about 200 hazelnut sticks for use as slalom poles. We got an old rain gutter, sealed both ends, and dipped the sticks in the gutters full of paint: three colors yellow red, blue). It was the thing to do, to have three colors of poles. We had to carry all the poles and put ski gear up the mountain. Sometimes I think we were idiotic for all we did to our bodies: hiking, skiing, and then playing soccer or running, but we believed in it as our training program for racing, and it made us strong".

PRACTICAL VALUE OF RUNNING GATES

Jack Rounds, former pro racer and technical rep for Rossignol, presently ski schools supervisor at Northstar-at-Tahoe, is high on the benefits of racing to improve your free-skiing. As he says, "properly running gates can really improve your rhythm and help correct rotational problems which lead to skidded, rather than carved, turns. But more importantly, it makes free-skiing seem easier. Imagine being can simulate ruts, and the more you do of each, running gates and skiing bumps, the easier each becomes".

Mike feels running gates encourages you to be more versatile in your skiing by "forcing you to create angles and quickness in your turning. Racing makes you turn, and depending on the course and circumstances, you must respond with the appropriate turn radii or you'll ski off the course". And, like Jack, Mike sees the connection between moguls and slalom skiing: "I find that skiers who run slalom gates for an hour and a half, say five runs of 20 to 30 gates (100 to 150 turns), who are then taken to a moguls. In fact, it's a great exercise for teaching bump skiing: Ski gates first, and then jump in to the bumps. You'll be quick, aggressive and surprisingly relaxed".

Taking full account of the practical value of properly running gates, the list of conditions it helps to correct includes: sluggish skiing: excessive skidding while turning; sloppy mogul skiing; rotational problems of the upper and lower body; timidity while skiing under adverse conditions (ice, slush, crud, etc.); fear of speed and speed control; slow reaction times to obstacles and other cirrus; erratic turning; lack of, or decreased excitement about, skiing; self-doubts as a skier; and most notably, the fear of falling.

FALLING

If you're inclined to examine your skiing and racing from the mind down-not a bad idea for the serious recreational racer consider this:

> A ski race is like a sprint in track. The difference between winning and losing is measured in hundredths a second. But unlike a sprint, falling is common, even likely, in skiing. Based on this analysis you might think that the primary objective would be a mistake for two reasons: First, as we have explained before, if your primary goal is to prevent a fall, you will reflexively be stiff and tense and will not ski well or fast. Second, in order not to fall, even if you are not tense, you must ski more slowly than your peak performance level. And since races are won and lost by fractions of seconds, you will be out of the running if you are skiing slowly enough to guarantee that you will not fall.
>
> Indeed, falling in a race course or while free-skiing or drilling has purpose and intention, even though at times you'd rather it had meaning for someone else. Nevertheless, falling gives you the opportunity to take yourself to the edges that wonderfully scary, and exceedingly exciting place where the "juice" is free, and where you're going as fast as you can. At this point you are still skiing smart, in touch with yourself just enough to stay in control, and remaining responsive to changing conditions and those it-could-never-happen-to-me surprises.

If you can't take yourself to the edge, you won't overcome the competition; those skiers are likely to be taking it to their respective edges. In racing, it is literally and figuratively an edge-to-edge shoot out. Falling helps you to discover the dimensions of your edge in varied conditions and teaches you to get up and go for it again.

"One thing is for sure," George nods, "you have a hard time learning anything if you're afraid of speed or falling down, because this means you're likely afraid of the fall line. You've got to overcome your fear of speed and falling down to progress in ski racing. The first thing you do is practice skiing fast on slopes you can ski without fear and then gradually move up to more challenging slopes retaining the speed". When Disk's kinds fall, he says simply, "Hey, no one is perfect. There are going to be a lot more races. And besides, it's part of the sport. Look at the 1984 Winter Olympics, Men's slalom. There were 104 of the best skiers in the world and only 47 didn't fall in one of their two runs. When you fall in a race, you just get back on the horse and go for it the next time out of the gate".

As Fritz says, "The best slalom skiers know they're going to fall at some time. The don't dwell in it, not is it written law, but most figure it's not out of the ordinary to fall two out of every five slalom runs." Of course, most hope the come in practice. Use your falls to teach you to race better and faster:

> During practice your attention should be on your falls. Because peak racing performance means that you must be carrying your speed right up to the limit of the forces of physics, you need to find that

limit. To know where that limit is, you must exceed it some of the time. If you do not fall very often in practice, you are not close enough to that limit. Conversely, if you are falling frequently in practice, you are too far over the limit. This limit is equivalent to the peak in your performance/arousal curve; for purpose of this discussion, speed replaces arousal.

Ever hang around the top of a race course? If so, you're well aware of the many emotions evident in everyone present: excitement, competitiveness, friendliness, guardedness, and quietness. The atmosphere is both intimidating and exhilarating. There are a lot of egos waiting to race and each wants to be its definition of the ultimate racer! On the recreational circuit it's mostly fun stuff; but when sponsors add prizes, racing becomes much more serious. For pro racers, it's a job.

Before going into more detail here's an overview, or a short plan of attack, on racing that you might want to stash in your pocket. Go into the race to have fun. At the starting gate take a deep breath and look ahead. When you start, push off hard and look ahead. Ski smart, stay early, and aim for speed. Be sure to drive through and past the finish. This last item is particularly important, yet at times it's taken to its extreme while at theirs it's completely ignored.

Something homers happened to a friend's daughter. Her skiing had been getting better and she wanted to start racing. Her dad took over to the race course and signed her up to run a real open GS course. She's a sharp young woman, and we talked about the race beforehand. Our two points of strategy: Relax and look ahead to the gates coming up, rather than the gate around which she was skiing. If she wasn't sure where to go, she should just follow the tracks in the snow where others had skied.

She had a fine first race, a little tentative on the steeper part, but well done overall. Her dad was proud of her. Instead of skiing through and past the finish, she made a nice stop in front on the uphill side of the finish and never actually went through the timing light; she wanted to ask me how she did.

We'll examine the view of our contributors and share their advice and other racing-related information, exercises, and drills.

To be sure, there's a great deal to recreational racing, and appreciate the description of the passion it can ignite in the citizen racer out for the challenge, of the gates, as described by Horst Abraham: "Part of the addiction to racing gates is the vicarious feedback that is provided instantly and continuously.... The fact that a skier finishes a course and the speed in which he completes that task will provide him with an intoxicatingly clear picture of his performance and progress". There's definitely a hook to recreational racing.

Once the more series recreational racer the high provided by the "intoxicating" personal experience, he or she seeks refinement in skills and technique. This skier trains year-round to be a racer, thinks of him or herself as a ski racer, and goes to racing camp in the off-season. Still, its skier may race only 10% of the time, even less for racers who free-ski 4 to 6 days a week.

Mental Attitude

Jack offers practical advice: "There are many mental states that can help the recreational racer, particularly relaxation, concentration, and the ability to focus on strategy, goals, and your line.

The critical mind-set for the recreational racer is the sense of being calm, and staying focused on the important changes in the course's rhythm. To do this, the racer must be able to ignore outside stimuli. The more the racer carriers a dead serious nervousness about racing, the more difficult it will be foil the racer to have a positive and confident attitude about his or her racing".

Christin maintains the origins of her confidence as a skier, and then as a racer, grew out of her passion for the spot. As children, she says, 'We loved skiing, and spent a lot of time working at it, slowly but surely. Figuring out that skiing wasn't a fight between me and the mountain was a critical step in my progress to higher levels of performance.

"When you're first learning, there's a lot of fighting and struggling to keep yourself together. As you get more miles behind you, begin to realize you can work with the terrain and really play with the mountain. This is when your skiing makes big leaps, and you approach the feeling of begin a high performance skier; a skier who's in control, and who's able to enjoy playing with the mountain. This same attitude carries in to your racing".

Former pro racer and head coach of North star-at-Tahoe's Junior Race Team, Chaz Kruck, expresses a similar view: "Unless you're physically unable to race, it's your mind that hinders your racing, because it's your mind that gets down on your body for not being able to learn the same skill Joe Blow's going to have problems learning new skills that are easy for you. Each individual is different; each racer is different. The most important things are that you remain dedicated and keep trying, and never give up"!

Pete Patterson feels that by seeking challenges in your skiing you acquire an adventurous mind-set sad becomes more versatile." Unfortunately, a lot of young racers learn to race before they can ski properly, and they just don't have the mind-set for wanting to ski a variety of terrain. As soon as they get out of their comfort zone (e.g., a smooth race course), they often shy away from it and become static. They practice the easy things, but don't work for challenges.

"Would-be racers ought to look for challenges in their skiing; Crued, ice, powder, steeps, poor lighting, and stormy skiing. In fact, some of the best days are those stormy days when very few skiers are out on the mountain and you those place in the trees with good snow and decent lighting and have a great time. Without challenges, you may lose interest in free-skiing, and you need plenty of free-skiing to perfect your racing skills".

Marks says simply, "If you have an attitude to challenge yourself every day of skiing, overcoming challenges is going to be come natural for you and translate in to higher levels of performance. Then, when it's time to race, you're not afraid. You accept the challenge and go with it. That's important. That's high performance skiing".

Both Mark's and Pete's comments remind me of

Christen's second run in giant slalom at the '84 Olympics at Sarajevo. In great position to win the gold, she began the course skiing like a winner. Then, five gates later, she slipped, her hip slamming in to the ground, but up she sprang, righted herself, and skied the course in championship fashion, finishing just 0.4 seconds behind the leader, teammate Debbie Armstrong, and winning the silver medal. This is an example of a brilliant run set up by Christin's versatility and history of challenging skiing.

Physical conditioning
Top recreational racers are skillful and strong both in legs and upper body, whereas the vast majority of weekend recreational racers have a broad range of skills and different levels of strength and conditioning. These difference are most evident when the difficult factor in courses is increased. This occurs when the terrain gets steeper or the gates are set either closer together down the fall line or back and forth across the hill to effect a curvy course. In these instances, technical skills are essential to maintaining speed in the course.

Another variable that increase the difficult if late season courses is the softening of snow to slushy conditions in which ruts easily develop, especially late ruts (ruts that have developed from too many skiers beginning, rather than finishing, their turns at the gate). And finally, there are hard, icy conditions, which may bring smiles to the faces of some racers and tears to those of others.

Mike emphasize the importance of physical conditioning to the recreational racer by contrasting a fit with a racer who lacks conditioning; "on very hard, icy conditions, the fit resort uses his skis like razors and doesn't drift sideways during his turns. This racer look strong and stable. A recessional racer who lacks conditioning, however, is a much different story when you put him on the same course: His legs wobble, his skis chatter, and drifts all over the course".

Mike continues: "Lack of physical conditioning makes the biggest difference when the conditions get together, even when the snow is softer. The racer who lacks conditioning loses his ability to effectively ski ruts (actually use the ruts), because he lacks the strength required to ensure he has the quickness demanded of him to use the ruts. In the most basic of languages, recreational skiers benefit from being able to hold a ski on its dagger for longer periods (like riding the downhill ski through a rut). To do this, the racer must be physically conditioned".

"You've got to train for racing, "says Pete, "especially at the World Cup level. Through your dryland, off-season training (i.e., running, hiking, weight training, gymnastics, climbing, cycling, etc..), you seek to become physically and things you need for high level competition. There's no easy way around it; it's a tremendous amount of work. You do it to get yourself ready and tough enough to complete at the level you must be to win."

He adds: "I think the most fun I had with off-season training was hiking in to the mountains and knowing that after I came out, I wanted to go back in. its was great fun for us carrying weight around the mountain and not even looking at it like training, but more like something we really looked forward to doing. Pretty soon, we realized how good it was for us". Christen, who grinned as Pete spoke, added, "There's something meaningful in enjoying pushing yourself and not seeking this as a drag. Rather, you see it as something that's fun and valuable, even though at times it hurt and was a lot of hard work".

A World Cup Perspective? Perhaps. Alternatively consider Jack's friendly perspective on the connection between recreational racing and physical conditioning for the infrequent recreational racer: "Although being in good shapes is essential to the top few recreational racers, racers running on more nationally standardized races can be quite successful on shorter courses while carrying a few extra pounds and not having strong quads. This is particularly evident in ex-racer types whose technical skills often compensate for the aggressiveness of a less-experienced racer.

"Still, any recreational racer who wants to get a powerful starts", says Jack, "needs good arm strength and a strong back plus, of course, the desire to leap a feet up into the air to better dive at that first gate. And, if you're going to skate all the way through some of the flatter course, it takes a lot of strength."

Chaz offers similar advice for novice racers, but sees a need for a bit more "juice" for the serious upper level racer: "you don't necessarily have to come in to the sport in racing fitness, particularly if you're learning basic skills. As you progress to the middle of your potential, and especially to upper levels of racing, yawned a year-round program with different types of training. This program includes summers conditioning, more intensive cardiovascular work in the fall, and a weight-training program to build the bulk you need for upper level moves like you see in World Cup technique. "For example, you see Ingemar Stenmark go down onto his right or left arm in a turn and then bounce back on to his outside ski. Think about the kind of conditioning he does: He jumps up and hits a basketball hoop 150 times consecutively to train for this sport, and that's only one of the exercises you can do for the same muscle groups to help break the monotony of training.

"If you don't train, it's going to show in those difficult situations in upper level racing where you get off the softer pack and on to some hard ice. This is where you get off the softer pack and on to some hard ice. This is where you will discover what you muscles are ask about and why you need them to keep your skis from skidding all over the place".

George views the training needs of the recreational racer in basic terms. "Even they must keep up with some sort of off season training. There are many sports they can perform as well as the running, weight training, and aerobics. They should do all of them: anything they enjoy, just keep moving all summer and fall. It needn't be as vigorous as the training we do, but even if they can do something three or four days a week, consistently, this is the key. Hiking in the fall is great. It strengthens your calves, ankles, and legs. The whole body is involved in hiking, and if I could give one recommendation for the recreational skier's dryland training, hiking would really be the one".

If you've been athletic throughout your life, you already know that training is probably the area of greatest commitment in athletics, competition the most personally rewarding-skill, they do go hand in hand.

Conditioning involves doing activities that makes your heart pump harder for an extended period of time by working your large muscles(i.e., those in your legs and upper body). The secret to a successful conditioning program is to see it as something that directly contributes to your dreams and aspirations. Don't ever do a conditioning program for anyone but yourself.

Skiing skills
One-time Olympic hopeful in the decathlon, expert surfer, and a top-flight racer, Steve Armstrong has over the years offered me many tips on upper level recreational racing. Although Steve is a man of few words who does most of his talking on the race course, I coaxed him in to giving me a contribution that he left would be most beneficial to serious recreational racers.

The three Hs. "The keys to advanced recreational racing are the three Hs: hands, head, and hips, plus the inside ski and outside arm. *Hands*: Keep them forward, pointing toward the next gate; this keeps you headed in the right direction. *Head*: when turning, keep your head over your outside or turning ski; this gets your ski where it's supposed to be, on edge. *Hip*: place your inside hip in to the hill when turning; this keeps your ski on edge throughout your turns. *Inside ski*: The more you lift it when turning (exaggerate if you must by bringing the knee of your inside leg up toward your chest), the easier and more natural it is for hip to fall in to the hill and your outside ski to hold its edge. *Outside arm*: Drive your outside arm around and through the turn; those gets you ready for the next gate and keeps you early".

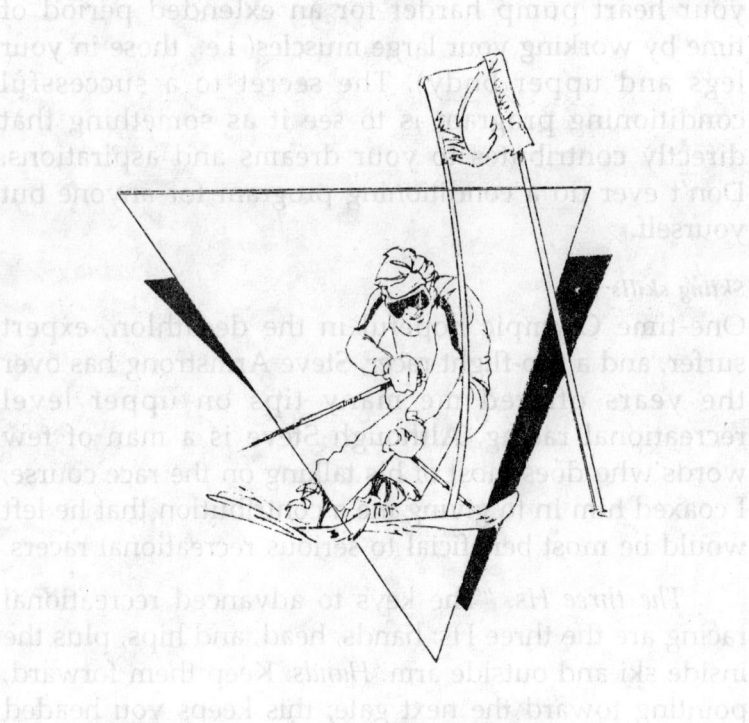

Figure 1: A dynamic GS turn

Developing Efficiency. Sometimes when you watch top racers move on skis, you know they're doing something incredibly efficient but exactly what it is a mystery to you. This is how Bill Show, former pro racer and head of the racing department at Heavenly Valley, California, impresses me when I took a racing clinic from him at squaw Valley this past season. Bill emphasize using quick foot action, flexible ankles, and knee movement to initiate turning, along with taking a slight or more exaggerated lateral step out put at the finish of one turn (in giant slalom), then immediately extending your legs and upper body in to the new turn by directing them down the fall line in the direction of the next gate.

As in most skill sports there are slightly different versions of efficiency. "In general", says christen," You want to be standing on the downhill ski, have a good pole plant, be relaxed, and ski relaxed. The latter will lead to flexibility, alertness, quickness, and the ability to recover from expected positions by instinctively utilizing basic skiing skills at high speeds".

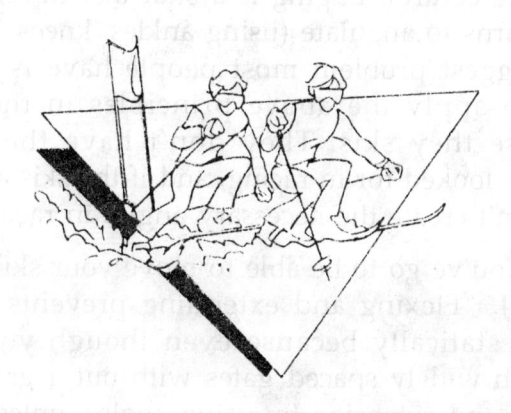

Figure 2: Take a lateral step to adjust your line to the next gate

She regards the decision to go fast as one that should be made only after the basics are soundly ingrained in your skiing. "Surprisingly, many recreational racers leave behind the basics when they think about going fast. They want so much to go fast that they come around and step off their downhill ski too early, instead of standing on it and letting it come around beneath them. They end up thrashing about and trying to go generate speed down the hill".

Flexion and extension. Dirt's view of important skills for recreational racing is decidedly aggressive. He speaks about the importance of flexion (down pressure in the turn) and extension (getting up and away from your skis by moving your center of mass down the fall line).

"Learn to use flexion to use flexion and extension to control the weight on your skis so you can move from ski to ski. Phil and Steve Mahre say that ski racing is like running: one foot then other. This is pressure control. Edging is a skill that develops when you learns to angulate (using ankles, knees, and hips). The biggest problem most people have is not being able to apply the above principles in their skiing because they skis. They don't have the dynamic balance looked for in racing, and if the skis aren't part, you can't create the necessary angles in racing".

"You've go to be able to move your skis around", says TJ. "Flexing and extending prevents you from skiing statically because even though you can get through widely spaced gates with out a great deal of flexion and extension by using angles, unless you're a great deal of flexion and extend you knees and ankles and use them as shock absorbs, you'll be bounced all over the course if conditions have gotten rutted and bumpy."

Jack's words of advice for both novice and serious recreational racers: "Novice: To enjoy skiing a races course, you need only have the ability to manage the hill it's on... with ease. Serious Competitive racers; To actually do well in a recreational race, it's important to be able to ski without skidding in your turns, pick the fastest line through the gates, and makes scissor steps or diverging steps at the end of each turn to begin racing".

The fastest line. Jack describes two kinds of lines: "On a flat GS course, a, late, straighter lines is often faster; on a steep course, an early rounder line is often faster". By a late but straight line we mean the flag (gate) is where you begin your turn. Aim right at the flag and then turn. In this kind of course, you couldn't make it in time because by then you'd be so late in the course, skiing too straight a line.

Skiing a straigter line on a flat course, you never really complete your turns. Rather, you leave your during ski in the fall line as much as possible and step off of it your new turning ski just before the original turning ski completes its turn. What you're doing is riding a flat ski between gates and rolling it onto an edge to effect directional changes right at the gate. In effect, you're making long-radius turns through the race course.

"Importantly, when skiing a flat course," Jack says, "you want to have maximum edging while in the fall line. To avoid slowing down when you leave the fall line, you want to decrease your edging, that is, ride a flattened ski. Staying on a maximum edge as you leave the fall line leads to skidding. A good way to make the transition from your edged ski to a flattened ski is to *feather* the edging pressure to your skis by relaxing this pressure a little a time as you leave the fall line. To maintain your line in progressively steeper race courses, you need increasingly more edge pressure as you cross the hill."

Chaz emphasizes the importance of being patient

with your line in a GS-type course; in fact, one of the signs that you may indeed by skiing the correct, smooth, round line is the sensation that you're moving very slow. With a smooth, round line in such a course your speed is going to build turn to turn because there's no resistance due to a lack of jerky moves or skidding. Don't ski a smooth, round line by aggressively attacking the slope if conditions and course rhythm don't call for this tactic.

"Instead of trying to ski a good line," says Pete, "a lot of recreational racers get into a course and all of a sudden think they have to go much straighter than they have been in training to go fast. They think the straighter they are, the fastest line is a steady line and knowing where you want to be on the course. It's important to look over the course, to study it. In a lot of recreational racing, skiers get up on the course, look down, and ski off with little idea of where the best line is."

Some skills are tougher to learn than others. Some of you reading this chapter aren't yet out there racing, whereas others of you have run a course or two with marginal or no success, but before we highlight their observations, we think it's valuable to consider George's perspective on learning: "Muscles tend to memorize certain moves, and to teach them something new by first having the muscles *unlearn* a movement pattern is extremely difficult. We would rather have skiers learn something new without thinking about changing old habits; the old habits will fall away if new, more efficient, and satisfying ones are learned." With this in mind you'll find that the following observations of difficult-to-acquire skills challenge you to learn rather than unlearn. According to Mike, turning the skis on command or in relation to the line being skied through the gates is one of the toughest skills for the new recreational racer. "If, for example, we start skiers down a very easy slope and out of the woods comes an elephant, believe me, they won't hit it, If, however, we remove the elephant and put a gate in its place it's a whole different story.

"The problem is really an inability to change direction without skidding; it's the weakest skill in many recreational skiers. While good racers steer their skis to an edge, novice racers put their skis on edge. By steering a ski to an edge (gradually changing body angles and correctly using flexion in relation to the hill), you bend the ski and thereby engage its design to direct your ski through the turn. Just putting the skis on edge and expecting them to turn leads to skidding."

Many top racers and coaches agree: Most skidding in the race course is undesirable and the result of inefficient turning skills and a poor or inappropriate line. it's difficult to accept that skiing a curvy line may actually be faster than skiing a straight line through a race course. "Personally, we fought it for years," says Mark. "I thought the fastest way between two points was straight, from gate to gate. Once you learn how the ski works and how to use those gates to your advantage, it starts to click that a smoothly skied line is fast. On a good line, there's no fighting with the course; it's like slow motion."

Christin elaborates on this theme: "Line is so difficult to learn because it goes against all of your natural instincts to try to go fast. You want to go straight down the hill, but you can't, regardless of your technical skills; you're on the wrong line and you can't fight the mountain. Things go wrong when you're off line; skiers fight it at all levels, including World Cup.

"I was involved in Pro-Am Skiing even one year where I helped Danny Sullivan, the race car driver, learn to ski gates. He was just learning to ski, but was a great learner. I told him all these things about how he'd have to start his turns above the gates and so on, and he understood immediately. He said it was just like race car driving: `You don't go into a turn at 150 mph, you have to bank out first and then come underneath, even slow down sometimes in order to gain more speed afterwards.'

"From there on teaching him was pure fun. He really had the picture of rolling into a turn. He knew from driving that you don't go into a turn cranking it. As in auto racing, in ski racing (giant slalom) you actually begin the turn well before turning, accelerate once in the turn—not to begin it—and apply pressure and power to control the turn. This is a difficult concept for new races to learn... but they must if they want fast times."

Jack is in agreement on the important of skiing the most efficient line, yet adds, "the ability to lift the tip of the inside ski and drop the inside hip into the hill at the end of the inside ski and drop the inside hip into the hill at the end of the turn, while staying real square (upper body) to the fall line [recall Armstrong's comments] is tough for recreational racers to lean. When they do, their race times and overall performance improve."

"It's the ability to balance on one ski and turn it in

both directions, the effective use of lower body rotation, and understanding the difference between slalom and GS turns," says Chaz, "that are tough for the recreational racer." There are drills that address the first tow problems in chapter 8, *single ski skiing* in "Lack of variety in turning," and the section on upper body rotation. With respect to the third, Chaz has an interesting way of discovering this difference. "It's all in the length of the turns. In a slalom course you will make short-radius turns with less time on your outside ski. In GS, it's just the opposite: You spend more time on your outside ski, thus, a longer radius turn.

"A good way to practice the difference of the two in your free-skiing is by counting and keeping the steady cadence one, two, three. You have a one-count turn, a two-count turn, and a three-count turn. Your have a one-count turn would be: 1, 1, 1, 1; right, left, right, left, each count being a turn. Your GS turns would be 1, 2, 3 right turn; 1, 2, 3 left turn.

"Try your GS turns as round and smooth as possible, realizing that in GS instead of in slalom, you'll feel your outside ski accelerating as it is coming to the number two in the count (the middle of the turn). Toward the number three count of the turn, you'll feel more work on your outside leg as you are fighting gravity and the force at the end of this turn. Then, at the number one count of the next turn, you'll feel relaxed as your ski flattens and glides.

"A good way to develop a sensitivity for these differences in turns is to go out free-skiing with the task of making a combination of count turns. Do four turns with a three-count; then four with a one-count; back to three-count. There's also a two-count turn.

Your task is to count aloud or to yourself as you turn, allowing your counting cadence to dictate your skiing. You don't want to be counting in a race course, though, unless it's a practice course. There's plenty else to concentrate on."

Try to incorporate these techniques into your race-specific skiing; (a) Ski bumps for a couple of hours and then use the race course for running practice gates to test your endurance and ability to ski the course with a measure of precision; (b) ski powder for several hours and then try the race course to test your versatility; and (c) free ski until the race course is bout to close and its ruts are fully developed, then ski the ruts hard for practice.

Sometimes, maybe too many times, move into the starting gate of a giant slalom course, thinking speed and aggressiveness; it's a wild feeling that comes over light off down the course looking for the underside of that edge, ignoring the fact that an efficient line might well be a faster way from start to finish.

Taking this same attitude of madness into slalom racing doesn't produce the same results. According to Fritz Vallant, "You need patience in slalom. In fact, it's one of the hardest things to develop. You just can't rush it in slalom; you can't be in too much of a hurry."

Taking this same attitude of madness into slalom racing doesn't produce the same results. According to Fritz Vallant, "You need patience in slalom. In fact, it's one of the hardest things to develop. You just can't rush it in slalom; you can't be in too much of hurry."

Indeed, there's plenty to concentrate on in racing: starting; maintaining momentum; focusing on the first two gates; watching your line; recovering; looking ahead; adjusting to rhythm changes in the course; and finishing. In general, you have to concentrate on your *racing strategy* while maintaining a large measure of patience.

Racing strategy

"Look ahead!" says TJ. "That's the only thing we'll say on race day; look ahead so you'll have an open mind and see what's ahead of you."

Dirk elaborates, "When you look ahead, you get that early line [i.e., turn well ahead of the gates] and achieve better balance. An early line is the key and by looking ahead you'll know when you don't have it. Even more, by looking ahead you won't hook your tips."

Look ahead, not to the gate in front of you, but to the gate beyond the gate you're approaching; how it is set will determine the line you take through the gate immediately in front of you. Further, looking ahead involves focusing your eyes on the fall line, hanging tough, and not being distracted by Mike's elephants.

Tactical advice. While all coaches and racers agree that looking ahead is paramount to good racing, a good deal of tactical advice is well. For example, Jack says, "If you want to win, you've got to think about your strategy. If it's a one-run race where you run in the order of your sign-up, you might want to consider the snow. If it's soft, you might want a few skiers to go before you to scrape away the loose snow. If it's a two-run race where both runs count, the order of running in the first race will be reversed in the second. You're got to think about where you want to run with respect to the snow conditions. "There's something else to consider, and that's the toughness of the hill and course when both runs count. You might want to take it easy on your first run, and then punch it on your next. There's no fun in blowing-out in the first run in a two-run race."

Confidence in your plan of attack. To Chaz, racing strategy is all in the line you take and the self-confidence you take with you into the race, especially when it's head to head racing. As Chaz sees it, "You have to have a heck of a lot of self-confidence if you're going to run head to head. When standing in the start, you've got to build yourself up to make your best run. Your concentration level should be high, and directed to the first and second gates. From here, you rely on what you have previously learned about the course from studying it.

"Even if you haven't done it before, you should try studying a course by at least 'slipping' it [sideslipping your skis through the course and around each of the gates]. Study its steepness, check for any rhythm changes, and determine how you'll go into and come out of these transitions. In time and with practice, you gain the ability to retain what you see on the course and use it.

"You see, there's war going on down there, and you're going to attack that course with all the strategy you can muster. Your knowledge of the course and the line you'll being skiing are going to govern your plan of attack. If you take too straight a line on a course that seems any bit steep to you, it's going to be way too fast and way too late. You'll probably skid through most of your turns. While the rounder line will feel slower, it may prove to be a faster line."

Fine-tuning your plan of attack. "Another consideration in your plan of attack, "Chaz continues," is how aggressively you're going to skate out of the start. If you skate right up to the first gate, you've got no time to set a line. If, however, you can blast right by the first gate before needing to set a line for the second gate, skate lime mad, but remember that skating is only efficient up to a certain speed.

"If the start is very steep, you might get only one skate after your start and be best off letting the skis run to prepare yourself for your first turn. Depending on how fast you are traveling, skating may not do you any good at the finish either. Sometimes the best thing to do is get into a tuck and sit back on your skis to allow them to run as fast as they can to the finish. If the snow is slow, however, or it's a flatter course, skating is going to be very important and you're got to fight all the way to the finish.

"A last strategy to consider is skiing the knoll. Any course is going to be steeper on the downside of the knoll, and whoever set the course is going to make this area of the course more turny that the rest of the course because it's going to put racers on a suicide mission if the gates are set too straight. So, a real good strategy to use as you approach a knoll, before you're at the knoll, is to start making your turns a little rounder than you had made earlier on the flatter part of the course. If you wait too long to change your line, you're going to skid a lot on those first couple of turns over the knoll, and whenever you're skidding, you're losing time."

Training strategy. Other areas of concern for the serious recreational racer are the kind of strategy to employ in training for a particular race and the general strategy you embrace throughout the racing season. Mark has an excellent perspective on this: Slowly work up to races, taking each day's runs close to where they need to be on race day but stopping short of it. "In this way," Mark says, "I'm hungry each day I train. I get to the point of being satisfied with my training runs, tired, but not having skied that perfect run. This keeps me sharp when I go back out the next day.

"It's important to stay fresh all season. I think a lot of it's trial and error. For me, there was one year when I had trained a lot early in the season and by March, I didn't have anything left mentally. My skiing was okay; I was solid, but I was just going through the motions. There was no spark, no life in me. I was flat.

"I have blown a couple of races because of inappropriate training, thinking In hadn't done enough coming into the races. I didn't have that feeling of being ready, of being sharp. A couple of days before one race, I thought I should get in one more hard stationary bike ride, and frankly, I burned out my legs. I got into the dual start and knew I wasn't going to beat that other guy; I just didn't have it."

Too much training. You hear World Cup skiers as well as recreational skiers talking about overtraining. It's easy to succumb to the inclination to overdo it; it can happen with activities unrelated to your training. Pete speaks whimsically about great powder days that led him astray; days when the fun of powder led to hours of play and stiffness a day later. Christin, too, remembers overtraining and says you can do it easily, "By simply skiing your buns off.

"You get so psyched up for a race and come out during practice thinking there are some things you've got to work on; thinking that you're not quite there but you desperately want to be there. So, you absolutely fry yourself by going out, training, and getting in the gates. Sometimes it really works, and you seem to ski a little better the next day. I can remember a lot of times when I got my skiing to be much better, but physically burned out my legs. All the technique and improved skiing that had resulted from the extra work was useless because I was drained.

"It's true," says George, "just a little extra training can throw you off. A lot of racers overtrain physically to compensate for being undertrained mentally. They lack confidence. They feel doing more is better. The confident racers take a couple of runs and know their timing is there. Those who doubt their timing go out and ski 10 runs trying to find it. When it comes to race day they've lost their sharpness."

Be confident and have fun. "The key to racing strategy," George continues, is confidence. When you're sure of what you're doing, and capable of doing, you perform well because you're able to train with minimum effort, thus conserving energy for varied training that will keep you fresh for each different event. The key to prerace training it getting the maximum confidence out of the minimum training runs."

Indeed, all racers can overtrain, though it may be that novice racers overtrain mentally and emotionally in addition to physically. Many feel unrealistic pressures to do well their first time out or to progress rapidly without training, coaching, or strategy. Fully cognizant of these struggles in beginning racers, Christin advises: "Seek your own level of performance on the race course. It doesn't matter if you go slow, it's fun just to make it through the course. You don't have to get out there and tear it up. The speed and your time are not the point at all. Having fun is the point, and negotiating the turns will provide it."

Starting. Skills aside, being relaxed in the start is important for many racers, whereas others use a reverse approach. "The way I get psyched up and ready to step into the gate is a bit unconventional, perhaps," says Chaz, "but what works for me is to think about something that makes me angry to the point where I feel fighting mad. Of course, I don't, but if you could imagine feeling like getting into a fight right there at the start, you'd know what I mean.

"It's that pumped up feeling where your eyes are open, adrenaline is flowing, and you're getting ready to fight. Think about something that's going to get you fighting mad, and take that adrenalin rush right into the starting gate. When you blast out of there, let that adrenalin propel you, never one letting up on the concentration you're directing to establishing your line by the first or second gate."

If you're more of an occasional recreational racer who comes out of the start rather tentatively, it might be that you are allowing this lack of momentum to set the pace of your race; this will most likely result in a lot of skidding because of a late line and a fear of carrying too much speed between gates. Why the tentativeness? A good deal of the time it's due to fear and intimidation of the starting ramp; unfortunately no strategy in the world can take away that fear. Increased exposure, on the other hand, will.

You'll never assume the attitude Chaz suggests unless you're over the fear and intimidation of the start. It's hard to get worked up only to step up to the wand and look fearfully down the starting ramp. You need to get out there and do some starts full blast by the first gate until you overcome this fear. Then, you'll be ready to look into specific strategy as suggested by Jack: "If the start is steep, pole two or three times *quickly and forcefully*. Make sure your poles are stuck in the snow at your heels as you push off of them, not in front of you. It's essential to make this poling extremely quick: 1-2-3! When the start is flatter, double pole and skate, making sure you're pushing off an edge and propelling yourself with each skating step."

If you observe ski racers, you know how they kick themselves up and project out of the start. They're using *kick starts* to build up as much forward momentum as they can before actually hitting the starting wand and triggering the timer. Kick starts aren't something you automatically do the first time, or first several years, in the gates; for the novice racer, this kind of start is definitely far less important than learning proper racing technique on the course itself.

Jack describes two kinds of kick starts. Both begin from the *ready position*: a low stance, knees flexed, your poles set firmly in the snow just the other side of the wand, and your shins approximately four to six inches from the wand.

1. Lift either leg approximately eight inches off the snow, keeping his ski parallel to the snow and the

other ski in firm contact with the snow. When you're ready to start, stomp down very hard with the elevated ski. Use your ski's hitting the snow to trigger you to lift straight up and forward, simultaneously using your arms to push you out onto the course.
2. Kick one foot back until it's extended behind you (knee relaxed) and only the shovel of the ski is in contact with the snow. When your leg is fully extended your arms straighten and push off to support your forward moving weight. At this point, you extend the stationary ski to match the kicked ski, which is actually on its way down. The swing of your two skis toward the wand provides complementary momentum to the work of your arms.

To elaborate on number two, it's important to straighten your back and lift your chin to maximize the pushing effect of the arms and poles that propels you through the wand. Further, when using this more active kick start, you want to use your kick to align your skis with the steepness of the ramp: The steeper the ramp the higher your kick; the flatter the ramp the lower your kick.

Time-efficient start. As you might imagine, race day is no time to practice your starts. In fact, if you haven't practiced a kick start of one kind or another, there's no sense in using a poorly developed one in a race. It'll only slow you down. Instead, get out quickly by making sure you have a *time-efficient start*. To do this, assume the ready position, inching your shins a bit closer to the wand. When you're ready to start, extend your body by pushing off with your arms, and straighten your legs, pushing out down the ramp, not up. The weight of your body should be on your arms. You lose time by going through the wand "flat" (i.e., standing tall and moving your skis through the wand and then down the ramp) and waiting until you're on the ramp to push with your poles. If you feel yourself tripping the wand before you've actually engaged your arms in pushing off with your poles, you're starting late. The clock has started timing your race before you've really started down the ramp. Pole yourself through the wand and if the course and your chosen line allow it, pole down the ramp nonstop for a time-efficient start.

You might want to try this variation of a time-efficient start: Do everything according to the preceding two paragraphs, but when you push off down the ramp with your arms, snap your lower legs back and let your legs follow your upper body down the ramp.

Recreational ski racing has been marketed as social racing for the friendly competition it inspires among skiers of diverse skills. Yet, ski racing at any level is still sport, although the work *recreational* softens the sports ethic of racing, which is bluntly, competition and winning. Whether you're competing against yourself, the clock, a buddy, or a group of strangers who all want to win the same prizes as you, physical performance during recreational ski racing is still subject to the influence of your psyche and the games it plays.

From many years of coaching and competing in several team and individual sports, developed these postulates regarding the *negative effects of the psyche on physical performance.*

1. If you feel fearful, frightened, or insecure, your body will be tense, static, and less responsive to unexpected stimuli.
2. If you're unable to concentrate on what your body must do, you may give it confusing signals and cause it to react unpredictably.
3. Each time your ego negatively questions or challenges your body's performance, your body is bound to falter.
4. Each time you must think about what you're about to do based on factors outside of yourself (e.g., your coach, other racers, the weather, the course, what you're wearing, the skis you're skiing, etc.), you're vulnerable to actually forgetting what to do.

The postulates regarding the *positive effects of the psyche on physical performance* include:

1. If you feel confident, your body will respond more naturally and spontaneously.
2. If you can focus your attention on the task at hand before ever attempting it, you will perform better without ever giving it a thought.
3. It you can focus on the essential character of your capabilities (e.g., skiing loose, skiing fearlessly, etc.) you will more readily execute movements that complement this character.
4. It's usually best to compete with an empty mind.

A good example of the latter two positive effects is Mark's World Cup slalom race at Vail in 1984. "I had a pretty good first run. At the start of the second run, I felt myself really getting worked up. I just backed up at the start, seconds counting off, and shook my head and said to myself, 'I'm doing this for fun; loosen up!' You're racing because skiing is fun. If you get to a point where you get so worked up over it that you're nervous and tight, you're losing the fun of the sport. I just relaxed that day at Vail, and it was the best I've ever performed."

Mark prevented the occasion of the race from becoming his psyche-o-drama. Instead, he took charge. Unfortunately, most of us, particularly inexperienced racers, seem to engage in psyche-o-dramas that diminish our ability, rather than improve it.

The psyche-o-drama occurs when we allow the fullest array of inputs (like those noted in the negative postulates) to cause us to question ourselves, mistrust our aspirations, and doubt our ability to execute the skills we know we possess. The psyche-o-drama does not occur when we use the positive influences of our ego, helpful mental directives, and the comments of others to uplift our physical performance.

Dirk identifies the bottom line of competitive racing: "In a ski race you're not competing against anyone but the mountain. In a way, this is really the best way to race, not thinking about what anyone else did. In reality, though, it gets competitive up there after a while. At these times there's no friendliness at the tip of a race course. When the race is over and they've beaten you or you've beaten them, you can be pals again. Next race: It's just like climbing into the boxing ring again. After all, why bother going out to race if you're not going for it? You don't have to race; no one's making you race. Go out there and go for the best time you can, yet ski within your own limits until you're ready to experiment with that edge." To be sure, recreational racing is a competitive sport, but for all that I've noted about its competitive nature, it's often the after-race and awards ceremony antics that make the competition friendly. Similarly, the help and advice that make the competition friendly. Similarly, the help and advice offered to new-entry racers at the top of the race course in the more standardized, nonprize races are both friendly and recreational. As TJ suggests. "When new at racing it may be best for you to think about being friendly at the top of a race course. You'll be more relaxed and probably ski better than you would if you were worried about everyone who might beat your time."

The psyche-o-drama effect in operation at recreational races on several occasions. Here's one example: Kathy knows she is a better skier than Jill, and Jill agrees but is reluctant to admit it. Still, Kathy won't jeopardize this understanding by accepting Jill's challenge to race (Jill is a better racer). Jill actually believes that beating Kathy means something. Of course Jill should win, because Kathy doesn't even like running gates. Taking advantage of Kathy's insecurity, Jill chides Kathy about the results of their race. Kathy is put on the most uncomfortable position of living up to her claims the next time they go skiing. Unreasonable tension has been placed on their skiing friendship by their skiing egos.

Here's another example: You're at the top of a race course, and Joe Jack (a good racer, but not great) is riding you about your new padded racing sweater. Jokingly (his ploy), he say things like "Do you ski as good as you look?" "Well, you look hot," If you're at all insecure about your racing, you might smile and shuffle away, wanting to avoid this guy; if you're "hot" and competitive, you might totally ignore him; or if you're inclined to a psyche-o-drama of your own, you might say, "Do we get to race each other?" "How do you keep from getting your arms bruised?" Or, "More appealing than your rages." Finally, if you're totally cool and secure, you'll converse with him about how much you like your new sweater and ask him how he's doing.

Understand, Joe Jocks are at every recreational race. You can usually locate them with your ears. Better to listen to a favorite fantasy or thought, and then go attack the race course.

Chaz offers a good example of a self-inflicted psyche-o-drama. "There's little as terrible as trying to ski a course when you've psyched-out yourself. There's a risk in watching too many other racers race. Somebody falling isn't a good image to let into your mind just before you're going to run. On the other hand, you might see somebody else who makes you take a second look and say, `Wow, that guy can race! I think he's going to beat me.' That's another bad thought to have in your mind in the start."

Clearly, whatever we let into our psyche can have an effect on our racing. This is likely why Jack says, "Watch the best; ignore the rest." I'd add only, "Fantasize, don't fatalize." Jack continues, "The ego is prominent in many racers, and problems can always occur where the ego is involved. If you are at a race where you know only a few racers, watch the best. Be aware of the guy who's pretty good racer, real well dressed, yet who loudly complains about the race, starting ramp, course, something [probably Joe's cousin]. Stay away from this racer; don't listen to him, he'll only be distracting. For sure don't watch weaker racers making mistakes. Be friendly with the good guys and your friends; they'll tell you things that may really help your racing."

If it's not already obvious, you don't race against another person in a dual course; though you start at the same time, each racer is timed separately by timing devices set up for each course. "Nevertheless," as Mike points out, "racing head to head adds a positive complement to racing against the clock. A racer next to you, especially a little ahead of you, provides incentive to go faster because you'd like to beat the other racer due to your competitive nature. Maybe you'll even take a few chances; instead of taking it to the edge, you may go beyond it. In this way, competition is healthy!"

The most important part of getting ready to race may be in feeling ready to race. Of course it's relative, but I'd imagine few feel the pressure of the start of an Olympic or World Cup downhill. Pete is a proponent of the *empty mind* concept when it comes to being ready for a race. "By the time a race has come around, you definitely know if you're ready. You can feel it. It's sure not the time to start thinking about the technical things you need to do. It's too late for that. That's what you work on in training.

"Once the competition is here, you focus on the race and on trying to bring yourself to a level where you're excited about the race. You feel concentrated and ready, and avoid dwelling on any negative aspects of your racing. You don't think about having problems with anything, including other racers. You just don't put any energy into psyching yourself out; it'll kill you in the starting gate. Filling your mind with thoughts about how poorly you're skiing, how tough the course is, how good the other racers are will only lead to poor performance. You want to be free of thought and full of excitement about the race so you'll be quick and skiing like you really want to ski."

An interview with Jean Claude Killy conducted some 20 years ago in which he mentioned a theme that is apropos to our discussion of psyche-o-drama and emptying the mind of thoughts. Probably many of you have and direct experience with this particular mind occupier. As he suggested in the interview, it's impossible to be a consistent winner in skiing when you're in love. How do you deal with such emotions? Constructively used, they can be a positive force in your racing.

The difference between mistakes and failures
Special attention must be directed here to the critical difference between *mistakes* and *failures* on the race course. If you recognize mistakes you make on the course as due to your own stupidity, you're interjecting failure into your racing, It's a difficult enough activity without adding new obstacles. If, however, you view mistakes as correctable errors in technique or strategy you're injecting success into your racing.

Know how to identify the mistakes you make in a race. Some examples are that you: were late at the bottom of the course; didn't get any extension; didn't look ahead; skied too much over your skis; let your arm get behind you; didn't anticipate the knoll; got too much air; or raced with a lazy mind (i.e., had no intensity). Any of these errors make your performance seem pretty grim; it is a wonderful skill, however, to be able to isolate the mistakes you make rather than seeing your race as a failure. Having the knowledge to identify correctable mistakes is great; if you can focus on what you did incorrectly, you can at least begin to think of strategies to correct the problems. This is much more constructive than getting down on yourself for making mistakes.

Unfortunately, this knowledge works better on paper where our mind can't censor what we perceive; or judge what we do. Too often the trap we spring on ourselves is self-criticism (e.g., "What a lousy skier") and name calling (i.e., "You jerk." "You fool."). The tendency for inexperienced recreational racers is to remember their mistakes and continue to put themselves down throughout the rest of the race; this leads to further mistakes. In this way, each racer experiences failure and builds emotional and physical obstacles to effective racing technique. The same is true for most competitive sports.

Seasoned racers make mistakes, too, but they adapt, adjust, and remain tough mentally; they ski the race course! Recall Steve Mahre's medal-winning run in the '84 Winter Olympics Men's Slalom. As Dirk saw it, Steve make as many as five mistakes in a row, including two huge ones in his second run, yet still finished the race and won the silver medal (Phil won the gold medal with a great second run).

George says flatly, "There's no question about it, you always make mistakes; of course not every time you ski, but as you progress in skiing you continue to make mistakes. If you didn't, you'd never get ahead. The key is to make the least amount of mistakes."

For the mistake of being late for a gate, you can make a corrective more (lateral step) to get you back on line. Similarly, you can learn the skills to make numerous adjustments to your mistakes as soon as they happen, but you must stay mentally resilient throughout the race to shed the mental interference and keep your mind alert to make adjustments. Sometimes, though, you find that you've had to make too many adjustments in a race, and this is reflected in your time. Sometimes you don't finish the race. In either of these cases, think of success in terms of brilliantly adjusting to your mistakes.

There's nothing wrong with admitting defeat when you blow out or the course, but not at the cost of your next race or your emotional well-being. Racers make mistakes. If you haven't figured out ways to adjust to these and would rather tough them out mentally, you're leaving room for failure. If, however, you're willing to use the *witness* in your racing and seek appropriate drills, exercises, and coaching from a race coach, ski school, or clinic, you're inviting in elements of success.

The witness

The *witness* is a handy concept that concerns the process of enlightenment. Though never intended specifically for ski racing, the witness does have an application to this situation. Who's going to argue with a concept that provides both enlightenment and faster race times? Here's the idea: Imagine that a witness resides atop your shoulder. This is a wonderful creature because it is completely nonjudgmental and has a vested interest in nothing else but recording what's going on as you ski.

This is an ideal partner to have along when you're running practice gates or free-skiing. This is what the witness might record during a practice race: moving slowly at start, early line, round turns, hit ridge, late over the knoll, lateral step adjustment, skidded, late again, arms forward, extreme extension, big lateral stop, throwing body downhill, charging hill, early line, fast finish.

Although there is certain valuation in an *early* line, *fast* finish, and *slow* start, these are not reflections of the value (i.e., whether it's good or had) but the product of what you're doing. Valuing statements might be *terrific* line, *outstanding* finish, and *terrible* start. Valuing statements trigger your ego to respond with feeling; nonvaluing statements point out what you're doing. Valuing statements make you feel something, thus altering your concentration of the course; nonvaluing statements tell you how to ski better.

If you want to give the witness a try, do so while free-skiing. Take a run and have the witness speak aloud though you (i.e., say what the witness observes). Practice this over and over again, first at slow speeds and then at progressively faster speeds. Once the witness works for in your free-skiing, take it into a practice course. Just try it out; don't make the witness a big production and don't make it a regular part of your racing. It'll create too much chatter in your head.

Keep in mind that in skiing, the witness is only a drill; it ids designed to help you identify correctable mistakes by learning to readily recognize what you're doing and where you're doing it in the race course, without having to constantly evaluate yourself as a racer. Of course, the witness will also help you to recognize correct technique, but if you get carried away with the good stuff, you'll miss the errors.

Correctable mistakes can lead to either success or failure; it depends on how you react to them mentally and whether you have the skills to execute the corrections.

Common problems and corrective drills
Many of these drills will apply to your racing technique as well, and when reference is make to them, perform them as designed, with racing at the back of your mind. It is essential to understand that while some of the drills are more or less isolated to one part of the body or one aspect of your skiing, the elimination of your difficulties is due to a combination of drills rather than a single drill or exercise.

As Chaz says, "Directing drills to one problem works for some people, but I've found the best way is to keep shaking up the drills and exercises. if it's an upper body problem, we work upper body and lower body, mixing them up. I've found that up to 50% of the time when I work the lower body (for an upper body problem) and get the lower body to function better, the upper body naturally does its job better."

The following problems and drills were identified by Mike, Chaz, Dirk, TJ, Fritz, Pete, and Jack.

Braking with skidding
Putting the brakes on is a common error among recreational racers. As Jack says, "They use their turn

to slow up, instead of using the direction in which they're traveling after they've turned to control their speed." Their turns aren't rounded or smooth; a rounded turn would be easier to control at variable speeds. Too much uncontrolled speed in a very controlled space (e.g., the gates) leads to putting on the brakes in self defense. You should never ski a race course defensively!

In addition to *hot wedges* ("Edge control"), Jack suggests a more advanced drill, *javelin turns*, to simulate at a slow speed the pressure and angles generated in a high speed GS turn. Javelin turns are done on an intermediate slope by beginning in a slight wedge. Ski slowly across the slope and one you've picked up some momentum, lift your uphill ski off the snow and point it across your downhill ski as you're traversing the hill. This is very aggressive pointing of your uphill ski. It should cross over the tip of your downhill ski about a third of the way from the tip, creating approximately a 30 degree angle at the crossing of the skis. To effect this angle, your uphill ski boot should be just in front of your downhill boot and facing down the hill, knees slightly flexed, and hands and arms waist-high and pointing down the fall line. (You may want to drag the tail of your "javelined" ski to add stability and allow you to get the fullest range of pointing.)

What you create with this drill is an alignment of your uphill ski with your center of mass as it faces down the fall line. By doing this, you exert pressures on your downhill hip and leg that keenly resemble the pressures you feel when moving over your downhill ski and dropping your hip into the hill while racing.

When you're ready to turn, move your javelined ski back just a bit and place it on the snow. Simultaneously lighten your downhill ski and you'll turn very smoothly on the old javelined ski; by being placed on the snow in a converged or stemmed position, the latter will immediately edge and become your new turning ski.

Lack of upper and lower body separation

Chaz expresses concern about skiers lack of aggressiveness, overrotation of the upper body, and failure to look ahead in the race course. This last difficulty can be addressed by learning to ski with your eyes ahead and off the snow: *target skiing*. An exercise he recommends for working on the alignment of the upper and lower body is to ski away from the sun on a gently slope and look at your shadow in front of you. "If you overrotate in your skiing, you will find that as you watch your shadow one of your hands will disappear in each of the turns. What you want to do is keep your hands steady in that shadow, out beside the body".

Lack of aggressiveness

Chaz offers an interesting perspective on aggressiveness. He's convinced that it is essential to racing, but concedes that in the absence of aggressiveness, an alternative would be to have superior skills that were reliable on the steepest of terrain. "If you could ski the steepest terrain with confidence, even without aggressiveness, most courses wouldn't seem that threatening." In a roundabout way, aggressiveness is a racing skill, too. If you don't have it, you must rely on superior skills.

Lack of pole plant rhythm

For slalom racing, Fritz emphasizes the importance of the single connected action of the skis rebounding, the pole being planted, and the shift to a new downhill ski; this complete action precedes each new gate of the course. it's combination of quick moves, accompanied by the arm of the pole-touching hand being moved into the body immediately and rhythmically after each pole plant. This will help skiers avoid catching their arms on gates when running a tight slalom course.

A drill for working on the rhythm of planting the pole and then moving in the arm is to ski an intermediate or lower run making short-radius turns. Plant the pole with each turn and after touching the pole to the snow, bring your arm in to your waist. If you're correctly skiing a series of short-radius turns, by the time you bring one arm in, the other will be engaged in a pole plant.

Lack of knee and foot action in slalom

Understandably, Fritz says, "Giant slalom is much easier to learn for beginning racers than is slalom." One of the reasons is that the former allows more wide open turns and more time to react and respond to your mistakes. Slalom is much quicker. Whereas in the giant slalom you use hips, knees, and ankles, in the slalom you use primarily knees and ankles, having time only to react, not think!

Here are three drills to word on using the knees the ankles in your turning:

1. Hold your poles out in front of you and across your body. Make short-radius and short-swing turns by pressing down and to each side with your

knees only! Don't use your hips; let your ankles flex forward to accommodate the action of your knees. With each flexing of the ankles and action of the knees, allow a light rowing of your poles to the side of the turn.

2. Along with another person, take hold of one end each of a 7-to 8-foot bamboo pole (or loop your poles together). Designate one of you to call out the cadence and sync-ski down an intermediate slope doing short-radius turns; the emphasis should be on turning with your knees and ankles.

3. Create a funnel corridor, or use a slope that's appropriately designed. Ski down making short-radius turns at the top moving toward more short-radius turns as you reach the narrowest part of the funnel. Again, emphasize turning with the knees and ankles.

In slalom, the knees and ankles initiate the turn while the feet are actively steering the skis throughout the turn. The angles created by the knees and ankles and the effect of these on the sidecut of a slalom ski, as well as its other properties of design, lead to dynamic turning.

Using the downhill ski properly

Something of concern to giant slalom racers in particular is the instrumental role of the downhill ski. Too often, skiers don't trust the downhill ski enough to just stand on it and ride it through a turn. If they would, their racing would greatly improve.

To become more familiar with the downhill ski's function, try this drill from Pete that's done primarily on the uphill ski. Traverse across an intermediate slope standing only on your uphill ski. When you are ready to turn, lead your upper body into the turn, plant your pole, and feel the uphill ski roll onto its inside edge ad become your new downhill ski. As soon as you turn across the fall line, move off the downhill ski and onto the uphill ski; repeat the drill. Continue for an entire run down the mountain.

Another of Pete's drills puts a heavy emphasis on your downhill ski. Go to an intermediate slope and make a series of long-radius turns top to bottom, stand only on your downhill ski at all times, and float the uphill ski off the snow. To add variety to both of these drills, do them in varied terrain including slush, bumps, steeper or gentler terrain, and ever several inches of new powder. Ice is not recommended.

10
SKI TOURING

As ski slopes become increasingly crowded, so more and more people are turning to the game of ski touring to escape the throngs. Many believe that the effort needed to climb up merely enhances our enjoyment and appreciation of the mountains. Originally ski touring was the preserve of the mountaineer, but as it has attracted a more diverse following so the emphasis has moved away from just using the skis to travel and climb peaks. Many now use ski touring techniques in order to reach good skiing, that being their primary objective rather than the ascent of the mountain. It is not for to pass any judgement on the relative merits of these two aspects of the sport, only to point out the directions in which it is moving.

Ski touring can be enjoyed at many levels, but as soon as you move above the tree line it is essential that you appreciate the severity of this environment. We suggest, therefore, that unless you are an experienced winter mountaineer or Alpinist you employ the services of a qualified Guide or go with very experienced friends. Not only are you confronted with the usual hazards of the avalanche, but also with the problems of navigation, safeguarding steep terrain, the use of crampons and ice-axe, and the problems associated with travelling in glaciated terrain. We are not trying to put you off, but it would be irresponsible of us to encourage you to partake in this very satisfying aspect of skiing real snow without making you aware of the needs of the sport. This chapter will familiarise you with the required techniques, but you should practise them under the watchful eye of an experienced friend. There are many variations to those we have described, but if you are conversant with these you will be able to operate safely.

UPHILL TECHNIQUES

These are the techniques that will allow you to move into a new world full of long empty powder slopes and high mountain peaks. Many enjoy the thrill of climbing up, whilst to others it is a necessary evil; whichever group you fall into the following point should help to make life easier. We examined the tools of the trade earlier, so let's now learn how to use them.

First you need to apply your skins. Dry the base of the ski as best you can; this can be quite difficult in a storm, but you should make every effort as it will save you problems later. If it is a skin with a hook, fix it to the tail first, making sure it sticks firmly as you go. When you reach halfway, fix the front in position then press firmly down on the skin along its whole length. Avoid getting any snow on the glue as it will not stick if you do. Skins without a hook must be started at the front; if you have difficulty making the tail end stick you can use an elastic hand or a specially designed hook which can be added to this type of skin. In some snows it may be necessary to rub wax into the skin to prevent the snow from sticking. It may also be worth doing this if you have a lot of moderate climbing to do, as it helps the ski to glide. With your skins applied to the base of your skis and the bindings in the uphill mode find a flat piece of snow. Practise walking along with a sliding action, moving your arms and poles as you would when walking normally. Try to develop the feeling that you are gliding along a little with each step. Lifting the skis will only tire you, so develop this gliding action before venturing uphill. Another way to reduce fatigue is to develop a rhythm, stopping only where the terrain dictates or after maybe an hour, depending on your level of fitness.

When you have mastered this, start to go uphill. Easy slopes can be tackled in the same way, but as the angle increases you will find it necessary to take a diagonal traverse, the steepness of which will depend upon the snow and your technique. Initially you will be able to turn at the end of each traverse by doing simple small steps uphill until you reach a more comfortable angle. Eventually, however, the slope will steepen to a point where this becomes impossible. It is now time to employ the infamous kick turn. Years ago every skier learned these very early in their ski careers regardless of their future intentions, but now many will never have been shown how to do them properly.

There are two types of kick turn, the uphill kick turn and the downhill kick turn, and there is much debate amongst tourers as to which is the most appropriate. We tend to use the uphill most of the time because it allows to continue with rhythm, and employ the downhill version only when the snow is very deep or when on steep slopes. Before we explain how best to learn these two techniques, let first illustrate how not to learn them. In the formative years of skiing career we were fortunate enough to ski with a number of experienced mountaineers whose joy was off-piste skiing. They were very patient and dragged everywhere enjoying, we think, the spectacle of developing the exclamation mark turn-straight down fall (!), straight down fall(!), On one particular occasion they spotted a beautiful untouched powder bowl, questions about why it had remained untouched were met by a whoop and a cloud of powder as they shot off down. When we finally arrived at the bottom by usual technique all we could find were a set of tracks. We followed them until to our horror they disappeared over a cliff. Before imagination went wild with images of them jumping over this precipice we spotted them down below. 'Just side slip down the runnel' they shouted, neglecting to tell that it was icy. We teetered down only to the met by a blank wall of rock. 'What now?' we shouted. 'Kick turn round and go the other way,' they replied. 'What's a kick turn?' came the inevitable reply. As they fell about in the snow, we could not quite decide whether it was in dismay or because they were laughing so much. The rest is, we are glad to say, history and we suggest you find more amicable surroundings in which to practise your first kick turns.

When ascending a slope the leader should level out the tracks at each change of direction, thus creating a platform on which to turn. Once you have done a few easy angled slopes, find a short steep but safe slope and see how steeply you can go up. You will need to use the climbers and make small steps ensuring that you distribute the pressure evenly over the whole ski base. If you experience difficulties you are probably either rolling your foot forwards and not keeping the pressure on the climber or rolling your foot slightly to one side and on to the edge rather than the skin, Use your poles for balance and hold the uphill pole on the shaft to avoid your shoulder aching. With practice you will be surprised at how steeply the skins will grip. If the conditions are very hard or icy you will have to use the harschisen. Remember that if they are attached to the binding they will not work if you use the climber, so you may also have to adopt a shallower traverse. In extremely hard conditions it may be necessary to stamp the harschisen down to make them bite. If you come across anything steeper or harder you will have to use ice-axe and crampons.

Ice-axe
The ice-axe has multitude of uses in the mountains and every ski tourer should carry one and be conversant with techniques needed to use it. We will look at the three most important uses in detail, self-arrest, step cutting and anchoring, but first we must look at how to carry the axe. When you are skiing through crevassed terrain it must be easily accessible for reasons that will become obvious when we examine crevasse rescue. The easiest place to store it is between your shoulder-bales and the sack. This sounds uncomfortable, but in fact is not. We always have the axe tied to a length of tope which forms a sling, which in turn is passed around shoulders so that we cannot drop the axe. When you are climbing with the axe you can either have the adze towards you, which is more comfortable, or away from you, which means the axe is then in the right position for self-arrest.

Self-arrest
Self-arrest is a system by which you can stop yourself after a fall and it must be practised. Find a steep

concave slope of hard snow which has a safe run-out. Ideally you should wear old waterproofs, gloves and a climber's helmet to protect yourself; do not use any crampons at this stage.

Once you have mastered all these techniques you should feel more confident on steep terrain. It is important to be aware, however, that even with good technique and a cool head it can be very difficult to stop yourself on slopes above 40 degrees.

Step cutting
Step cutting, even amongst many mountaineers, is a sadly neglected skill. Many of our most spectacular peaks were originally climbed by climbers cutting thousands of steps. The technique was superseded by the crampon, but is still of value in case you lose or break a crampon.

Self-belaying
Finally, you can use the axe to anchor yourself to the mountain. When you are climbing up or down place the axe firmly into the snow before you move, then if your feet slip you can hold on to the axe for support. This is known as self-belaying and provides a safe technique for moving quickly over fairly steep ground. You can use the axe to anchor with in several other ways which we will look at in detail later.

Crampons
Cramponing should be practised first on easy terrain so that you get used to wearing them. We are not going to teach you how to go up vertical faces as that is beyond the scope of this book and the type of crampon that most of us carry for touring is not suitable for this usage. The main thing to remember is

to walk with your toes slightly apart so that you do not spike your own calf muscles and try to get as many spikes into the snow as possible. Slacken your boots so that your ankles are as flexible as possible; this will allow you to keep your feet flat against the surface even when it gets quite steep. In some snow conditions the snow will stick to the crampons, balling up underneath. This condition can be quite hazardous and the snow should be cleared by either kicking hard into the next step or by knocking your boot with the ice-axe shaft.

This is not an exhaustive list of techniques, that it covers all the situations that you are likely to come across on normal tours. For more advanced techniques we feel you should follow a course of instruction from qualified people.

Ropework
These of you unused to handling ropes, prepare for some mind-twisting fun! We have kept the number of knots that you have to learn to a minimum and with a little perseverance you should soon master them. They can be learned in the comfort at your home and indeed it is far better that you familiarise yourself with them there than half-way down a crevasse!

The techniques that we have described are those needed to operate in crevassed terrain and to protect someone who is about to test-ski a potential avalanche slope. We have not described the ropework needed to ascend and descend rock ridges, or steep snow and ice, as feel that these situations are beyond the normal concept of ski touring.

The Rope

Basically, there are two types of rope available: hawserlaid rope and kernmantle rope. The former, although cheaper, is rarely used nowadays because it is much harder to handle, so will confine myself to discussing the kernmantle variety.

Let's start by considering the length of the rope. If you buy a climbing rope it will normally come in two lengths: 45 metres and 50 metres. If you are skiing in a party of two or three we think it is essential that you use the 50 metres length. The reasons for this will become evident when you read the section on crevasse rescue. If you are skiing in a larger party, providing you have at least 9 metres of rope between each person you should be safe. Large parties may decide to cut their rope into short convenient lengths thereby spreading the load throughout the group, this does, however, reduce the versatility of the rope.

Climbing ropes generally come in three diameters: 11mm, 9mm and 7mm. the first is usually considered to be too thick and heavy for touring, and we feel that the last, although strong enough, can be difficult to prussik up (prussiking, as you will see, is one of the major rescue methods) and so our own preference is for 50 metres at 9mm kernmantle.

For the expenditure of a little extra money you can get ropes that have been treated to prevent them soaking up water. This makes sense because a wet rope is an a extremely heavy item to carry on a tour. The rope should be stored away from direct sunlight and should always be dried naturally. Respect your rope do not stand on it in ski boots or in skis, and replace it according to the manufacturer's recommendations. Finally, to not be tempted to buy or use anything but a proper climbing rope. Climbing ropes are specially constructed to survive the rigours we subject them to any they will carry a UIAA label identifying them as such.

Slings and Karabiners
Each party member should carry two 8 foot 1 inch (120 X 19mm) tapes (strength is 2,500kg). These can be of the sewn variety or you can tie them with the tape knot, do not try to sew them yourself. Every member should also carry four 2,500kg screwgate karabiners (UIAA approved), one of which should be the pear-shaped or HMS variety, one pulley and two prussik loops.

Harnesses
The advantage of wearing a harness over just tying the rope around your waist is that there is no chance of the rope riding up over your diaphragm causing you to asphyxiate. There is, however, the extra cost and weight to consider. Before the advent of harnesses tourers either carried a prussik already attached to the rope that they could stand in or they constructed a harness out of the rope. There are two types of harness available: the UIAA approved full body harness or the lighter sit harness. Sit harnesses do not have approval because in the event of a fall they do not allow the subject to hang in the best possible position. However, with the method of tying on to the rope that we will show you this problem is easily overcome. Whichever you choose, keep it light and simple and preferably of a design that has leg loops which undo so that it can be put on over ski boots.

INDEX

Abraham, Horst, 254
Aerial turn, 91
American Teaching Method, 67-68
Ankel flex, 143
Athletic skiers, 7
Axial motion, 46

Banked turn, 91
Butterfly turn, 98
Balaclava, 165
Binding, 179
    toe piece, 179
    heel piece, 180
Brack skidding, 289

Cardiovascular fitness, 9
Climbing steps, 21
Centred skier, 68
Counterrotation, 85
Charleston step, 93, 100
Crossed ski turn, 98
Converging turns, 147
Chase skating, 154
Counter turn, 217
    demonstration, 217
    special tips, 218
    movement of, 218
    smooth slopes, 219

Down hill, 43
Drills exercises, 110
    basic position on skis, 111

walking/gliding on skis, 111
turning in position, 111
straight schussing, 112
side stepping, 113
diagonal side stepping, 113
schussing down, 113
bending under ski pole arches, 114
getting up after fall, 114
snow plough stop, 116
Diverging turns, 134
Discovering platforms, 136

Every day drills, 118
    warm up, 119
Excessive skidding,
Edge control,
    lack of, 148

Foot swivel off, 88
Foot pedals, 143
Falling leaf, 151
Float ski, 213
Free-skiing, value of, 246

Graduated-length method, 66-67
Gradually tighten grip, 103

Hôpe turn exercise, 55, 64
Hocky stop, 151
Hot wedges, 153

Index

Heavier crud, 209

Inner skier, 68

Javelin traverse, 96
Javelin turn, 97
Jean-claude killy, 171

Kick turn, 19
Kangaroo's-struck, 78
Knee wiggles, 95
Kinesthetic hint, 124

Linked parallel turns, 54
Long leg, short leg, 155

Modern skiing methods, 63

New learning approaches, 68
    ski schools, 69

Pendulum-type fashion, 3
Parallel fan, 53
Professional Ski Instructors of American (PSIA), 67, 74
Pole Push side slip, 152
Pole, 183
Pole-sensing exercise, 205
Power skiing, 229
    texture, 230
    depth, 230
    resistance, 230
    balance point, 230
    guide/ride, 235
    common mistakes, 236
    general tips, 242

Reactional skiing, 5
Rounds, Jack, 250
Round-Finished turn, 148
Recreational racing, 245
Running gates, practical value of, 250
    falling, 251
    mental attitude, 255

    physical conditioning, 257
    skiing skills, 261
Racing strategy, 271
    confidence attack, 272
    fine tuning, 273
    training strategy, 273

Skiing, fundamentals of, 1
Short-swing turn, 146
    technical skills, 1
    physical attitude, 2
    mental powers, 2
Ski feel, 7
Ski-Snow awareness, 7
Skiers, types of, 9
    skeletal bracing, 10
    higher performance skier, 11
Skidded turns, 12
Skiing, principles of, 15
    natural positions, 15
    total motion, 15
    unweighting, 15
    axial motion, 15
    edge control, 15
    weight transfer, 15
Side step, 21
Snow plow turn, 33
Skating, 37
Single swing, 98
Skiing tools of, 162
    clothing, 162
    basic design features, 164
    materials, 166
    glasses/goggles, 168
    boots, 168
    skis, 173
Skiing steeps, 187
    pole plant, 191
    edging, 191
    rotation steeps, 191
    machine-groomed steep, 194
    angles using, 195
Special situation skiing, 201

Shotswing turns, 220
    rhythm, 220
    special tips, 221
    wide-track, 222
    feet weight, 225
    separated skis, 225
    intermediate slopes, 227
    narrow ski runs, 228
Ski touring, 295
    uphill techniques, 296
    ice-axe, 299
    self-arrest, 299
    step cutting, 300
    crampons, 300
    rope work, 301
    harness, 303

Traverse side step, 22
Traversing, 35 Taylor, clif, 66
Tail-wagging, 85
Tip roll, 101
Tows technique, 102
    rope tows, 102

Upper body, 159

Wide track, 67
Wedge hoppers, 136
Wedge progression, 140
World cup technique, 260
Witness, 287

Zigzag manner, 22